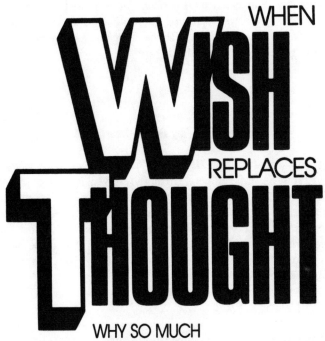

WHEN

WISH

REPLACES

THOUGHT

WHY SO MUCH
OF WHAT YOU
BELIEVE IS FALSE

Steven Goldberg

PROMETHEUS BOOKS
BUFFALO, NEW YORK

Portions of this book appeared in *American Anthropologist, Chronicles, Ethics, Humboldt Journal of Social Relations, International Journal of Sociology and Social Policy, National Review, Policy Review, Psychiatry, Reflections,* and *Society.* Permissions are gratefully acknowledged.

Published 1991 by Prometheus Books.

95 94 93 92 91   5 4 3 2 1

Library of Congress Cataloging-in-Publication Data

Goldberg, Steven
    When wish replaces thought : why so much of what you believe is false /
by Steven Goldberg.
        p.   cm.
    Includes bibliographical references and index.
    ISBN 0-87975-711-6
    1. Social problems. 2. Subjectivity. 3. Knowledge, Sociology of. I. Title.
HN28.G58   1992
149'.73—dc20   91-25086
                                                                    CIP

Printed in the United States of America on acid-free paper.

For
Liz, Alan, and Joan

The life which is unexamined is not worth living.   —Socrates, *Apology*

The moment a man questions the meaning and value of life, he is sick . . .
—Freud (Letter to Marie Bonaparte, August 13, 1937)

Acknowledgments

In addition to those to whom this and my first book are dedicated, there are a few people who were so generous that they deserve special mention:

Michael Cooperstein and Carol Saltus, whose comments often directed attention to whole areas that I had left unexamined and that demanded analysis.

Helen Hans, William Helmreich, Francis Wilson, and Jack Winter for comments on specific subjects discussed in this book and for general suggestions about its presentation.

Ibtihaj Arafat, Pnina Bright, Neil Epstein, William Fishbein, Willie Flower, Ernest van den Haag, Henny Helmreich, Jeffrey Rosen, Faith Scheer, Susan Thomas, and Ruth Wolff all offered suggestions so illustrative of their individual gifts that it is unfair that space requires they be grouped in a way that camouflages the uniqueness of each of their contributions.

Paul Kurtz, Bob Basil, and the good people at Prometheus, who are among the few in publishing who really do believe that every voice has a right to be heard and without whom this book would not have seen the light of day.

Steven Goldberg
New York, New York
November 16, 1991

Contents

PART 1: WHY WE BEHAVE AS WE DO

1. Introduction: What This Book Is and Is Not   13
2. Does the Death Penalty Deter?   25
3. What Is Normal? The Question of Homosexuality   47
4. What Does "Cause" Mean? The Causation of Homosexuality   65
5. The Theory of Patriarchy: Why Do Males Rule?   73
6. Black Athletic Superiority: Why Are Blacks Better Athletes?   121
7. What Good Are the SAT's?   131

PART 2: WHY WE VIEW THE WORLD AS WE DO

8. Are Stereotypes True?   151
9. Is Astrology Science?   155
10. Is There a Feminist Science?   169
11. Is Freudian Theory Science?   177
12. Is There a Correct Use of Language?   193
13. When Logic and Science Are Not Enough: The Question of Abortion   197
14. Sociology: Uncommon Sense, Common Sense, or Nonsense?   205
    Index   213

Part 1

Why We Behave As We Do

1

Introduction
What This Book Is and Is Not

I

This book is an attempt to understand aspects of how the world works and our method for understanding how the world works. Save for a few chapters that address purely logical aspects of social questions, these chapters all concern the causes of behavior—the factors that facilitate and encourage specific forms of behavior and the factors that retard and discourage such behavior. These chapters are not concerned with moral assessments of the behavior or political prescriptions for social policies.

This book addresses empirical (and related logical) questions that are capable of eliciting the strongest of emotions. These emotions are capable of generating a substitution of wish for thought. It is the purpose of this book to demonstrate the fallacy and error in "answers" to the questions addressed, fallacy and error that would never infiltrate explanations of unemotional issues. In many cases this book attempts to offer alternative explanations that are without fallacy and error.

This book assumes that acceptance of the faulty explanation is never justifiable on political or moral grounds, and that no claim of a (putative) social or political consequence of the acceptance of a correct explanation ever justifies rejection of that explanation.

This book is not an attempt to persuade the reader to accept one or another side on any moral or political issue. It is axiomatic (at least in the world of the empiricist) that "is cannot generate ought" and that no explanation of the world can entail a moral or political view of the world. Moral and political views require something in addition to logic and fact, some subjective impulse giving direction. Nature, the logic that gives order to nature and makes nature comprehensible, and the science that attempts to explain nature—none of these can provide the subjective impulse required to give the direction that defines the moral or political view.

Thus, for example, one can accept all that I write on the causation of differences of male and female behavior and feel that this suggests that we *should* have a sexual equal rights law. A view of this sort might give priority to a need to limit the behavioral advantage for attaining high positions that flows from male physiology in a world where aggressive incompetence often attains a higher position than does cooperative competence. It might do this to meet the demands of a sense of justice or to increase economic efficiency or to accord with some other impulse and goal.

One can, on the other hand, accept all that I write on the subject and feel that this suggests that we *should not* have a sexual equal rights law. A view of this sort might give priority to a need to emphasize sexual differences in order to give focus to the amorphous tendencies the infant brings to a world in which role models are hard to come by. It might do this to facilitate the development of strong integration of personality or to render concordant aptitude and ambition or to accord with some other impulse and goal.

Nothing I write favors one of these views over the other. However, all that I write—to the extent that it is correct—sets limits on the empirical claims that one making a moral or political argument can make. It is perfectly legitimate—I believe preferable—for one who attempts to explain how the world *does* work to ignore all questions about how the world *should* work. But one who would tell us how the world *should* work is committed—if one wishes us to believe that one's recommendations can be effectuated in the real world—to refusing to misrepresent how the world *does* work.

II

For reasons of readability, in this section I refer to all positions to the right of center as "conservative" and all to the left of center as "liberal." This is not meant to distinguish the political conservative from those further right or the political liberal from those further left; indeed, the things I say here tend to be more true as one moves further from the center in each direction. It is simply a way of avoiding repetition of the phrases "those to the right" and "those to the left."

I emphasize all this for two reasons:

(1) It may well strike the reader that my work seems often to reach conclusions that are more acceptable to the conservative than to the liberal.

It is true beyond question that these chapters—though not the empirical approach that infuses them—will be welcomed more by the conservative than by the liberal. But the reason that this is the case has nothing to do with any tendency of mine to favor conservative moral or political views. The reason is rooted in a difference between conservative and liberal arguments.

Possibly because the roots of conservatism, both historical and contemporary, are often embedded in religious soil, the conservative feels at home with arguments that are clearly based on assumptions that are, from a logical and scientific point of view, arbitrary and subjective (i.e., founded on values).

The liberal, whose positions are, in reality, no less and no more subjectively anchored than are those of the conservative (or anyone else making a moral or political argument), has been far more greatly affected by the empiricism that stresses the distinction between the scientific and the moral-political. The liberal is far more often loathe to acknowledge the subjective nature of his argument because he feels in his bones that, once the subjective nature of his assumptions is exposed, no one will feel compelled to accept his argument.

Now, I am, by nature, just like the liberal in this regard. I tend not to write about the weakness of conservative arguments because the conservative usually acknowledges from the start the subjective assumptions that, for empiricists like myself, render his argument incapable of persuading anyone who does not already accept his assumptions. Once your opponent acknowledges that his attack dog is dead, there is no reason for you to shoot his attack dog.

Many liberals—precisely because they feel, as I do, that the subjectively rooted argument is inherently impotent—are far more likely to offer muddled empirical explanations in an attempt to camouflage the subjective roots of their arguments. The chapters of this book are analyses of these muddled empirical explanations (and of related logical questions). One can, of course, accept the analyses and continue to favor the liberal subjective impulse over that of the conservative. At that point, however, the liberal argument is, from an empiricist point of view, analogous to that of the conservative in that it is acknowledged to be subjectively rooted and no longer amenable to either validation or refutation in logical and empirical terms alone.

Thus, for example, one of the conservative views of the death penalty argues simply that an eye should be taken for an eye (even if doing so does not deter others from taking an eye) and acknowledges that it cannot persuade one who believes that an eye should *not* be taken for an eye.

Many liberals, on the other hand, abhor acknowledging the subjective nature of their argument. They are far more likely to refrain from making an argument symmetrical with that of the conservative (the argument that sees the death penalty as wrong *even if it does deter*). They feel the need to argue that it has been demonstrated beyond reasonable doubt that the death penalty does not deter. While its conclusion that the death penalty does not deter may or may not turn out to be correct (it is still an open question), the argument that these liberals present is demonstrably fallacious and offers no reason to believe that its conclusion is correct.[1]

I believe that such fallacious arguments, presented as explanations, infuse social science today and are responsible for millions of people accepting explanations of the world that have no logical consistency, are discordant with the empirical evidence, and either fail to explain that which they claim to explain or offer explanations of that which does not exist (that which, therefore, is not in need of explanation).

The exposure of the logical and empirical inadequacies of such explanations—and, in some cases, the presentation of explanations that seem to me far more concordant with the reality they attempt to explain—is the purpose of this book.[2]

Were it not the case that the fallacious arguments dominate the American universities and infuse their textbooks, I would probably have not written these chapters or even been particularly aware of the existence of attempted explanations that the chapters attempt to refute. But such fallacious attempts at explanations are routinely taught to students by professors who either fail to see the obvious incorrectness of the "explanations" or see it and continue to give the explanations to their students on the grounds that the *consequences* of the students' believing the correct explanations would be undesirable.

The issues capable of engendering in a great number of academics an emotional need sufficient to override even the most basic constraints of logic and empirical method tend to fall into four categories: (1) issues concerned literally with life (abortion) and death (the death penalty); (2) issues concerned with male-female differences or sexual orientation (male-female roles, male-female performance on mental tests, stereotypes, and homosexuality); (3) issues concerned with race (black athletic performance and stereotypes); and (4) issues concerned with intellectual and scientific authority and legitimacy (prescriptivism in language, and the scientific claims of the feminist, the astrologer, and Freud).

Thus, for example, many sociologists present patently fallacious and misrepresentative "explanations" of male-female differences that deny a physiological basis to differences in male and female modes of thought and behavior. They do so because they fear that acknowledgment of such a physiological basis would predispose the students to accept views of males and females that the professors find unpalatable or politically undesirable. These professors defend as "humane" that which we used to call lying.

In any case, as the reader has already realized, there is something in this book for everyone to dislike. The liberal will dislike the arguments made in the individual chapters, arguments that, if they are correct, refute empirical arguments favored by the liberal. Conservatives will dislike even more an approach that refuses even to discuss many conservative arguments as soon as it becomes clear that such arguments are founded on subjective premises. In fact, it has been my experience that nearly every reader of my work has concluded that I am *really* on the side that he or she opposes. Conservatives believe that I am *really* liberal and liberals believe that I am *really* conservative. (In the case of my earlier work on abortion, virtually every reader was certain that I was on the side he or she opposed—this despite the fact that the entire purpose of that work was to argue that the issue is entirely one of the definition of the fetus, so that neither side can possibly demonstrate a logical or empirical superiority.[3])

Should conservative ideology come to dominate in academic and intellectual circles, then it will be *conservatives* who gravitate toward the fallacious, exhibiting the mental flaccidity against which even common sense cannot immunize one. For power confers feelings of moral superiority and intellectual infallibility on those who serve a psychological and ideological master, whether one of the right or of the left, and this is the seed of destruction that grows within one whose goal is not truth.

(2) It is not merely that these chapters are not conservative; they are not

liberal either. Logical analyses and empirical explanations are not "conservative" or "liberal"; they are (relatively) correct or incorrect. Nature will give you a lift only if you are going her way and any bias, whether rooted in psychological need or political leaning, that detours the journey will take one away from truth. Fortunately, as we shall see, bias *per se* (i.e., the bias of an author, rather than the effects of this bias in his work) is irrelevant. It is only the effects that matter.[4]

In short, it is the assumption of this book that the arguments of both the Right and the Left invariably attempt to smuggle in values hidden under empirical facts, and it the purpose of this book to expose such intellectual crimes.

III

There is a sense in which the empiricist approach utilized here can legitimately be labeled subversive. All social, cultural, and political ties derive their strength from subjective assumptions of right and wrong, good and bad, worthwhile and worthless, that are socialized into the members of a population from early childhood. Values can be studied objectively, but they cannot derive their power primarily from the intellect.

The sorts of questions and objectifications that constitute the empiricist's arsenal—and that are the point of education—are ultimately life-threatening to every social, political, and religious set of beliefs and values because all such beliefs and values are grounded in the subjective. Culture is in great part the set of subjective values shared by the members of society.

It is usually the case, of course, that those who share cultural beliefs vastly outnumber those whose attempts at objectification threaten those beliefs. And it is usually the case that the power of culture—the power of early socialization and the threat of ostracism of those who do not acquiesce and accept the subjective assumptions as objective—dominates, at least in the short term, any attempt at objectification. But it may be that *inherent* in modern society is a process of objectification that renders permanently weak the cultural ties that society requires if it is to be strong. In (correctly) distinguishing the subjective and arbitrary from the objective, modern society may even render unavoidable its sowing the seeds of its own destruction. (The process of this objectification in the United States and its effect of undercutting American values is the subject of my next book).

If the reader infers that I believe that (higher) education (as opposed to mere indoctrination into the set of subjective beliefs that both the right and the left pass off as education) is the enemy of culture, then the reader can rest assured that he has correctly understood all that I have written to this point. The most lovable thing about truth is that it is true. But a close second is that it is subversive; no authority system, and certainly no political administration, loves truth for its own sake, because truth by its nature fails to ratify the values that give an authority system power. It is the great glory of the American system of authority that this fact is not seen as justifying the suppression of truth.

The reader who wishes to know the psychological impulse that drives an author to write what he writes will find it here. All groups require an acceptance of their subjective beliefs by those who wish membership. This is what makes the group a group and, to the extent that such beliefs are of a normative and moral nature, is as unobjectionable as it is inevitable. But when the group demands, of those wishing acceptance, acceptance of patently nonsensical or fallacious *explanations* and patently misrepresented or bogus *facts*, then the group makes denial of truth condition for acceptance. And every group does this to a greater or lesser extent.

For people with my constitution, this demand is intolerable. (The chapter on prescriptivism makes clear this constitution's acceptance of the intellectually justifiable beliefs and rejection of a prescriptivist group that attempts to smuggle in along with its intellectually justifiable beliefs beliefs that are agreed upon but are not intellectually justifiable.)

To be sure, the empiricist is a person, and as such he or she, like everyone else, has strongly held subjective feelings of what is good and what is bad. But the empiricist does not pretend that these are anything more than feelings, that they could in any sense be ultimately validated by objective reasoning and evidence, or that there is any reason why the reader should accept, or even care about, an empiricist's (or anyone else's) feelings about what is good and bad.[5]

IV

It is important to distinguish here subjective beliefs about the good (e.g., the conservative's emphasis on liberty as good or the liberal's emphasis on treatment of the worst-off as good) from empirical questions about such beliefs. "Premarital intercourse is bad (or good)" is a subjective value. "Societies that believe that premarital intercourse is bad economically outperform societies that don't" is an empirical claim that is unobjectionable to the empiricist. It is unobjectionable because the question of whether this claim is correct or not is amenable to empirical study.

Likewise, a question concerning "which moral beliefs must be held by the members of a population if their society is to survive" is an empirical question. Unfortunately, centuries of attempts to address this question have uncovered nothing more than the obvious candidates anyone would know (e.g., the population must believe that physical violence against another member is wrong under most conditions).

The empiricist may often write about logical fallacy and misrepresented evidence in arguments serving a subjective impulse, but once these are exposed, he has nothing more to say; he sees the belief that remains as both invulnerable (immune to logic and evidence) and impotent (incapable of using logic and evidence—the only valid weapons of persuasion—to persuade anyone who does not already share the belief). The empiricist can be invaluable to one whose interest is in how things work. He can be helpful to one whose interest is moral or political insofar as he can clarify logical issues and address relevant empirical ones.

But once this is accomplished the empiricist is worthless. He has nothing to offer those who wish to know good from bad. For the empiricist is one who does not know good from bad.

There is no reason to despair over this. Morality (and its practical manifestation, politics) is the enemy of truth. And so is immorality. Both spring from impulses that subordinate the satisfaction of curiosity to the fulfillment of some other impulse, some impulse that subordinates the discovery of truth to that of another physical, emotional, or moral pleasure. There is, of course, no alternative to this and one who is committed only to an amoral life of satisfying curiosity (assuming that such a thing were possible) would be an especially inhuman monster. But to acknowledge the necessity and superiority of a life infused also with other passions and with morality is not to deny that these are, by their nature, the enemies of truth and the passion to find it.

V

It must be acknowledged that even empiricism is rooted in the subjective belief that our sense perceptions are in some sense accurate. Likewise, it must be acknowledged that, like all attempts to render a continuous nature discrete, empiricism encounters difficulties when attempting to demarcate the nonempirical from the empirical, the illegitimate from the legitimate, and the like. But this introduction is not in any sense an attempt to provide a rigorous defense of empiricism; it is merely a statement of the impulse—the empiricist impulse—that informs all of the chapters of this book.

Thus, one can dismiss empiricism, just as one can dismiss all discussion of all types by taking refuge in a solipsism that denies the existence of anything other than one's own thought. Such views, while tenable, have little persuasive power because, whatever the subjective assumptions or other difficulties that dog empiricism, empiricism offers its ability to make predictions. Systems concerned with good and bad and right and wrong offer *nothing more*, from an empiricist point of view, than tautological restatements of their initial subjective assumptions.

In fairness, it must be said that most of what is written by those who deny the validity of the empiricist's refusal to accept the groundedness of the subjective does, in practice, conform to the constraints imposed by the empiricist. For example, discussions of freedom that focus on such issues as the psychological and social effects of democracy, the behavioral consequences of freedom of speech, and the like clearly do meet the constraints imposed by the empiricist.

Another example: Consider two people arguing about the morality of homosexual behavior. To the extent that one offers merely a sophisticated version of "homosexual behavior is just as morally valid as heterosexual behavior" and the other a similarly sophisticated version of "homosexual behavior is immoral" or "homosexual behavior is immoral because the Bible says it is," there is nothing for the empiricist to say.

However, it is likely that the former will say something like, "homosexual behavior is, unlike thievery, a 'crime without a victim' " and, therefore, not immoral.

The latter might respond by claiming that society is the victim of the behavior even if the participants participated voluntarily. The former would claim that society doesn't suffer if the participation was voluntary. The latter, exploiting the weakness of the concept of a "crime without a victim," would point out that bribery is voluntary (i.e., neither party wishes to become a complainant), yet clearly victimizes society.[6]

Here the former will acknowledge that an act can injure society (and therefore can be immoral) even if the participants participate voluntarily and gladly. He will agree that, as an attempt to *qualitatively* differentiate a *category* of crimes, the concept of "crimes without victims" fails. But he will argue that, in the case of homosexuality, society is *not* harmed.

At this point the argument may become one for which empirical investigation is relevant. It will behoove the opponent of homosexual behavior to demonstrate convincingly that some harm comes to society from homosexual behavior *per se*, or from the social acceptance of homosexual behavior as morally unobjectionable. In other words, at this point there is agreement on the criterion for an assessment of morality (i.e., what "harmful" entails), and that criterion is empirical.

In any case, even if the reader is a non-empiricist who disagrees with all that I have written to this point, he need not fear that his non-empiricism will lead him to reject anything in the chapters of this book. For the empiricist's rejection of the fruits of non-empiricism is not balanced by a non-empiricist's rejection of the fruits of empiricism. For example, the empiricist will see discussions of "virtue" as astonishingly erudite but nonsensical, and therefore inherently of no value. But even those who see such discussions as being of greater value than any empirical enterprise do not question the appropriateness or value of the empiricist's analysis of logical and empirical questions. The non-empiricist may challenge particular logical and empirical analyses, but he does not see the logical and empirical analysis as *inherently* meaningless. He may feel sorry for the empiricist, whom he sees as ignoring that which is of most beauty and most importance in favor of that which is less beautiful and less important, but he does not see the empiricist's work as being *inherently* without beauty or importance. Thus, he may find that he agrees with all that is written in these chapters while disagreeing with all that has been written to this point and with the justification of the approach that infuses these chapters.[7]

VI

Those who serve a political master often feel the need to dismiss logical and empirical analyses they see as failing to serve their ends, and they often accuse the one making the analysis of bias. Thus, at the risk of my belaboring the obvious, it is necessary to make a few relevant points.

Even if the author of a logical analysis or empirical explanation *is* biased, it is only the fallacy or error (including biased selection of evidence) caused by the bias that is relevant and that renders the analysis or explanation incorrect. If the author is biased, but his bias does not engender fallacy or error, then the bias is irrelevant. Eratosthenes may have had a tremendous psychological need or political bias leading him to favor a belief that the world is round, but this did not render the world flat or Eratosthenes' argument that the world is round incorrect.

All this has been known for millennia and recognized as the fallacious *ad hominem* argument. To the extent that the biases of the author of an explanation cause him to commit fallacy or error, his explanation can be shown to be incorrect merely by exposing the fallacy or error. But this is the *only* way in which his explanation can be shown to be incorrect: Accusations that the author is biased are irrelevant—and would be even if the accusations were true—except insofar as the bias has engendered fallacy and error in the analysis; if there is such fallacy and error in the analysis, its exposure is sufficient to refute the analysis, and it would make no difference whether the fallacy and error are the result of bias, unbiased incompetence, or incomplete information. Similarly, the accusation that a claim about how the world works will have unfortunate consequences—even if correct—has nothing to do with the correctness of the claim. This has been recognized for as many millennia in the fact that the *ad consequentium* argument is fallacious.

I make these points because works concerning logical and empirical issues that easily arouse emotion invariably elicit from some the charge of bias. This charge is always either without force or unnecessary. The charge of bias is without force if it is not accompanied by the examples of fallacy or error that is the evidence of the bias. It is like an accusation of sophistry or misrepresentation that fails to identify any fallacy or error. The charge of bias is unnecessary if the bias has engendered fallacy, error, or misrepresentation whose exposure is alone sufficient to refute the biased claim. In the case of an accusation of bias, as in the case of an accusation of libel, truth is a complete defense.

For this reason and, more importantly, because to do less is to cheat the reader, I have done my best to present all of my reasoning and all of my evidence in as clear a way as I know how, so that the reader may discover such fallacy, error, or misrepresentation if they are there. This is the least the reader has a right to demand.

If this introduction seems to offer a defense against an illegitimate attack that the reader has not even made, I can assure the reader that such criticisms are today the norm for work that addresses the controversial subjects I address. It is the norm for the truthfulness of claims to be dismissed because of the (putative) social or political effects of an acceptance of the truthfulness of the claim. It is the central tenet of this book (and, I believe, of *any* discussion of the world that is to avoid self-parody) that the consequences of a claim that something is true are entirely irrelevant to the issue of whether the claim is true. Even if, for example, it is true that "if people believe that the death penalty deters, we're more likely to get capital punishment" and one agrees that capital punishment is a bad thing whether it deters or not, this has nothing to do with the empirical issue of whether or not the death penalty does deter.

The likelihood that no reader would invoke consequences as an argument against the logical and empirical claims made in this book is infinitesimal. Many readers, of course, will find all that I have said too obvious to merit discussion and would not consider raising the *ad hominum* and *ad consequentium* objections. To them I apologize for wasting their time with this introduction.

I apologize also for the occasional—but I hope not annoying—repetition of an analogy or explanatory sentence. I chose to risk repetition because I assume that some future readers will read just one of these essays out of an interest in its specific subject and that such readers would not have read the analogy or explanatory sentence.

NOTES

1. Incidentally, as has often been pointed out, the biblical injunction concerning "an eye for an eye" had the purpose of limiting retribution, of denying the victim the right to act on a desire to take *two* eyes for the eye he had taken by his assailant. The wisdom of even this advice is not self-evident: the victim might ask why his assailant took his eye and whether the irrationality that drove his assailant might not manifest itself again. The victim might conclude that taking just one of the assailant's eyes would leave the assailant with an eye—and the ability to come after the victim's second eye. But I digress.

2. There is a second reason these chapters often take issue with liberal, rather than conservative, positions: American academic social science tends to be liberal. Most contemporary academic analyses—both the worthwhile and the worthless—are liberal because most academic analyses are liberal. Among the strongest of academic liberal impulses in the social sciences is that which dislikes analyses finding physiological factors of causal importance to emotion, cognition, behavior, and the institutions that reflect these. This liberal aversion is understandable and springs—at least in part—from humane motives; faulty physiologically rooted theories have played a disgraceful part throughout history in justifying murderous behavior—from slavery to extermination. But it was not the purposes and consequences of these theories that rendered them untrue; they were rendered untrue by their incorrect reasoning and misrepresented "facts." (The purposes and desired consequences may have been the reason for the fallacious reasoning and the misrepresentation, but this is irrelevant. We shall discuss this a bit more below.)

Among the issues that most easily elicit strong feelings are those that fall under the "nature vs. nurture" rubric. A great many liberals—for reasons that speak well of them—favor the view that hereditary-physiological differences between individuals play little role in individual differences in temperament, cognition, behavior, and institutions reflecting these. This view collides with research over the past two decades—work in the brain sciences, studies demonstrating the tendency of adopted infants to reflect as adults characteristics of their biological parents, and the like—that has made it clear that inherited characteristics influence individual psychology and behavior far more than many would like, and far more than is reflected in the environmentalism favored by large numbers of educated people who went to college when behaviorism, Marxism, and other overly environmentalist explanations were far more tenable.

A number of the chapters in this book take exception to analyses that insist, against the evidence and the logic that explain it, that hereditary-physiological factors are of little causal importance to emotion, cognition, behavior, and the institutions that reflect these.

3. Like many social scientists, I am "conservative" in the sense that, like the political conservative, I see social life as entailing myriad intuitions, understandings, and ways of doing things that—while ultimately empirically analyzable—defy easy explanation and serve society in ways that argue against our jettisoning them too easily.

However, unlike many conservatives, I usually find the nexus from this social truth to political action too long to enable us to base the latter on the former. Thus, most political disputes strike me as analogous to the Right's refusing to permit the government to erect a street light because doing so would run counter to human nature, and to the Left's attempting to abolish the institution of the family by Tuesday because it doesn't like the family anymore. Moreover, the conservative often seems motivated by fear, a fear of his own uncontrollable emotions projected onto a barbarian mob breaking through the gates; the conservative's greatest tendency seems to be his remarkable ability to endure other people's pain. The liberal often seems motivated by guilt, in some cases a free-floating guilt that everything is his fault, and in others an ostensible guilt that is in reality fear of the anger of those who are less fortunate than he is; the liberal's greatest tendency often seems to be his remarkable ability to confuse wish with reality.

The modes of argument of both the liberal and the conservative tend to demonstrate the reality that the less justified one is that one is correct, the more certain one will be and the more vociferous will be one's argument. Society is endlessly complicated and its members represent a seemingly infinite manifold of variables, making accurate prediction virtually impossible. Nonetheless, those who make short-term social and political predictions—the tests of the validity of social and political analyses—invariably speak with a certainty that would embarrass the logician or mathematician. Indeed, it often seems that the probability of the correctness of a claim is inversely correlated with the degree of certainty of the claimant. The followers of both Friedman and Marx speak as if their views had received empirical validation equivalent to that leading us to accept Newton and Einstein. But a speaker's *conviction* that he is correct adds not a scintilla to the likelihood that he *is* correct. (It is only fair to acknowledge here that *I* have a virtually uninterrupted string of woefully incorrect political predictions and that is why the reader will not find here a single short-term social, economic, or political prediction.)

But none of this matters. The chapters in this book make logical and empirical arguments that must stand on their own, and it is irrelevant whether the one making such arguments and the one reading such arguments are monarchists or anarchists.

4. A good rule for everyone—particularly those who have strong political or moral feelings—to follow: If an empirical investigation comes to a finding you like, rethink and double-check everything. The empiricist is no less prone than is anyone else to the human sources of bias, but the empirical approach is devoted to preventing such sources of bias from biasing result and explanation.

5. I am, of course, speaking of the scientific level here. One *does* very much care about a friend's or lover's feelings about right and wrong and good and bad. It is the concordance or complementariness of such feelings with one's own that underlies the close relationship.

6. I believe that it was Murray Rothbard who first made this devastating criticism of the "crimes without victims" concept.

7. While a general empiricism is probably the century's most influential philosophical tendency, it is currently derided by those who search for empirical "natural moral laws" and discuss subjects like "the meaning of freedom," searches and discussions that the empiri-

cist sees as inherently futile and endlessly circular, respectively. Derision, however, is not refutation, and the singular power of empiricism—a power derived from its noncircular nature and its ability to generate prediction—seems to me as strong as it ever was.

2

Does the Death Penalty Deter?

This chapter consists of two parts. The first attempts to demonstrate the fallaciousness of the widely accepted argument that concludes that the death penalty does not deter certain capital crimes. It does not argue that the conclusion is necessarily incorrect, but that the argument given to support it gives us no reason to believe that its conclusion is correct.

The second part of the essay—which necessarily recapitulates certain portions of the first—is a more theoretical analysis of the general question of what social factors encourage, and what social factors discourage, behavior (particularly murderous behavior).

PART 1

The question of the death penalty is one of the most complex facing the social sciences. It conjoins extraodinarily difficult empirical, moral, and political questions, none of which has been satisfactorily answered. As a result, there is a strong incentive, and tendency, simply to assert an answer to the empirical question most see as central: Does the death penalty deter people from murderous behavior more than imprisonment for life does?

"Deterrence" to the criminologist refers to the deterrence of *other* people besides the murderer, people who, if the death penalty does deter, will not murder if there is a death penalty, but who will murder if there is not a death penalty. In other words, if the death penalty does deter, this means that it prevents murders; the society's murder rate is lower than it would be if there were no death penalty. If the death penalty does not deter, this means that no one is dissuaded from murdering by the death penalty (or that the death penalty persuades as many—say, suicidal—people to murder as it dissuades); the murder rate is as high as it would be if the death penalty were not invoked.

The fact is that we do not yet know with anything approaching confidence whether the death penalty does or does not deter. The question is clearly an empirical one amenable to answer and it is likely that sophisticated statistical techniques will eventually permit us to find an answer. For now, however, we have only tentative evidence; as a result, conclusions about whether the death penalty deters are usually illegitimately determined by one's psychological and moral leanings, factors that have nothing to do with the question of whether the death penalty deters.

In academic circles, particularly those somewhat removed from the actual study of the deterrence issue, and in the media, psychological and moral resistance to capital punishment usually leads to the assertion that the death penalty does not deter, an assertion that is, indeed, made by many—but far from all—academics.

Here I shall argue that the reasoning on which these academics base their conclusion is a fallacious one. Their conclusion (that the death penalty does not deter) may or may not be correct, but it does not follow from their arguments and, so, their arguments do not give us any reason to believe that their conclusion is correct. The following are the incorrect assumptions that both underpin and infuse such arguments.

1. *Since many murders result from emotional impulse (e.g., the angry husband who kills his wife), the death penalty could have, at best, only the slightest deterrent effect.* If the death penalty deters, it is likely that it does so through society's saying that certain acts are so unacceptable that society will kill one who commits them; the individual internalizes the association of the act and the penalty throughout his life, constantly increasing his resistance to committing the act. There is no *a priori* reason for assuming that this process is less relevant to emotional acts than rational acts; most husbands, when angry, slam doors, shout, or sulk. The fact that the death penalty has not deterred the husband who *does* kill his wife does not cast doubt on the role of the death penalty in deterring those husbands who *don't*. After all, neither the death penalty nor anything else deterred the husband who does murder his wife, so the question is not what deterred the person who did murder (nothing did), but what deterred the person who didn't.

Note that there is no implication here that the potential murderer consciously weighs the alternatives and decides that the crime is worth life in prison but not death. Those who argue that the death penalty doesn't deter are quite correct in saying that those who are in the process of "deciding" whether to commit a murder do not often rationally calculate the alternative payoffs and decide that the crime is worth life in prison but not death. But no serious theory of deterrence claims that such rational calculation of punishment (as opposed to no rational calculation or calculation only of the probability of getting caught, clearly a far more important variable than that of the punishment received *if* caught) plays an important role. Thus, the issue of rational calculation of severity of punishment is irrelevant to the central question of deterrence. If the death penalty deters, it is, in all likelihood, primarily because it instills a psychological resistance to the act, not because it offers a rational argument against committing the act at the time that the decision is being made whether or not to commit the act.

2. *There is no evidence that the death penalty deters.* This is simply untrue. Professor Isaac Ehrlich and colleagues utilizing his statistical techniques argue that there can be little doubt about the ability of the death penalty to deter. Ehrlich concludes that each additional execution prevents about seven or eight people from murdering. All statistical arguments on the death penalty are, however, excruciatingly complex and leave room for counterargument. Some critics, for example, have argued that increased likelihood of execution leads juries to convict fewer people, thereby offsetting the deterrent effect of execution.

So here let us assume, for argument's sake, that there is no empirical evidence one way or the other. The more important point is that there is a crucial difference between there being no evidence that two things are correlated (in this case, an inverse correlation between the death penalty and the murder rate) and there being evidence that two things are not correlated. The latter means that we have good evidence that the two things are not related; the former means simply that we have no evidence.

Now, it is quite true that we must have some sort of evidence in order even to entertain the idea that two things are related. Our reason for not believing that tall Italian men are smarter than short Italian men is not simply that we have no direct evidence, but also because we have no informal evidence suggesting that this is true—and so we do not bother even to investigate the possibility. It is the lack of relevant informal evidence that permits us to ignore the difference between not having evidence that the hypothesis is true and having evidence that the hypothesis is not true.

But in the case of penalties, we have an enormous amount of both informal and formal evidence—from everday experience of socializing children and limiting adult behavior and from such "experiments" as increasing the fees for parking violations—that, as a general rule, the greater a punishment, the fewer people will behave in the punished way. Thus, it is perfectly reasonable to expect that the death penalty would have a more dissuasive effect than would life imprisonment and there is no *a priori* reason to believe that the increase from the threat of life imprisonment to that of death fails to dissuade anyone from committing murder.

On the other hand, it certainly is possible that the relationship between penalty and behavior breaks down at some point and that the increase from life imprisonment to death does not increase resistance to murder and does not lower the murder rate; this is the belief of those who argue that the death penalty does not deter. My purpose here is merely to point out that it is simply incorrect to say that we have no evidence suggesting that the death penalty does deter and that the question of whether the death penalty does or does not deter is an open question awaiting further evidence.

Finally, nearly every popular article, and a good many academic articles, invoke the experience of the British with public hanging of pickpockets as proof that the death penalty does not deter. The argument sees the fact that pickpocketing continued long after the introduction of (public) hanging as demonstrating that the death penalty has no deterrent effect. It demonstrates no such thing, of course. At best, it demonstrates that not every pickpocket was dissuaded from pickpocketing, a fact no one would doubt. Even if it could be shown (which it can't) that all practicing pickpockets continued to pick pockets at the same rate, this would still not address the more important question of whether some people who had not yet become pickpockets were dissuaded from doing so by the death penalty. I have no idea whether they were, but neither do those who assert that the death penalty had no deterrent effect.

3. *States imposing the greatest number of executions have the highest murder rate.* This is true, but the implication that this fact somehow demonstrates the inability of the death penalty to deter is false because the fact is irrelevant. It is just as reasonable—though no more reasonable—to argue that the high murder rate in these states is precisely the reason that these states most require the death penalty and that the murder rates in these states would be even higher if they did not impose the death penalty. Clearly other factors (the presence of a father, local attitudes toward violence, and the like) are *more* important than the death penalty in determining murder rates—and, clearly, these tend to encourage murder more strongly in states like Florida that have both high murder rates and the death penalty. The question of whether the death penalty deters is the question of whether the death penalty deters when these other factors are held constant. The fact that the states that impose the greatest number of executions have the highest murder rates is irrelevant; the question is whether these states would have an even higher murder rate than they now do if they did not impose the death penalty (and whether the states with a low murder rate and no death penalty would have an even lower rate if they did impose the death penalty).

4. *You can't do anything about crime until you do something about the causes of crime.* This argument is as silly as it is ubiquitous. It is, of course, true that you can't do anything about an effect (in this case, crime) unless you alter one necessary condition—or reduce one predisposing factor—of the cause. But this one factor can be the punishment factor in the causal formula of crime. In medicine it is often the case that a disease can be prevented by our blocking one necessary condition for the disease when we otherwise understand it not at all.

To argue that you can't do anything about crime until you do something about poverty is—to use Ernest van den Haag's devastating analogy—to play the fireman who refuses to turn on the hose because "you can't do anything about fire until you do something about the cause of the fire." To put out a fire you need merely remove one necessary element of the causation—oxygen; to the extent that the death penalty deters (if it does deter), it works even better than water on a fire; it prevents the effect from even occurring.

Poverty is a cause of murder (or crime in general) only in that it is a facilitating factor that must be complemented by other factors if the effect (murder) is to occur; the vast majority of poor people do not, after all, murder anyone. But, to the extent that it is a facilitating factor, alteration of one of the complementing factors (the severity of punishment) can certainly reduce the frequency of the effect without altering the degree of poverty. There are many good reasons for reducing poverty, but for the reduction of crime, reducing poverty is not necessary and is about as difficult a solution as one could imagine.

If the death penalty deters, it does so by replacing a necessary weakness of the internal resistance to murder with an internal resistance sufficiently strong to prevent murderous behavior in a situation that would otherwise elicit such behavior. If the death penalty deters, it does so without affecting any additional element of the cause of murder.[1]

5. *The death penalty will inevitably be imposed on a few innocent people.* This is, of course, true. But it is also true that, if the death penalty deters, the number of innocent people whose lives are saved will, in all likelihood, dwarf the number of people—nearly all of whom are guilty, but a few of whom are wrongfully convicted—who are executed. Moreover, even the opponent of the death penalty who emphasizes wrongful executions is willing to sacrifice thousands of lives each year for the social advantages of motor vehicles. Realizing this, the opponent differentiates between the death penalty and the use of motor vehicles on the grounds that:

6. *In the case of the death penalty, it is the state that takes a life.* This is an objection that seems to be an argument, but is, in fact, merely a restatement of the basic *ad hoc* moral objection to the death penalty. The state's taking a life of one who has been convicted of a capital offense is what the death penalty is. The objection based on its being the state that takes a life is as invulnerable as is the response to it that says, "so what—the 'state' in a democratic society is merely another way of saying 'the people.' "

The objection *does* successfully render irrelevant to the opponent's position the fact that, if the death penalty deters, it saves lives. In other words, the opponent of the death penalty who bases his opposition on the fact that it is the state that takes a life is basing his argument on a moral assumption and not on the question of whether the death penalty deters. Like other moral arguments against the death penalty, this one can be maintained even if the death penalty *does* deter, because it would find the death penalty unacceptable even if it deters. But, like other moral arguments against the death penalty, it has no power to convince those who do not accept its initial assumption ("the state may not take a life," "capital punishment—like torture—is wrong even if it does deter," etc.).

It is fair, however, to point out that those basing their opposition to the death penalty on the fact that it is the state that takes a life are, *if* the death penalty deters, maintaining their belief by sacrificing the (innocent) people who will be murdered because the death penalty is not invoked.

Incidentally, capital punishment is *not*, as is invariably claimed, "state-sponsored murder." "Murder" is, by definition, illegal killing. Capital punishment is no more "murder" than is legal imprisonment "kidnaping."

7. *The death penalty exchanges "real lives" (those of the executed) for "statistical lives" (those of the people who will not, if the death penalty deters and is invoked, be murdered).* Even if one grants this dubious distinction, this defense is available only to the pure pacifist. The most justified military action makes

just this exchange when it sacrifices some of society's young men to avoid a probable greater loss.

8. *If we do not know whether the death penalty deters, we should not use it.* If the death penalty deters, it deters the murder of people who are, in addition to being innocent, in all likelihood more numerous than the murderers who are executed. Thus, if society does invoke the death penalty on the assumption that the death penalty deters and is incorrect in this assumption, it unnecessarily accepts the deaths of a relatively small number of (nearly always guilty) individuals (i.e., individuals who are executed).

On the other hand, if society refuses to invoke the death penalty on the assumption that the death penalty does not deter and is incorrect in this assumption, then it unnecessarily accepts the deaths of a relatively large number of (innocent) people (i.e., individuals who are murdered who would not have been murdered had society invoked the death penalty). Consideration of this casts doubt on the intuitively plausible claim that, for as long as it is not known whether the death penalty deters, it should not be used.

9. *The death penalty is "uncivilized."* If the death penalty deters, then, by definition, it results in a society in which there are fewer murders than there would be if the death penalty were not invoked. The opponent of the death penalty can, of course, render this fact irrelevant and immunize his argument by detaching it from deterrence altogether; he can assert that the death penalty is wrong even if it deters. He can, in other words, see the death penalty as analogous to torture for theft: the association of torture with theft would no doubt deter some people from theft, but it would still be unjustified. This is what is implied in the rejection of the death penalty on the grounds that it is "uncivilized" or that it "increases the climate of violence." Ultimately, these defenses of opposition are as invulnerable to refutation as they are incapable of convincing anyone who does not already accept their assumption that the deterrence of murders would not justify the use of the death penalty.

One might ask, however, what, precisely, are the definitions of "civilization" and "climate of violence" that would see as "more civilized" or having "a lesser climate of violence" a society in which more (innocent) people are murdered than would be the case if the society did not refuse to use the penalty that would prevent their murder.

10. *It is those who oppose the death penalty who act out of humane motives.* Motivation is irrelevant to the correctness of an empirical claim. However, since nearly every article on the subject accords to the opponent of the death penalty the right to claim a greater humanity (a right the opponent invokes with alacrity), it is worth noting there are alternative views of the opponent's motivation.

One such view is that the opponent's opposition flows not from feelings of humanity but from the fact that the opponent can picture the murderer being executed, while he cannot picture the statistical group who will, if the death penalty deters, be murdered if the death penalty is utilized, but who will not be murdered if it is not. The picture of the execution is capable, as the murder of the statistically expected victims is not, of eliciting guilt, and fear of anger and aggression, with which the opponent cannot deal. The opponent rationalizes his avoidance of these with feelings of humanity, which bolster self-esteem and avoid awareness of his true motivation.

It is as reasonable—but no more reasonable—to see this as the opponent's motivation for his opposition as it is to accept that his opposition flows from his self-proclaimed greater humanity.

Incidentally, the commonly heard demand of the opponent that one who supports the death penalty must be willing to perform the execution himself is without merit. Many of the opponents would not have the stomach to perform a medical operation even if they knew how; would they claim that this argues against the correctness of the operation?

11. *A theory of deterrence.* It seems likely, though not demonstrated, that throughout life we internalize society's view of the relative wrongness of acts—and develop a relatively stronger or weaker resistance to such acts—in part on the basis of the relative strengths of the punishments the acts elicit. If society says that an act is so wrong that it will kill you for committing it, most people develop a stronger resistance to the act than they would if society sees the act as worthy of only life imprisonment (just as the child develops a stronger resistance to an act for which he is spanked than one for which he is less severely punished). It seems likely, though not demonstrated, that the death penalty engenders—in most people most of the time—a stronger resistance to an act than does life imprisonment. In other words, it seems reasonable to suppose that for some (marginal group of) people the difference between the death penalty and life imprisonment will determine whether they do or do not murder when they encounter an emotional or practical situation in which murder is an option.

This process takes place long before the time of the act. As we have seen, there is no issue of calculation at the time of the act of the difference between punishments; there is, therefore, no reason to believe that acts of passion are inherently immune to the ability of the internalized resistance to prevent the act. The person who yells or sulks, rather than kills, does so because he has a sufficiently strong resistance to murdering. Some of the people who yell or sulk, rather than murder, would murder if their internalized resistance were nurtured by perception of a weaker social punishment.

To be sure, for most people most of the time, a social reinforcement of a crime by life imprisonment—or, indeed, a significantly weaker punishment—is more than enough to engender an internal resistance sufficient to prevent the crime. And, to be sure, other factors (social frustration, the absence of a father, the likelihood of being caught, etc.) are more strongly related to crime than is the difference between the death penalty and life imprisonment (though most frustrated individuals, fatherless sons, etc., do not commit crimes). But these factors are irrelevant to the question of whether the death penalty deters and will be unless alteration of these other factors can reduce the crime rate to zero. The question of the death penalty is whether the presence of the death penalty renders the murder rate lower than it would be when the other factors are at any given levels.

Like the opponents of the death penalty, I hope that it turns out that the death penalty does not deter. If this should happen, we will avoid the terrible choice that deterrence forces upon us. Unlike the opponents of the death penalty, I do not fool myself into thinking that this hope speaks well of one's character. After all, it is a hope that is willing to sacrifice the possibility of saving innocent people in order to avoid personal psychological pain. This doesn't count as altruism where I come from.

PART 2

One who opposes the death penalty can terminate all discussion simply by asserting that it is morally unacceptable for a society to take the life of one of its own, and that it would be unacceptable even if it could be demonstrated that the death penalty deters some who would murder if their society did not invoke the death penalty. (This is, of course, the position on torture taken even by most proponents of the death penalty.) Likewise, one who supports the death penalty can foreclose further discussion by asserting that an eye must be taken for an eye even if the taking of an eye does not deter anyone any more than would a lesser penalty. Each of these positions is as irrefutable as it is incapable of persuading anyone who does not already accept it.

The question of deterrence is, however, paramount, not merely for those whose position would be based on the death penalty if it does deter, but would not if it does not—but also for those who favor and those who oppose the death penalty for any reason and wish to see their view become public policy.[2] For it seems inevitable that public policy will be derived from the assessment of the death penalty's deterrent effect. Therefore, even those who support or oppose the death penalty categorically for purely moral reasons, and for whom the question of deterrence is irrelevant, tend to argue their positions in terms of the ability or lack of ability of the death penalty to deter.[3] This has led to a situation in which the discussion of the death penalty has become—like the discussions of homosexuality, abortion, and pornography—a discussion in which both the proponents and opponents have raised to the level of high art the attempt to bypass logic and invent knowledge in order to make reality congruent with wish.

Those who would deny the ability of the death penalty to deter almost invariably invoke a line of reasoning founded on two errors. They argue, quite correctly, that the murderer often acts out of irrational motivations and conclude, incorrectly, that this somehow indicates that the death penalty does not deter. The two errors are:

(1) concluding that the death penalty does not deter those who have not murdered from the fact that it has not deterred those who have murdered. It is not necessary to demonstrate that the death penalty has not deterred the murderer. Of course it hasn't; by definition, the murderer is one who has not been deterred by the death penalty or anything else. *The crucial question is not what deterred the murderer (nothing did—that's why he or she became a murderer), but what deterred those who were deterred (i.e., not the murderer, but the rest*

of us). This, incidentally, makes clear the error of the argument that claims that the fact that many murderers think they will not be caught (so that they do not care what the penalty is) demonstrates that punishment does not deter. Unless one wants to be committed to the silly argument that murderers differ from nonmurderers only in that they think they won't be caught, he or she must ask what deters those who feel that they wouldn't be caught if they did murder, but who *don't* murder.

(2) the assumption that acts motivated by passion are immune to deterrence by the threat of penalty. This assumption is merely *asserted,* despite the fact that it runs counter to all human experience. It is true by definition, as we have just seen, that acts not deterred by the threat of penalty are not deterred by the threat of penalty. But every day millions of people feel anger; something prevents nearly all of them from murdering to satisfy their anger. *There is, in other words, no reason to assume that the penalty for murder plays no role in deterring those who feel murderous feelings but do not murder; nor is there reason to assume that there is no one who is deterred by the threat of execution who would not have been deterred by a lesser penalty.* As we shall see, the increased deterrent effect of increased penalty need not imply any conscious calculation on the part of the potential criminal; the difference between a lesser and greater deterrence may exert its influence over the long term by emphasizing the seriousness of the criminal act and increasing the strength of the internalized resistance to that act.

Until the opponents of the death penalty can offer an alternative theoretical explanation of what deters the rest of us, it is unlikely that the assertion that the death penalty does not deter will be very persuasive. One need not, of course, accept an element as a "causal" factor simply because he cannot offer an alternative explanation, but when he denies an explanation that is both in accord with common sense and persuasive, it behooves him, if he cannot present an equally persuasive alternative explanation, to demonstrate that the element that is presented as the causal factor he denies cannot be the causal factor.[4] Opponents of the death penalty implicitly acknowledge this when they attempt to demonstrate that the death penalty is not a factor causing a lower murder rate (i.e., when they attempt to demonstrate that the death penalty does not deter).

For example, these opponents have pointed out, quite correctly, that some societies that do not invoke the death penalty have lower murder rates than some that do, and have implied that this fact somehow demonstrates that the death penalty does not deter. It does not. The fact that society A has no death penalty and a murder rate half that of society B (which does invoke the death penalty) can just as legitimately, but no more legitimately, be interpreted as demonstrating that the death penalty does deter and that if society B did *not* invoke the death penalty it would have a murder rate of, say, four times that of society A. One might, in other words, argue that the very factors that generate the high murder rate in society B necessitate the use of the death penalty. This is seen more clearly if we consider what would happen if we invoked the death penalty for all individuals who commit murder, except nuns. We would find that nuns had a far lower murder rate than did the rest of the population; and even though they comprised the only group that was not threatened with the death penalty, this can hardly be argued to demonstrate that the death penalty does not deter. (If we had the death penalty *only* for nuns, we would find that nuns had a lower murder rate; this can hardly be argued to demonstrate that it does deter.) Here, in our case, it is obvious that the determinative factor is the internalized social values of the individuals and the strength with which the values have been internalized and not (primarily) the presence or absence of the death penalty. We should note, however, that the fact that another factor (in this case the values that activate or obstruct murderous behavior) is a greater influence on the murder rate than is the presence or absence of the death penalty in no way affects our discussion of the death penalty, nor does it indicate that the death penalty does not deter; the question is whether fewer members of the general population commit murder when they are socialized in the presence of the death penalty than when they are not and whether fewer nuns commit murder when *they* are socialized in the presence of the death penalty than when *they* are not and not whether other factors deter. In other words, if the death penalty does deter, the fact that other factors are more effective in inculcating a strong resistance to socially forbidden behavior is irrelevant and will be unless it can be demonstrated that these other factors could reduce the murder rate to zero.

Criminologists have attempted to eliminate the problem of contaminating factors by using statistics on American states, sections of states, and regions for comparisons of every conceivable combination of factors. However, while some comparisons have increased our understanding of the relative importance of various factors to murder rates (as in their demonstration of the immense importance of differing regional values to differing murder rates), I think that they encounter a problem that is insurmountable, particularly if the suggestion of how capital punishment might deter advanced in this essay is correct. All of these American states and areas are in a society that has traditionally emphasized the importance of the prohibition of murder by invoking the death penalty, and this emphasis may well have been internalized even by the populations of those states that have not invoked it. It is likely that the majority of Americans do not even know whether their respective states have the death penalty. What they do know— through movies, television, and stories—is that being convicted of murder is associated with hanging and electrocution. The crucial question is whether, for a marginal group of people, this association has engendered an internal resistance to the emotional and environmental incentives to murder that is sufficient to deter while an association of murder and life imprisonment would not have been sufficient.

The question of whether the death penalty deters, whether execution of the murderer prevents some people from murdering while a lesser punishment of the murderer does not, is an empirical question. I do not think that any of the empirical studies concluding that the death penalty does not deter have avoided the difficuties I have mentioned. I do not wish here to present an empirical argument claiming that the death penalty does deter. I wish to present a theoretical explanation of how the death penalty deters *if* the death penalty does deter. To be sure, if someone does present empirical evidence that overcomes the difficulties I have mentioned and that does indicate that the death penalty does not deter, then these theoretical considerations are worthless. (There is little that is of less use than a theoretical explanation of a nonexistent empirical reality.) But I would suggest that in the absence of such empirical evidence the theoretical considerations do make it seem most plausible that the death penalty does deter and that, for the reason given in footnote 4, the burden of "proof" falls on those who argue that capital punishment does not deter.

A determinative factor affecting the degree to which murder will be committed in any given society may be the strength with which the value prohibiting murder is inculcated in the society's individual members, and this strength may be a function of the penalty with which the society backs up the value. It may be that individuals give values an internal weight concomitant with the weight they perceive the value as being given by their society, and this perception may judge the weight given to the value by the society in terms of—among other things—the weight of the penalty with which the society backs up the value. This seems a reasonable explanation of why and how most individuals develop an internal resistance to murder that is sufficiently strong to deter them from acting on the basis of the emotional forces (such as anger) and the environmental forces (such as poverty) that encourage murder.

I cannot stress strongly enough that there need be no element of rational calculation on the part of the individual for us to accept the deterrent capacity of the death penalty.[5] The death penalty deters—if it does deter—not because the potential murderer weighs the potential murder against the penalty and decides that life imprisonment would be a cheap price to pay but execution is too high a price. He is deterred by the death penalty—*if* he is deterred by the death penalty—because he has perceived, from childhood on, that murder is the most serious of social offenses.[6] He has accepted this assessment of the seriousness of murder and has internalized it because (among other reaons) his society has emphasized the importance of this value by penalizing it with a penalty stronger than that which it imposes for any other crime.[7] The death penalty deters—if it does deter—primarily by deterring today's child from becoming tomorrow's murderer; it deters—if it does deter—by engendering in today's child a resistance to murder that prevents him from ever seriously *considering* murder in the behavioral calculations he makes as an adult.

There is no reason to believe that the internal resistance is inoperative when the incentive for murder is emotional rather than environmental. When most people feel extreme anger they yell, or punch a refrigerator, or stifle their anger. Most people do not invoke murder in the service of their passions; their internal resistance to murder is sufficient to deflect their passions to a permitted object. In some cases the strong sanction prevents the individual from consciously considering the environmental possibility, or feeling the emotion, that would serve as incentive for murder, while in other cases the sanction channels consciously considered possibility or felt emotion into nonmurderous behavior; in either case the sanction is responsible, in some individuals, for the prevention of murder. If this is all correct, if one develops a stronger resistance to committing murder when there is the death penalty than when there is not, if the additional strength of resistance thus engendered prevents some people from murdering, then we are justified in believing that the death penalty deters, and that it deters crimes of passion as well as rational crimes.

We might see this more clearly if we consider shoplifting rather than murder: The two-year-old who spies a bit of shiny costume jewelry will "shoplift" without guilt; he is unaware of the negative social sanction on such behavior. The four-year-old child, who is aware from previous observation and experience that shoplifting is considered bad, will consciously weigh alternatives before deciding whether or not to shoplift the jewelry. The twelve-year-old child, who has fully internalized the values and sanctions relevant to shoplifting, will (in most cases and most of the time) not even consider stealing the jewelry. For the twelve-year-old shoplifting is not, as it is for the four-year-old, a question of weighing satisfactions against penalties. In most cases, most of the time, *the thought and possibility of shoplifting do not even enter the twelve-year-old's mind.*

Observation and experience certainly seem to justify the conclusion that the degree to which children internalize the value against shoplifting is, *ceteris paribus,* a function of the severity of the negative sanction (be it formal punishment or a harsh word). Mild sanction, such as verbal parental disapproval, will be sufficient; these children will reach the point where the thought of shoplifting will seldom even enter their minds. But there will be some children who will not sufficiently internalize the value of the importance of the value against shoplifting if it is not supported by physical punishment, while they will sufficiently internalize the value if physical punishment emphasizes the importance of the value.[8] Can this not all be said of murder and capital punishment as well as of shoplifting and physical punishment and of the adults children become as well as of the children?

It is worth noting that if the death penalty does deter in the manner described here (i.e., if the death penalty increases the strength with which the social sanction is internalized and if rational calculation is of no relevance), then we would not (necessarily) expect the abolition of capital punishment to engender an immediate increase in the murder rate. The increase would not be expected to begin until the new generation (those socialized in the absence of the death penalty) reached adolescence.

If our description of the way in which individuals develop the resistance to emotional and environmental factors encouraging murder is correct, society inculcates in the individual the value prohibiting murder (or any other value) on the basis of its "saying" (through its severe punishment) that the value is a very important one and *not* primarily through the *immediate threat* of punishment. One might argue that threat is always the initiator in the development of the individual's perception of the strength of a value, and this might well be correct, but it is important to note that this is very different from the assertion that threat deters at the time of the act. We who do not murder refrain from murdering because of the strength of the internalized value that one does not murder and not because the present threat of punishment is so great that present fear of punishment precludes our committing the murderous act.

Thus, the fact that some pickpockets picked pockets at the public hanging of pickpockets, a fact often cited as if it demonstrated the inability of the death penalty to deter, demonstrates only that some individuals who have chosen to become pickpockets will not be deterred by the death penalty. It does not even demonstrate that no pickpockets were deterred (but only that not all were, a fact no one doubts). But even if we grant that *no* pickpocket will be deterred by the death penalty we have granted only that the *pickpocket* (i.e., the person who has already chosen to be a pickpocket) has not been deterred. The important point is that the pickpocket story avoids the central question: Does the execution of pickpockets, public or private, reduce the number of people who choose to become pickpockets? *If* it does, *if* fewer people become pickpockets when pickpockets are hanged than when they are not, then we can conclude that the death penalty does deter. We can conclude that, *ceteris paribus,* the death penalty caused a marginal group of individuals to develop an internal resistance to pickpocketing that was sufficiently strong to deter them from pickpocketing at all (i.e., from becoming pickpockets), while a lesser penalty would *not* have caused them to develop a sufficiently strong internal resistance. We can conclude that we refrain from committing crimes because (among other reasons) we *feel* that the crimes are too bad to justify our committing them and that the strength of this feeling is a function of the strength of the penalty. (I have no idea whether the number of pickpockets decreases or not when pickpockets are hanged, but neither do the people who invoke this irrelevant fact about hangings and assume, with no justification, the conclusion they claim to be proving.)

The argument I have presented does not distinguish between the emotional forces that motivate an individual to murder and the environmental forces that encourage murder; I can see no *a priori* reason to assume that the mechanism responsible for the development of the internal resistance to the passions that encourage murder is different from the mechanism responsible for the development of the internal resistance to the environmental forces that encourage murder. I see no reason to assume that the mechanism responsible for one's resisting the impulse to murder out of anger is different from the mechanism that is responsible for one's resisting the incentive to murder for profit. However, if one wishes to treat these separately, nothing that I have presented need be altered. The psychiatrist who is interested in the emotions that, as Freud tells us, would "murder even for trifles" must ask why the vast majority of people possess internal resistances to such emotions sufficient to dissuade them from acting on the emotions;[9] he must ask whether there exists a marginal group of people who develop an internal resistance that is sufficiently strong to keep them from murdering when the seriousness of murder is societally emphasized by the death penalty, but who do not develop a sufficiently strong resistance when society does not so emphasize the offensiveness of the act.[10] The sociologist, who is more interested in the environmental forces that encourage murder, must ask why most people resist such environmental incentives to murder (why, for example, most poor people do not murder);[11] he must ask whether there exists a marginal group

38 When Wish Replaces Thought

of people equivalent to the one just mentioned.

It is worth noting that an objection to the death penalty that rests on the heinous possibility of the execution of an innocent person can be seen to reduce to the dubious objection against "murder" by the state: Those who raise this objection acknowledge that the number of innocent people who are executed is infinitesimal when compared to, say, the sixty thousand people per year we are willing to sacrifice in order to have the automobile. Those who raise this objection distinguish between automobile deaths and the loss of innocent people that, given human fallibility, will accompany the administration of the death penalty, by invoking the fact that only in the latter case does the *state* take the innocent life. But this acknowledges that the objection is not the loss of innocent people (which they accept in exchange for the automobile), but the loss of innocent people in which the state takes an active role. Thus, this objection is, in reality, the objection against "murder" by the state (in this case the "murder" of those mistakenly convicted and executed). This objection is as silly as an objection that the state's incarceration of the kidnaper is "kidnaping" by the state. Certain state acts—such as the execution of political dissidents—are unquestionably *morally* reprehensible, but such acts are not murder if they conform to set state laws prohibiting murder; "murder" can have no legal meaning other than "*illegal* killing," so "murder by the state" is a contradiction in terms when the state is legally permitted to execute the person who is executed. (An administration's imposition of execution that ignored legally required mechanisms would, of course, be murder.)

I do not know whether the death penalty deters, but I do know that it makes sense that it would and that the arguments attempting to demonstrate that it does are not unpersuasive. Given the nature of a modern society with its heterogeneity infusing every aspect of social life and its encouragement of diversity and freedom of speech, it does not seem likely that, save perhaps the society in the throes of religious or revolutionary rebirth, any society will ever again be able to count on the strength of a single shared cultural and familial authority to maintain even the minimal amount of social control necessary for a society to survive. If we cannot rely on shared values and familial authority as the sole sources of social control it behooves us to understand the mechanisms that serve to permit society to survive. Such understanding is rendered impossible if we categorically assume the correctness of an explanation that may well be incorrect. This is what we do when we assert the inability of the death penalty to deter.

I suspect that we would all *like* to believe that the death penalty does not deter. This relieves us of the weight of a moral decision. The strength of human reaction reflects perceived proximity, and most of us feel the responsibility inherent in supporting the execution of real murderers more intensely than the responsibility for a hypothetical group of victims who—if the death penalty does deter—will be murdered if our opposition to the death penalty prevails but who will not be murdered if our opposition fails and the death penalty is maintained.[12] Our seeming sympathy may well be an act of moral cowardice, an acceptance of a position that caters to fears of potential guilt rather than to responsibility to real, if unnamable, people. For if the proponent of the death penalty is incorrect in his assumption that the death penalty deters and is successful in his efforts to convince his society to invoke the death penalty, he is responsible "merely" for the deaths of guilty individuals who, if deterrence is the rationale for execution, should not be executed. If the opponent of the death penalty, on the other hand, is incorrect in his assumption that the death penalty does not deter and is successful in his efforts to convince his society to refrain from invoking the death penalty, *he* is responsible for the deaths of *innocent* people. Moreover, the number of innocent people who would not have been murdered if the deterrent of the death penalty had been invoked will be far greater than the number of innocent people who could conceivably be executed as a result of the mistaken conviction of innocent individuals for crimes they did not commit in a society that invokes the death penalty—and considerably greater, in all probability, than the total number of individuals who will be executed (guilty plus executed by mistaken conviction) in a society that invokes the death penalty. An awareness of this reduces considerably the persuasiveness of the position that argues that since we do not know whether the death penalty deters we should not invoke it.[13]

A Theoretical Postscript

The strength with which values are internalized is a determinant of the degree to which members of a society resist pressures leading to the commission of crime (educational and economic discrimination, for example). It would seem time to discuss the crimes committed by members of oppressed economic and racial groups in more penetrating terms than those utilized in the superficial observation that poverty fathers crime. Poverty does, under certain conditions, father crime, of course, and the pressures leading to the commission of crime are far greater for the members of these groups than they are for members of groups for which the rewards of crime are available through legitimate means and in whose members the mechanisms that strengthen an individual's internal defenses against the emotional and environmental factors generating crime are more strongly represented. As long as some of the members of oppressed groups feel that they are outcasts in American society, some of the members of these groups will fail to internalize the prohibitions against crime that are inculcated in the other members of the society. But if the commission of murder is the victory of the environmental factors and the emotional forces that encourage murder over the internal forces that reflect social prohibition for every other group, then it is for members of these groups also, and our ignoring this is to treat the members of these groups as irredeemably alien as well as to limit our understanding. Without question the external factors encouraging crime and the internal anger they generate are infinitely greater for blacks than for whites, but other groups in other societies, and blacks in former times in our own, have been equally oppressed, and yet they did not always have high crime rates. Indeed, even now the overwhelming majority of blacks do not commit crimes, despite the fact that they suffer the same outrages as do those who do commit crimes. This all suggests that crimes committed by blacks, like those committed by every other group, reflect not only the external factors encouraging crime and the anger that such factors engender, but the nature of the values of the group itself and the strength of the mechanisms by which the group inculcates its values in its members—mechanisms that are the same for blacks as they are for every other group. It should be remembered that, whatever the fears and fantasies of the white majority, the overwhelming number of victims of black crime are blacks, and it is they who are suffering as we pretend that it is only factors that are external to the black group that contribute to black crime.

The predictable response to the *Moynihan Report* on the black family was the fallacious attempt at refutation that argued that most black families were not female-headed. This was, of course, true, but it misses the point of the report—which is that a far larger number of black families are female-headed than are white families. In every society it is an adult male who serves as the threat and the model by which internal resistance to the external and internal pressures encouraging crime is developed in the maturing male. If these pressures are greater for the black than for the white, it is especially important that the methods by which black resistance can be strengthened be discovered. To the extent, and it is a very great extent, that external factors encourage black crime and weaken the development of internal resistance, these external factors must be changed (as, for example, by reducing economic discrimination and those factors that encourage the deterioration of the black family), but to the extent that it is black values that contribute to the weakening of the internal resistance to the pressures encouraging crime in individual blacks it is only blacks who can bring change. It seems to me that only the black nationalists have understood all of this fully and have seen that, for example, to deny the pathological effects of the absence of the father from many black families (that is, the effect of increasing crime by weakening the forces that engender a strong internal resistance to crime) is to argue that blacks develop this resistance in some other way than do all other human beings and that, therefore, they are not human.

A Legal Postscript

One might argue that, even if the death penalty does deter, it is unjust in that, in practice, it is invoked primarily for the lower economic classes or for racial minority groups. If the members of middle- and upper-class groups are executed less often for the commission of the same crimes for which members of the oppressed groups are executed, then this is patently unjust, but it is an injustice that should be corrected not by abolishing the death penalty (it is equally unjust to put the former in prison for ten years while putting the latter in prison for life), but by equalizing the punishment. This seems to be the reasoning invoked by most of the justices of the Supreme Court in a recent decision on the death penalty. Indeed, it would seem the only possible justification for considering as "cruel and unusual" a punishment that was accepted and common when the Eighth Amendment was written and that is still favored, I assume, by a majority of the population. (If it is not so favored, then the legal question is academic; even if the death penalty does deter, it will not, and should not, be invoked if a majority manifests its moral abhorrence in legislation banning it; the question of whether it is "cruel and unusual" becomes irrelevant.) Thus the Court-imposed moratorium on capital punishment would have seemed to have been justified when the death penalty is unfairly imposed and when there is doubt about where the public stands (though one might argue that the Court must assume that present public opinion is reflected in present laws no matter how old such laws are as long as such laws are fairly applied), but one would be hard put to find a justification for a future Court's ruling that the death penalty, fairly imposed and based on recent legislation, was "cruel and unusual."

If members of lower-class groups are executed more often than members of the middle- or upper-class groups, but only in proportion to the greater number of capital crimes they commit, then there are a number of ways in which this fact can be viewed, but, while these views will differ on whether the situation is just or unjust, none is a strong argument for the abolition of the death penalty on theoretical grounds. If the crimes that are punished by death can reasonably be argued to be more serious than those that are not (violent murders as opposed to embezzlement, for example) and if equally serious middle- and upper-class crimes (treason, for example) are also punishable by death—if, in other words, capital crimes are not capital crimes merely because they are crimes committed by the lower class—and if all individuals who commit these crimes are treated equally, then, in a narrow sense, no injustice is present. However, one might argue that this situation is unjust in the wider sense that the groups that commit these crimes do so as a result of environmental forces over which they have no control. To a point this is unquestionably correct. However, such an environmentalist view is sustainable only if carried all the way through to describe all punishment of all types. It is to argue that all punishment is unjust because it assumes free will when there is none. Correct or incorrect, this view is perfectly logical, but no society could predicate its legal system on the central deterministic assumption; for even if all crime is in reality completely determined, i.e., even if there is no free will, the view of crime held by the members of the society (i.e., whether criminal acts are seen as the result of free will or as the effect of only deterministic factors) will be a crucial factor in determining the amount of future crime. Thus, whether or not there is, in reality, free will, the societal view of whether or not there is free will will be a monumentally important factor affecting human behavior and the amount of future crime.

NOTES

1. In testing this hypothesis we must define "internal resistance" in terms independent of the act of murder. It would be tautological to use as evidence for the claim that A

had a stronger internal resistance to murder than did B the fact that A did not murder in a situation in which B did murder. There are many such independent measures (for example, psychological tests of "strength of conscience," "superego development," "social concern," and the like.

2. Three oft-heard arguments can be seen to reduce, in all respects relevant to this essay, to one or the other arguments referred to in the opening paragraph. (1) The argument that the death penalty is bad because it "creates a climate of violence" or "reduces the value put on life by members of society" is either (A) arguing that the death penalty does not deter (indeed, that it *increases* the murder rate) or (B) arguing that the death penalty "reduces the value put on life" or "creates a climate of violence" in some sense that is not reflected in the murder rate and that, therefore, it is bad even if it does deter. I must admit that I have never understood in what sense the death penalty could be said to "reduce the value put on life" or "create a climate of violence" if it does deter or why anyone would care if the value put on life were reduced (or if there were an increase in the climate of violence) if this did not mean that there was, in fact, more violence. (2) The argument that the death penalty is good for the retributive reason that it reasserts the moral, social, or legal order is arguing that an eye must be taken for an eye and that the death penalty is good even if it does not deter. I must admit that I have never understood in what sense retribution could be said to reassert the moral, legal, and social order if the retribution does not even deter or why anyone would care if the moral, legal, or social order were reasserted if reassertion does not have even the empirical result of deterrence. (3) The argument that the death penalty is good because it supports the desire of a member of the society that, if he is murdered, society will avenge the injustice he suffered by meting out (what he sees as) justice is (in respects relevant to this essay) arguing that an eye must be taken for an eye.

3. Two important points of usage: (1) "Deterrence" refers to the ability of a penalty to prevent *others* from taking an action; it does not refer to the deterrence of the person being penalized from taking such action in the future. In this chapter I assume that the alternative to the death penalty is life imprisonment—under conditions that would preclude the person being penalized from again taking the prohibited action (murder, kidnaping, etc.). (2) I do not like the jargonistic-sounding "positive sanction" and "negative sanction," but the connotations of these terms are more desirably inclusive than are "reward" and "punishmnent" (which, while arguably denotatively the same as the terms I use, connote relatively more formal sanctions).

4. It is, in general, true that since most empirical variables are not closely "caus-ally" related, the burden of "proof" is on one who claims a close relationship between two variables. This is, however, a rule of plausibility and not a rule of logic. It is important to keep the difference in mind when we consider the argument (made by those who deny that the death penalty deters) that places the burden of "proof" on those who claim that the death penalty deters. The burden of "proof" would be on those who claim that the increase from life imprisonment to death does *not* have the effect that every lesser increase has.

5. Those who are temporarily or permanently mentally disturbed have impulses and desires that are, quantitatively or qualitatively, different from those of most other people. But there is no evidence against, and much evidence for, the belief that such people are affected by the early internalization of the prohibitions we have discussed. The psychotic murderer, like the normal person who murders, has, of course, failed to sufficiently inter-nalize the prohibition against murder. But, again, this proves only what need not be proved (because it is true by definition); the murderer is one who was not deterred from mur-

dering. The question is: What deters those, psychotic or normal, who *are* deterred?

6. I assume here that we are considering the usual situation (murder for profit, for example) in which the seriousness of the crime as represented by the possible punishment of the death penalty is complemented by the other elements that lead to an individual's accepting the importance of the value and giving it this weight. If other factors tend to counteract this process—if, for example, murder in a particular society is punishable by death, but murder of a wife's lover is traditionally considered virtually justified—then the members of the society will not, despite the presence of the death penalty, resist the pressures to commit this crime with the strength with which they resist crimes in which the presence of the death penalty is complemented by other factors tending to emphasize the seriousness with which the society views the crime. (In this essay I ignore a number of other considerations that are important in any empirical assessment of the deterrence. For example, it must be remembered that "murder" is socially defined—killing is the act—and one society might define a particular type of killing as "murder" while another will not. Likewise, one society's murder rate might be far more accurately reported than another's. Such considerations are of practical importance in testing the hypothesis that the death penalty deters and in assessing the theoretical points made in this essay, but they are irrelevant to the hypotheses and theoretical points themselves.)

7. It is possible, of course, that this reasoning is all correct, but that one weighs internalized values only in relative terms so that the internal resistance to the emotions that would utilize murder (and to the environmental factors that encourage murder) would be equally strong if life imprisonment were the most severe penalty invoked by the society. Or it is possible that absolute severity is crucial, but that it is so only up to a maximal threshold (ten years' imprisonment, for example) past which the individual's internal resistance no longer increases its strength. However, one is not justified in *assuming* that either of these possibilities in reality obtains.

8. There is, of course, a third category of children (those who will shoplift whether there is physical punishment or not). There is even a fourth category, children who will shoplift *only* if there is physical punishment (because, for whatever psychological reason in any given case, these children are attracted to the punishment). If the fourth category were larger than the second (i.e., if more were attracted than deterred by physical punishment) this would be identifiable from the fact that shoplifting would be *positively* correlated with physical punishment and no one would argue in favor of physical punishment as a deterrent. However, for the reason given in footnote 9, it is highly unlikely that more are attracted than deterred by an increase in punishment. (In theory, one could impose physical punishment only for category 2 individuals, but this is both impossible until such individuals can be identified, but this would be impermissible in a democratic society.)

9. Throughout this essay I have assumed that if the death penalty deters, then the number of people who are deterred is greater than the number of people who are *encouraged*. I think that all human experience indicates that punishment in general deters a greater number of people than it encourages. (Whether the death penalty is in this respect like all other punishment is the question of the deterrent capacity of the death penalty. However, the psychiatrists are no doubt correct in arguing that there are some people who are encouraged, even if the psychiatrists tend to overestimate the numbers of such people because such people are so overrepresented among the psychiatrists' patients. If such people do equal in number those who are deterred, then, of course, the death penalty does not deter. This will be reflected in the empirical evidence that would demonstrate that the murder rate is not reduced by the death penalty. Thus, this psychiatric argument against the death penalty is, at bottom, an empirical assertion that the death penalty encourages more people

than it discourages and that, therefore, the death penalty increases the murder rate. It is on this prediction that the psychiatric argument rests.

10. One could, logically, but most implausibly, argue that all individuals have internal resistances of identical strength and that individuals differ only in the strength of the forces (emotional or environmental) that motivate them to murder. However, logical or not, this view is too implausible to warrant serious consideration; clearly some people have stronger consciences or stronger superegos than others.

11. See "A Theoretical Postscript" for a discussion of the role of environmental pressures leading to murder.

12. Motivation has, of course, nothing to do with correctness of argument. But it is often the opponents of the death penalty who introduce the issue of motivation—without, I suspect, realizing that an examination of motivation casts more doubt on the goodness of the motivations of the opponent of the death penalty than on those of the proponent. This becomes clear when we consider the question frequently asked of the proponent by the opponent: would *you* "pull the switch." Now the proponent might well answer that he would not pull the switch; nor would he shoot a man who was about to kill a small child. The fact that he *could* not perform an act is not sufficient to demonstrate that the act *should not* be performed by someone who is capable of performing the act. What the opponent's demand that the proponent pull the switch *does* indicate is the psychological importance (to one's attitude toward the death penalty) of a fear of guilt. For if the proponent is one who would have difficulty pulling the switch (as any human being should), the opponent is often one who does not merely have difficulty, but whose position on the death penalty is determined by the source of this difficulty: the fear of guilt. This is not surprising; a fear of guilt is far more easily elicited by picturing a murderer about to be executed than by trying to picture a statistical group of people who will—if the death penalty does deter—be murdered if there is no death penalty but who will not be murdered if there is a death penalty.

13. One might argue: *(a)* that no matter how great a likelihood we may someday be able to attach to the *hypothesis* that the death penalty deters, the death penalty necessitates the *certain, tangible* deaths of *specific* individuals; *(b)* that *ipso facto,* the lives of these individuals must be given priority over the lives of the members of a *hypothetical* group of *unknown* individuals who will, in all probability, be murdered if the death penalty is not invoked (but who will, in all probability, not be murdered if the death penalty is invoked); and *(c)* that the certainty of the deaths resulting from the death penalty (that is, executions) morally precludes our invoking capital punishment no matter how much larger the *hypothetical* group than the group comprised of the executed, and despite the fact that the hypothetical group is comprised of innocent individuals while the group of the executed is comprised almost entirely of guilty individuals. This argument can be seen to be either irrelevant to this essay or unsatisfactory even if we disregard the distinction between guilty and innocent individuals. For one who so argues will be forced either: *(a)* (if he argues that certainty must *always* take priority) to deny the acceptability of every military action—in which case his argument is virtually identical with the moral assertion that the state may never take a life, a position that renders irrelevant the question of deterrence, but one that both leaves him responsible for the murders that deterrence would have prevented (if the death penalty does deter) and fails to convince anyone who rejects its moral assertion; or *(b)* (if he is not willing to take the pacifist position and is not willing to argue that certainty always takes priority over probability) to admit that the death penalty will be justified if our future knowledge does enable us to attach to the hypothesis that the death penalty deters a probability equal to that for which he would

consider a military action justified even though such an action accepts *certain* deaths as justified by the probability that more lives are ultimately saved. If he takes this latter position he is merely saying that the death penalty is not *now* justified because the evidence does not *presently* allow us to attach to the hypothesis that the death penalty deters a high enough probability to morally justify our invoking the death penalty; he would have to admit that someday we may be able to attach a high enough probability to justify its invocation and that the death penalty is not, *ipso facto,* immoral. This is, incidentally, the position I take. I would not consider the (admittedly very forceful) argument that only God has the right to deny the possibility of worldly redemption (a denial inherent in the invocation of the death penalty) sufficiently strong to justify our ignoring a high probability that by refusing to invoke the death penalty we are condemning innocent people to death.

3

What Is Normal?
The Question of Homosexuality

The twentieth-century mind is cast in the mold of empiricism. Perhaps empiricism has not succeeded in actually severing the moral from the scientific, but it has driven in a wedge so deep that by now the modern mind's propensity for distinguishing between the two is virtually intuitive. Whether we delight in the feeling or abhor it, many of us do feel that the very nature of moral questions precludes the possibility that moral statements can have the persuasive force possessed either by statements of a purely logical nature or by statements susceptible to empirical falsification. Invocation of moral assertion is not sufficient to persuade a mind that traces a moral conclusion back to its beginnings and finds a subjective premise that seems to expose the moral argument as an exercise in subjectivity.

To be sure, there are many philosophers who object to the empiricist distinction. They stress our inability to construct a criterion that clearly demarcates the scientific from the moral. However, while the philosophers who offer these and similar arguments often argue that analysis of scientific statements to their fine structure will expose buried normative assumptions, they do not, for the most part, argue for the possibility of an objective morality. Most philosophers argue only for the impossibility of a truly objective science. They too feel the power of the empiricist arguments and refrain from claiming natural justifications for moral conclusions.

This has led to a rather peculiar situation. Today the arbitrary feeling of moral arguments causes many people not merely to refrain from making moral arguments, but from even suggesting that scientific considerations can be relevant to assessments of behavior. There is, for example, a tendency, particularly pronounced in sociology and the popular educated press, for denying that the concept of normality can be anything more than a manifestation of arbitrary social, moral, or individual values. This view sees our terming "abnormal" any behavior that is not clearly destructive or self-destructive as having no meaning other than that we dislike the behavior. It sees rationalization of prejudice and discrimination not merely as a misuse of the designation "abnormal," but as its only purpose.

Now, no one would deny that an assessment of behavior as "abnormal" is not a purely scientific endeavor. Science is the attempt to find general empirical relationships, and no assessment of normality is necessary or possible. But to acknowledge this is very different from accepting the completely arbitrary nature of an assessment of normality. Scientific considerations alone cannot assess the normality of a behavior, but any assessment of the normality of a behavior must, for reasons we shall soon examine, rest on an understanding of the causes of the behavior. An assessment of normality is like a scientific question in that the causation of the behavior to be assessed is determinative to an assessment of the normality or abnormality of the behavior; it is unlike a scientific question in that an assessment must be made. The assertion that the assessment is arbitrary, that it is rooted only in subjective values, ignores the former consideration.

HOMOSEXUAL BEHAVIOR

Consider homosexual behavior. The prevailing view is stated in rather pure form by historian Martin Duberman:

> The deepest morass is found in discussion of the "causes" of homosexuality. Much of the scientific literature concentrates on this question, though homosexuals, sensibly, are learning to eschew it as presently unanswerable, as a political tactic designed to perpetuate barbaric legal and social discriminations, and as a convenient intellectual outlet for heterosexual condescension. . . .
>
> Most scientists bring to their research a culturally derived model of normal behavior that influences the nature of their feelings. . . .
>
> The model is a moral, not a scientific construct—as even a cursory glance at cross-cultural data reveals. . . . [The] Judeo-Christian model of "normal" sexuality can hardly accommodate the evidence that Arab women in certain Red Sea areas take black female lovers, that among the Keraki anal intercourse is thought essential to the health and character of the growing boy, and that prominent Siwan men in Africa lend their sons to each other for purposes of sodomy.[1]

This reasoning is attractive to large numbers of people in a time when moral restraints on individual behavior are about as popular as shingles. It has been criticized primarily by those who invoke questionable assertions of nature's intent or moral arguments rooted in biblical injunction. Such criticisms fail to impress the modern mind, to say nothing of the modern mind with an emotional commitment to opposing them. Thus, whatever the logical inadequacy of the position that sees an assessment of homosexual behavior as abnormal as being nothing more than a statement of individual taste or social disapproval, the position has been sufficient, when couched in somewhat more sophisticated terms, to convince even a majority of the American Psychiatric Association.

However, it is worth noting that a poll of thousands of APA members taken after the APA vote found that two-thirds of those polled feel that homosexuality is a disorder. The difference between the original vote and the poll may merely reflect a theoretical distinction between two types of abnormality; if this is the case, then—despite the fact that the APA vote is invariably invoked as evidence that the members find homosexuality normal—the original vote did *not* indicate that the members considered homosexuality normal. More likely, the difference between the vote and the poll indicates, as Arno Karlen has suggested, that many members publicly argued that homosexuality is normal (and voted this way) while privately believing homosexuality to be abnormal.[2] Many members do, in fact, admit privately that they did this. They justify this in terms of humanitarianism. It used to be called lying.

"ABNORMAL" BEHAVIOR AND ABNORMAL CAUSES

The term "abnormal," as it is used by the general population and as it should be used by the psychiatrist, psychologist, sociologist, and philosopher, does *not* mean merely socially or morally unacceptable or statistically unusual. Robbing banks runs counter to social and moral norms and stamp collecting is statistically abnormal, but no one refers to these behaviors as "abnormal." While many could not articulate their meaning (they would use words like "strange," "screwy," and "unnatural"), when most people describe a behavior as "abnormal" they mean that the behavior springs from irrational sources, or to put their perception in one of a number of possible modern terms, they perceive the behavior as representing a displacement or mischanneling of emotions that generates a need that can be met only through behavior that forces one to suffer the unnecessary pain of social ostracism. (They do not mean that eliciting the ostracism must be the purpose of the behavior, but that the irrational need is sufficient to cause the individual to behave in ways that encounter social ostracism.) Thus, they do not call the behavior of the nearly nude African warrior "abnormal"; they understand that this behavior is explicable in terms of the values and sanctions of the warrior's society. They *do* call the behavior of the American who behaves similarly in Times Square "abnormal"; they sense that the causes of the American's behavior (the causal situation that engendered the needs that can be met only through inappropriate behavior, and the irrational needs themselves) are abnormal. To be sure, a society can incorrectly view a given behavior as flowing from abnormal causes (as with the society that sees left-handed behavior as abnormal), but the error lies in the incorrect perception of the behavior as having abnormal causes, not in the meaning of the term as the members of the society use it.

In arguing that a social assessment of homosexuality as abnormal is incorrect, virtually all of the homosexual spokesmen *assert* the very thing they must *demonstrate*. They assert that an assessment of homosexuality as abnormal is as unwarranted as a similar assessment of unpopular political behavior, a religious refusal to eat pork, or left-handed behavior. They ignore the fact that the crucial distinction between such behaviors and homosexual behavior is the normality of the causal factors that generate the behaviors. Unpopular political behavior is (usually) generated by a philosophical and intellectual worldview that is not in any psychological sense abnormal. A refusal to eat pork is the result of socialization by the religious subgroup into which one was born. The tendency to use the left hand is owing to physiological and experiential factors that cannot reasonably be termed "abnormal" in any but the statistical sense. These behaviors have all at one time or another been strongly negatively sanctioned, forcing the individuals who manifested these behaviors to suffer the pain of social ostracism. But these behaviors were not psychologically abnormal, though they were incorrectly assessed as such by society, because their causes were not in any sense psychologically abnormal. The pain of negative sanction was not in these cases "unnecessary," but was, given the incorrect social assessment, an unavoidable result of behavior that was rooted in normal situations that did not engender a mischanneling or displacement of emotions. Homosexuality is not, in the case of the large majority of American homosexuals, rooted in intellectual belief or social values; the biographies of nearly all homosexuals speak of a childhood awareness of the propensity.

The homosexual spokesman argues, in effect, that homosexuality is analogous to left-handedness. If he is correct, if homosexuality is the result of an interplay of physiological and environmental factors that can reasonably be seen as normal, then he is quite correct in saying that homosexuality is normal and that society is terribly wrong in its assumption that homosexuality is abnormal.[3]

But the homosexual spokesman cannot merely assert that this is the case. For necrophiliac behavior, like homosexual behavior, is seen as abnormal by society. Necrophiliac behavior, like homosexual behavior, is negatively sanctioned by society. Necrophiliac behavior, like homosexual behavior, is not inherently (i.e. regardless of social sanction) destructive or self-destructive. Necrophiliac behavior, like homosexual behavior, is (I assume) found in many or all societies. (For some reason many people seem to feel that, if a behavior is present in other societies or other species, that somehow demonstrates its normality; they would never make this argument for physical diseases.) Necrophiliac behavior, like homosexual behavior, is often seen by those manifesting it as being perfectly normal and as not being a source of unhappiness. Assuming that the homosexual spokesman would agree that necrophiliac behavior is abnormal in some sense other than merely that the society considers it such, clearly the spokesman's problem is that he must present us with a distinction between homosexuality and necrophilia that would permit us to consider the former as normal and the latter as abnormal.

NORMAL AND ABNORMAL DISTINCTIONS

The distinction cannot be one of those just enumerated, because they fail to distinguish one behavior from the other. The distinction that would be most plausible, and the criterion that we all tend intuitively to use anyway, is the normality of the cause. The spokesman must argue that homosexuality is normal because it flows from causes that can be considered normal, while necrophilia is abnormal because *it* flows from causes that must be considered abnormal. In other words, an assessment of the normality of the behavior must be based on an assessment of the normality of the cause.[4] The eschewal of questions of causation that Professor Duberman finds laudable would have the homosexual spokesman avoid the only procedure by which he could offer us a reason for assessing homosexuality as normal.

The central logical point of this essay should now be clear: the homosexual spokesman can challenge the *logical* adequacy of an assessment of homosexuality as "abnormal" *only* if he is willing to make this same argument against an assessment of necrophilia or coprophilia as "abnormal." I assume that he will not be willing to do this because, in doing this, he would sacrifice the last measure of reason. The homosexual spokesman's purpose is to demonstrate that homosexuality is normal; to do this he must distinguish between homosexuality and those behaviors (necrophilia/coprophilia) that no reasonable person could argue to be normal. He must, in other words, acknowledge that it is meaningful to call some behavior "abnormal"; and in so acknowledging, he surrenders the possibility of successfully challenging an assessment of "abnormality" on logical grounds. If he is to persuade anyone that homosexuality should be assessed as normal, he must demonstrate that there is an empirical difference (in cause or function, for example) between homosexuality and necrophilia/coprophilia sufficient to justify our assessing homosexuality as normal and necrophilia/coprophilia as abnormal.

Now, here it must be acknowledged that—because any assessment of normality has the nonscientific component we have discussed, and because the normality of a behavior must be assessed on the basis of the normality of the cause (our reason for terming left-handed behavior "normal" and necrophiliac behavior "abnormal")—the homosexual spokesman can, with logical impunity, accuse my entire argument of being tautologous and of invoking a Platonist idea of normality. He can argue that the nonempirical component of an assessment of the normality of the cause of a behavior makes my entire argument circular. But again, he can use this approach *only if he is willing to deny the meaningfulness of an assessment of abnormality for necrophilia and coprophilia on the same grounds.* I assume that he will not be willing to do this; to do this would be to surrender both reasonableness and the possibility of persuading anyone.[5] He is far better off surrendering the logical challenge and attempting to find an empirical distinction between homosexuality and necrophilia/coprophilia that justifies viewing the former as normal and the latter as abnormal.[6]

I do not, of course, mean to imply that homosexuality is morally, psychologically, or in any respect comparable to necrophilia and coprophilia other than in the logical sense invoked here; my point is merely that in the logical respects mentioned here the three are analogous, so that one cannot make these arguments for the normality of homosexuality unless one is willing to make them also for necrophilia and coprophilia.

I hasten to emphasize that I am not implying that any particular negative sanction is good or right. If a society permits one to eat popcorn and punishes the eating of peanuts with death, we would consider the latter sanction horrible. But we would still wish to know what factors were capable of engendering a motivation for eating peanuts that was so strong that one was willing to risk death. We would acknowledge that there was nothing inherently abnormal about eating peanuts (after all, we do it in our society and no one seems to be hurt by it); we would, however, no more accept the peanut-eater's claim that his death-defying behavior was a "mere alternative" than we would accept a similar explanation from an American who preferred dachshund to turkey. We would not assess the peanut-eating behavior as abnormal simply because the behavior was negatively sanctioned in the peanut eater's society. *Behavior is not abnormal simply because it is different and negatively sanctioned. (It may be moral and heroic.) But it is obvious that a behavior's being different and negatively sanctioned is not, as the example of necrophiliac behavior demonstrates, proof of its normality.* There is no question that our society has imposed on homosexuals burdens that are unconscionable even if, perhaps particularly if, society's assessment of abnormality is correct. But it is the very strength of the oppressive attitudes, unfortunate as they may well be, that forces us to ask *why* an individual behaves in a way that is so strongly punished and why he abjures the heterosexual behavior that is rewarded. It is on an answer to this question that an assessment of normality must be based.

ANTHROPOLOGICAL EVIDENCE

That the homosexual spokesmen are, on some level, aware of all this is clear from their invocation of the anthropological and physiological evidence. Now it is simply untrue that the Siwan, the ancient Greeks, or any other society positively sanctioned adult homosexual behavior equivalent to the homosexual behavior of the American homosexual. Positively sanctioned homosexual behavior is, in all societies, limited to a minority, to certain periods of life, or to highly defined rituals. But let us, for argument's sake, accept the assertion that there are societies in which general homosexual behavior is not negatively sanctioned. What does this prove? I am certainly willing to acknowledge that homosexual behavior is capable of giving pleasure, that people will satisfy their capacity for pleasure whenever the pleasurable behavior is not discouraged, and that in a society that did not discourage homosexual behavior, a large number of individuals would at least occasionally partake in the pleasures of such behavior. However, if there is one thing that the homosexual spokesman has demonstrated beyond a shadow of a doubt, it is that in America we do not positively sanction homosexual behavior. Thus the explanation (capacity for pleasure and positive sanction) of the homosexual behavior of the large majority of Siwan males (those who would not so behave if the behavior were negatively sanctioned) can no more apply to the homosexual behavior of the American than can the explanation that is perfectly satisfactory for the homosexual behavior of prisoners (the explanation that stresses an absence of women). Homosexual behavior in a society that negatively sanctions homosexual behavior must have some cause that is not only *not* positive sanction, but that is powerful enough to override negative sanction.

The reader might wonder whether my requiring the presence of negative social sanction for an assessment of abnormality—a requirement that is necessary but not sufficient (as the examples of unpopular political behavior and the negatively sanctioned eating of pork make clear)—does not leave us in the position of declaring all positively sanctioned behavior "normal." The simple answer is "yes"; positively sanctioned behavior may be dysfunctional, unjust, immoral, or cruel, but it seems to me that obfuscation is the only result of terming "abnormal" behavior that can be explained by positive sanction. The homosexual behavior of those Siwanese who would not behave homosexually if the behavior were negatively sanctioned is an example of behavior that cannot reasonably be termed "abnormal." Similarly, an individual's anti-black prejudice that reflects (but is no stronger than) a prejudice that permeates a culture cannot reasonably be termed "abnormal"; an individual's prejudice that is stronger than that which can be explained by the individual's social environment is abnormal in the terms we discuss.

There is also a more complex answer to the question: Do not my criteria declare all positively sanctioned behavior "normal?" I could argue that I leave open the possibility of other criteria that would assess as "abnormal" not only the negatively sanctioned behavior I discuss, but also some positively sanctioned behavior that my criterion leaves unassessed. As long as such alternative criteria find "abnormal" the negatively sanctioned behavior that meets my criterion, there is no logical objection to their also finding "abnormal" positively sanctioned behavior that my criterion does not assess. However, my preference is for accepting all positively sanctioned behavior as "normal" and attacking detestable positively sanctioned behavior (such as socially supported racism) on grounds of dysfunction, stupidity, and the like. To insist on calling detestable, positively sanctioned behavior "abnormal" strikes me as childishly attempting to load disliked behavior with every bad adjective, even those that do not apply.

THE CAUSATION OF HOMOSEXUALITY

There is still much that we do not know about the role of physiology in the causation of homosexuality. Many social scientists fail to understand that physiological causal factors are irrelevant to an assessment of normality unless the physiological factors are *sufficient* to explain the homosexuality (i.e., environment plays no important role). If this were the case, one *might* argue that homosexuality is analogous to left-handedness. The problem with this approach is that virtually all of the evidence argues against there being such a determinative physiological causal factor and I know of no researcher who believes that such a *determinative* factor exists. All of the recent neuroendocrinological evidence indicating the role of physiological factors indicates that such factors play a predisposing, not a determinative, role.

It is far more likely that there are physiological factors that play a pre-dispositional and interactional role. Such factors, hereditary homosexual propensities or hormone imbalances resulting from fetal accident, would engender in those affected a capacity for homosexuality that will not be realized unless it is complemented by necessary postnatal environmental situations: likewise, one who meets the environmental conditions for homosexuailty, but who lacks the physiological predisposition, will not become homosexual. Thus we could not conclude that a given homosexual lived in an environment that was more "homosexual positive" than a given heterosexual; the heterosexual's environment might be identical to that of the homosexual, but the heterosexual lacked the physiological propensity. Knowledge of this possibility might (and should) eradicate much of the guilt felt by parents of homosexuals.

The third, and only other logically possible, category of causation is that which sees physiological differences between homosexuals and heterosexuals, whatever these differences might be, as being purely a *result* of postnatal environment. This view sees the physiological alteration as occurring in virtually any individual who encounters the necessary environment. While a chemical intervention on the physiological mediator between the environment and the homosexual propensity might conceivably allow for prevention or alteration, the causation is seen by this view as being "physiological" only in the trivial sense that nearly all thought and behavior are in some way reacting to environment and are mediated by physiological factors.

Thus, physiology is relevant to an assessment of normality only if the physiological factors are determinative. If the physiological factors are either predispositional or mere effects of environment, then the necessary environmental situation(s) is the determining factor in an assessment of normality.[7] Homosexual behavior can no doubt be the effect of a number of discrete and separate causal sequences, and it is possible that some of these are normal (for example, that leading to the homosexual behavior of the Siwan) while others are abnormal (for example, that described by the Freudians). This means merely that we must assess the normality of each individual's homosexual behavior independently.

It is worth noting that the contemporary penchant for collapsing all relevant distinctions has led some to subsume both homosexual and radical feminist arguments under the rubric "sexual oppression." In at least one crucial respect these two arguments are very different: the discovery of a (determinative) physiological factor would be the best thing that could happen for one who argues that homosexuality should be considered normal; the greater the role of physiology, the more reasonable it is to see homosexuality as normal. However, for the radical feminist the issue is not one of an assessment of the normalcy of behavior, but the empirical roots of (differentiated male-female) behavior; the increasing and overwhelming evidence of a neural and hormonal basis of masculine and feminine motivational tendencies casts great doubt on the radical feminist assumption that such propensities are due primarily to the differentiation of socialization. This evidence suggests that, to a great extent, such socialization *conforms* to the reality of psychophysiological differentation.[8]

THE FREUDIAN EXPLANATION

The search for environmental causes proceeds on the assumption that there is a sequence of steps, and various researchers have emphasized various steps. Thus, some researchers emphasize an early fear of competition that leads one to avoid identification with the male role and its competitive demands. Others emphasize adolescent homosexual encounters. Still others emphasize a social ostracism that "labels" a behavior and thereby forces an individual to develop a self-conception that is wrapped around a nucleus of the labeled behavior. (We do not, however, speak of one who likes bowling as suffering from bowlerality.) It is conceivable that any or all of these steps are *necessary* for the development of some or all homosexuality; investigation of each is desirable. But an approach that emphasizes any of these (possibly *necessary*) steps is, by its nature, incapable of providing us with an explanation that could conceivably be *sufficient*. For such explanations beg the central question of why those who become homosexual have such fears of competition, why those who become homosexual choose adolescent *homo*sexual experiences, or why those whose homosexual propensities are labeled have *homo*sexual propensities. These approaches fail to provide a sufficient causal explanation because they leave unidentified the initial causal factor(s) that generates the childhood fear of competiton, choice of adolescent experiences that are *homo*sexual, etc. And it is on an assessment of the normality of the initial factor(s) that an assessment of normality must be based.

Whatever its other problems, the Freudian explanation of homosexuality cannot be criticized as begging the question. Whether correct or incorrect, it provides us with an explanation that does not leave unanswered the question of first cause (assuming one is willing to take the parents as givens), and, because it is a sufficient explanation, it can meaningfully—whether correctly or not—assess the behavior as abnormal on the basis of a causal factor that is abnormal. (The Freudian does not *have* to see the familial factors he presents as sufficient—he might see a physiological propensity or homosexual encounters during a critical childhood or adolescent period as being necessary if homosexuality is to develop—but, unlike those offering the environmental explanations mentioned above, he *can* offer his explanation as sufficient without begging any questions.)

It is not easy to state the Freudian explanation of homosexuality; one must state the explanation in terms both wide enough to encompass many subtly different theories and narrow enough to avoid oversimplification. I think it fair to say, however, that all "Freudian" explanations see male homosexuality as devolving from a refusal of the boy to identify with the father. The familial realities usually seen as responsible for this refusal include the mother's (perhaps warranted) contempt for the father, an unusual bond between the mother and child that is not complemented by a paternal authority that would ensure that the child transfer identification with the mother to identification with one who the mother would love (the father in other families), a resulting rage on the part of the child toward the parents, and extreme feelings of guilt, shame, isolation, and distrust. One need not, of course, accept an explanation simply because he can offer no alternative. But if we have an explanation that is logical, plausible, and relatively free of anomaly, it behooves one who denies its validity to demonstrate its inadequacies.

(Incidentally, it seems to me probable that a test of the Freudian hypothesis must consist of identifying parents exhibiting the qualities seen as facilitating homosexuality and then seeing if the children of these parents grow up to be homosexual more often than do children of a control group of parents. Difficult as this test is, practical considerations rule out the validity of the more common—and much simpler—attempt to discover the past familial realities of current homosexuals. The necessity of the more difficult test is practical; homosexuals are extremely sophisticated test-takers and cannot be expected to fail to see the implications of questions about their relationships with their mothers and fathers. It is amazing that *any* homosexuals acknowledge the sorts of difficulties posited by the Freudians.)

The Freudian says that most homosexuals grow up in the familial environment claimed by the Freudians to facilitate homosexuality. He does *not* say that most people who grow up in such an environment become homosexual. He predicts that, in a random population, there will be an important correlation between being a homosexual and growing up in a homosexuality-facilitating familial environment; he does *not* predict that there will be an important correlation between growing up in such a familial environment and becoming homosexual. The reason that the correlation does not work strongly in both ways is that there are other necessary conditions for homosexuality that must be present in addition to the familial situation. (An analogy makes this clear: there is a strong correlation between being a professional basketball player and being tall, but only the slightest correlation —introduced by the pocket of non-randomness representing professional basketball players—between being tall and being a professional basketball player. Moreover, even the weak correlations are expected only if we assume all other variables to be normally distributed.) I make this obvious point because some critics of the Freudian hypothesis seem to think that the fact that most children who grow up in the familial environment seen by the Freudians as homosexuality-facilitating do not grow up to be homosexuals is a refutation of the Freudian hypothesis that most homosexuals grow up in such an environment. This is no refutation.

The homosexual criticism of the Freudian explanation has not focused primarily on the central premises of the explanation itself (the familial configuration); it has tended merely to assert away the considerable evidence summarized by Fisher and Greenberg.[9] The homosexual criticism has concentrated on the Freudian implication that the pathology associated with homosexuality (the isolation, distrust, guilt, and shame) is inherent in the development of the homosexuality.[10]

PATHOLOGICAL DEBATES

Freudians argue that the very nature of the development of homosexuality is such that psychic distress is intimately bound up with the familiar relationships that generate the homosexuality.[11] While not denying that social attitudes exacerbate the homosexual's pain, they believe that eradication of the negative sanctions would not eradicate the pain. Gay activists seem undecided as whether to argue that homosexuals *do not* demonstrate any greater pathology than do heterosexuals or whether they *do*, but that the greater pathology is owing to the social sanctions of an oppressive society and to parental attitudes that reflect these sanctions. If they take the former tack, they undercut their claim that society's values harm the homosexual by loading him with excess guilt and shame. If, on the other hand, they acknowledge that homosexuals do exhibit a greater pathology, they rest their argument on their ability to demonstrate that the pathology is owing to the social sanctions; a failure to do this would leave us with no alternative to concluding that not only is homosexuality rooted in abnormal cause and negatively sanctioned (this would be sufficient for an assessment of abnormality on the basis of unnecessary pain), but also that homosexuality entails pain and pathology even when it is not negatively sanctioned.

It is not possible to recapitulate the entire arguments here, but it is worth noting that virtually every homosexual spokesman who has argued that homosexuals demonstrate no greater pathology has rested his case on an article by Evelyn Hooker without noting that Professor Hooker *selected for* individuals who did not manifest any of a number of signs of pathology. Her subjects, who in any case numbered only thirty, were selected on the basis of never having been arrested, not being in therapy, not being glaringly effeminate, not being unemployed, and being suggested as subjects by the homosexual community. Such selection was perfectly valid for Professor Hooker's purposes, but to invoke this study as demonstrating that homosexuals demonstrate no greater pathology than heterosexuals is like selecting a sample of thirty six-foot-tall women and six-foot-tall men and concluding that women are as tall as men.[12]

Moreover, even the argument that Professor Hooker's sample demonstrates that at least *some* homosexuals do not demonstrate any more pathology than most heterosexuals is dubious. Other studies *have* been able to discriminate homosexuals from heterosexuals on the basis of indicators of psychological distress; it would, then, seem likely that Professor Hooker's criteria were not sufficiently sensitive to expose pathological symptoms that do, in fact, exist even for members of her homosexual sample group. When two *different* tests disagree on the presence of a factor, the plausible assumption is that one test is capable of discriminating the factor while the other is not. An absurd example makes this point: Let us say that two researchers wish to find out if it is true that men are taller than women. One researcher measures men and women and concludes that men are taller. The other researcher asks men and women questions about American history and concludes that, because the sexes do equally well, men and women are equal in height. The tests do not cancel each other because it is obvious that only the former test measures that which it claims to measure. (If *no* test is able to discriminate the factors it claims to discriminate, then, of course, we must consider the possibility that the factors do not exist. If the *same* test sometimes finds what it is looking for and sometimes fails to do so, then we have a problem.)

INTOLERANCE AND PAIN

When the homosexual spokesman argues that homosexuals *do* exhibit more pathology, but that this pathology is owing to the negative sanctions, he makes an argument that is more plausible to most people (at least those who are not impressed by the Freudian explanation). B t he makes an argument that is not supported even by evidence provided by those who strongly sympathize with the plight of the homosexual. Martin Weinberg and Colin Williams[13] compare differences between homosexual and heterosexual reports of "unhappiness" and "lack of faith in others" in the United States (with its strongly intolerant attitudes towards homosexuality) with differences in reports in The Netherlands and Denmark (which have far more tolerant attitudes). The authors "do not find, as societal reaction theory implies, smaller differences between the homosexual and general population samples in the more tolerant societies." In other words, *the distress does not decrease as tolerance is increased.* Some have, rather astonishingly, argued that all that this indicates is that tolerance is not sufficient and that the homosexual's pain, which they continue to attribute solely to the social sanctions, can be reduced only by positive social sanction. This is logically possible; there could, in theory, be a necessary threshold of positive response—below which fall both mere tolerance and intolerance—so that mere tolerance will permit as much pain and pathology as will oppressive intolerance. But this is about as implausible as an argument can get. One would expect at least some diminution in the pain and pathology as tolerance is increased. It would seem far more plausible to explain the absence of a correlation of pain and intolerance with an explanation, like that of the Freudians, that sees the pain as having its roots in factors that have little to do with the social sanctions. (In a society in which homosexual behavior was positively sanctioned and in which most or all men took part in the behavior, the Freudian would not predict much of a correlation between pathology and homosexual behavior; the causes of the behavior, for the large majority, would not include the psychodynamic factors that lead one to follow a homosexual path despite negative sanction.[14])

NON-SCIENTIFIC IMPLICATIONS

I have suggested that human beings will, *ceteris paribus,* behave in ways that are rewarded and will refrain from behaving in ways that are punished, so that when someone behaves in ways that are punished, while refraining from behaving in ways that are rewarded, we must ask *why?* I have further suggested that when someone behaves in a way that is punished because he has needs that can be satisfied only by such behavior *and* when this is all rooted in a situation that a reasonable person would see as abnormal, then we assess the behavior, *correctly,* as abnormal. This assessment is correct even when the social sanction is indefensible and even if the behavior is self-destructive and painful only because of the indefensible social sanction; the exectuion of peanut eaters is morally heinous, but the assessment as abnormal of peanut-eating behavior that risks death may be *correct*.

It need not matter—for the determination of political, legal, or educational policy—whether homosexuality is abnormal. The determination of policy is never entailed in either scientific considerations or in considerations of normality such as those discussed here. Policy decisions require moral and emotional choices that are outside the area negotiable by the means utilized in this essay. This would be true even if we were virtually certain of the causal factors that generate homosexuality and even if homosexuality were shown to be clearly abnormal. For example, if we were to conclude beyond a reasonable doubt that most homosexuality results from the causes postulated by the Freudians, we might conclude that homosexuality was abnormal but that factors over which we have control have little relevance, so that it would be an exercise in social cruelty to exacerbate the homosexual's pain with policies that had no salutary effect (for either the homosexual or society). If, on the other hand, we concluded that some homosexuality is the result of a causal sequence that requires adolescent homosexual experience,[15] then, even if the causal sequence contained no step that was abnormal (i.e., even if the homosexuality were normal), we might feel that, in the case of minors, society is abdicating its moral responsibility in permitting "gay" college dances that condemned some to lives of social ostracism.

My suspicion is that the homosexual does not want merely the rights that should always have been his. Nor does he want merely the empathy and openness we offer (or should offer) anyone with or without physical or psychological problems. The homosexual wants social affirmation of the normality of his behavior. For the reasons we have discussed, we cannot give this affirmation unless he can give us a causal factor for homosexuality that can be considered normal. If he cannot do this, he asks us to affirm as normal that which fails to meet the criteria for normality we invoke in all other cases. To do this we would have to deny truth and live a lie. Nothing can justify our doing that.

I realize that some will feel that debate over the concept of normality, at a time when homosexuals suffer a social ostracism far greater than can conceivably be justified, is both callous and as absurd as the debate over angels dancing on the head of a pin. To such critics I can merely reply that this alleged scholastic enterprise was absurd *not* because it obsessively attempted to conform explanation to logic; an explanation *should* conform to logic. The critic feels, correctly, that the theory about angels was absurd because it attempted to construct a theory when there was nothing to explain. That such is not the case here, that the critic does not consider "normality" and "abnormality" absurd in this way, is clear from the fact that he uses the term "abnormal" to describe necrophilia in his arguments. That the critic does not, on an emotional level, consider this debate absurd is indicated by the fact that he has been willing to endure this essay to its final period.

NOTES

1. *New York Times Book Review,* December 10, 1972.
2. See Arno Karlen, "Homosexuality: The Scene and Its Students," in *The Sociology of Sex,* James Henslin and Edward Sagarin (eds.), New York: Schocken, 1978.
3. Whether or not homosexual behavior so generated is *moral* is, of course, a philosophical and sociological question that is irrelevant here.
4. While it would take us too far afield to do so here, it can be shown that the argument presented in this essay can, *mutatis mutandis,* be made in terms of alternative methods of determining normality—methods that replace my criterion of normal/abnormal *cause* with an emphasis on need, function, reason, purpose, or compuslion. There are important differences among these criteria, but the differences do not obviate the need to distinguish between normal behavior and abnormal behavior such as necrophilia.

For example: an approach that emphasizes *needs* rather than causes—while it does have the attractive element of emphasizing that behavior can come to satisfy needs that are different from the (now irrelevant) needs that originally generated the behavior—still must ask why an individual satisfies these needs with behavior that elicits negative sanction. In other words, we may, at least for argument's sake, accept the assertion that homosexual behavior serves sexual and affectional needs identical to the needs served by heterosexual behavior for most people; still we must ask why the homosexual selects negatively sanctioned behavior to satisfy those needs. If this selection was determined by a situation that is abnormal in the sense we have discussed, then the behavior can legitimately be termed "abnormal." The same point can be made about the paradigms stressing function, reason, or purpose.

The distinction between normality and abnormality that is based on noncompulsiveness/compulsiveness (rather than normal cause/abnormal cause) raises an additional point. While I doubt that the two methods for distinguishing normality from abnormality would often disagree on assessments of actual behavior, I prefer the cause criterion because the compulsion criterion has difficulty with noncompulsive behavior that is generated by a displacement or mischannelling of emotions; surely noncompulsive necrophiliac behavior is abnormal. (The "compulsion" theorist cannot argue that the very existence of necrophiliac behavior indicates a compulsion that is necessary to override the enormous sanction against necrophilia; this approach accepts tautology and risks labeling *all* strongly negatively sanctioned behavior "abnormal.")

5. Note that the point made in this paragraph—that a criticism of circularity can be sustained only if applied to necrophilia/coprophilia as well as to homosexuality—applies for whatever criterion one chooses. Thus, selection of some criterion other than cause (for example, need, function, reason, or purpose) cannot avoid an analogous requirement of distinguishing between homosexuality and necrophilia/coprophilia if the former is to be considered normal.

6. In granting that the necessity of distinguishing normal from abnormal cause permits a criticism of circularity by one who is willing to take the unreasonable position that it is meaningless to call necrophilia/coprophilia "abnormal," I am not suggesting that there is any particular difficulty in distinguishing normal from abnormal cause. There will, of course, be difficult borderline cases in any nonpurely analytic attempt at categorization. But in the overwhelming majority of cases it is easy to distinguish normal cause from abnormal cause. The distinction is seen clearly in the example of the near nudity of the African warrior and the American mentioned above. Similarly, I would certainly acknowledge the reasonableness of seeing as "normal" any homosexuality rooted in *purely* physiological causes and seeing as "abnormal" any homosexuality that is owing to fa-

milial situations such as that described by the Freudians. My point above, however, is merely that one who refuses to grant any such distinction, on the grounds that any such distinction must have a nonempirical element, can sustain the criticism that all such distinctions rest on circularity, unreasonable as may be the position in which this puts one.

7. It should be noted here that there is not complete agreement on the role of physiology in heterosexuality either. This is not relevant here because the points made here hold whichever view of heterosexuality one subscribes to. No one doubts that the propensity for reacting with sexual emotions is rooted in central-nervous-system and hormonal factors; the disagreement concerns the role of physiology in determining the heterosexual *direction* of those emotions. Some researchers believe that there is a physiological predisposition to heterosexuality, while others believe that heterosexuality is owning to learning, example, and positive social sanction. If one takes the former view, then he would want to know what factor overrides the physiological predisposition to heterosexuality. If the answer is simply that homosexuals are born with a different physiology, then the behavior is normal; but if they were born with a physiology that leads to homosexuality only if it is complemented by a necessary environmental factor, then an assessment of the normality of the behavior would be based on an assessment of the normality of the necessary environmental factor. If one takes the latter view, that the heterosexual direction is entirely environmental in origin, then one would want to know what environmental situation led to the homosexual's acting in opposition to learning, example, and positive sanction; and it is on an assessment of the normality of this situation that he would assess the normality of the behavior.

8. For this analysis, see my *The Inevitability of Patriarchy,* revised edition (London: M. T. Smith Ltd., 1977—or the fully updated edition to be published by Open Court in 1992).

9. Seymour Fisher and Roger P. Greenberg, *The Scientific Evaluation of Freud's Theories and Therapy* (New York: Basic Books, 1978).

10. The issue of "latent homosexuality" is irrelevant to the argument I make in this essay; here we speak only of active homosexual behavior. However, it is worth mentioning that the oft-heard criticism that the concept of "latent homosexuality" is without meaning because it is ungroundable or untestable is a criticism that is without merit. Let us imagine a test that is administered to sixteen-year-old boys who have had no homosexual experience. Let us say that those boys who score above eighty on the test turn out, with great statistical significance, to become adults whose sexual preference is solely homosexual. Let us say that those sixteen-year-olds who score between sixty and eighty do not tend to select homosexual contacts, but do tend to remain unmarried and do tend to exhibit the defensive behavior that the Freudian associates with barely suppressed homosexual desires. We might further imagine that these individuals are found to be the first to accept homosexual contact under unusual environmental situations. It seems to me that this is the sort of thing that the Freudian has in mind when he speaks of "latent homosexuality" and, it seems to me, that this is, in theory, perfectly valid even from a purely operationalist point of view. Even if the Freudian could not, in fact, begin to approach the predictive capacity of our imaginary test, this would cast no doubt on the logical or theoretical validity of the concept.

11. No doubt some heterosexuals demonstrate far more pathology than do the vast majority of homosexuals, but this proves nothing; one cannot demonstrate the normality of one person's behavior by showing that another person's behavior is even more abnormal.

12. A similar fallacy permeates *Homosexualities,* the recent and much-publicized Kinsey Institute work by Alan P. Bell and Martin S. Weinberg. Bell and Weinberg divide

their sample of homosexuals into five categories (Close-Coupled, Open-Coupled, Functionals, Dysfunctionals, and Asexuals—the latter two categories constituting forty percent of the categorizable homosexuals in the sample. The authors conclude that stereotypes about homosexuals are unwarranted because they apply only to the latter two categories. Even if we assume that the pathologies observed by the stereotypes are limited to homosexuals of the latter two categories (a dubious assumption, as we shall see in the next paragraph), this would not at all demonstrate the incorrectness of the stereotype. Bell and Weinberg's argument is analogous to calling all women between 5'4" and 5' "little women" and all women shorter than 5' "tiny women" and then concluding that the stereotype that sees women as shorter than men is incorrect because it applies only to "little women" and "tiny women." Stereotypes are always statistical and one can no more demonstrate their incorrectness by disregarding those members of the stereotyped group who are responsible for the stereotype than one can demonstrate the incorrectness of the stereotype associating greater height with men by disregarding all women under 5'4".

Moreover, all Bell and Weinberg show us is that *they* are incapable of finding the pathology associated by the stereotype with homosexuality in homosexuals of the first three categories. Other researchers, using methods for discriminating pathology that are *different* from those used by Bell and Weinberg, claim to be able to find the pathology in all categories of homosexuals. The most plausible conclusion is that the methods of those researchers are capable of discriminating pathology, where Bell and Weinberg's are not.

13. Martin S. Weinberg and Colin J. Williams, *Male Homosexuals* (New York: Oxford University Press, 1974).

14. There are a number of theoretical points that are not possible to consider here. I should, however, make three points that are discussed at length there. (1) All that I write here applies to "bisexuality" (assuming that there is an adult who is strongly sexually attracted to both sexes in a single period of time, a dubious assumption). The question of the normality of bisexuality is more complex because one can make the argument (unavailable to the exclusive homosexual) that bisexuality "maximizes pleasure." Here I can merely point out that in the case of "bisexuality," as in the case of homosexuality, we must ask the basic question on which as assessment of normality rests: What situation engenders a motivation so strong that it forces one (or "allows" one) to behave in a way that is so painfully sanctioned? (2) I do not like the term "homosexuality"; it obfuscates the fact that homosexual behavior is an effect that can be the result of any of a number of discrete and separate causal lines, some of which may be normal and some of which are in all likelihood abnormal. However, while the term is not necessary for theoretical purposes, avoidance demands such stylistic infelicity that I use the term here. (3) Throughout this essay I refer only to *male* homosexuality. We have far less evidence on female homosexuality, and it is not clear how relevant the evidence on males is to females. The criterion for assessment of normality represented here is, of course, equally applicable to male and female homosexuality.

15. I am not suggesting here that it is possible for adolescent experience to render an otherwise average boy a homosexual. I am suggesting that it is possible that there is a minority of boys who, having met the earlier physiological and environmental conditions necessary for homosexuality, will become homosexual if exposed to "gay" dances and the like, but who will not become homosexual if homosexuality is not positively sanctioned at this critical period of the boy's life. I have no idea whether there is such a minority, but neither do those who merely *assert* that homosexuality is *always* set before adolescence. While at least *some* of the necessary conditions for homosexuality clearly must be met before adolescence, it is not at all obvious that, in all cases, *all* of the necessary conditions must be met before adolescence.

4

What Does "Cause" Mean: The Causation of Homosexuality

I.

Fifty years of research into the causation of male homosexuality has not engendered a consensus even approaching unanimity on the precise nature of the interaction of factors, or even the factors themselves, that can explain homosexuality. Nonetheless, it is probably fair to say that the modal view posits hereditary-physiological factors (including physiology-affecting fetal environmental events) interacting with familial-environmental factors.

In practice, researchers tend to emphasize either the former or latter elements, depending on their training and subdisciplines. But most think it likely that both types of factors play a role and that each influences the other.

While there is a minority of researchers who claim that homosexuality can be explained without reference to nonenvironmental factors, I know of no one in the field who argues that homosexuality can be explained without reference to environmental factors. To say that environmental elements play at least a partial role in the development of homosexuality—to say that an hereditary-physiological factor may be necessary, but is not sufficient, to engender homosexuality—is to say that the hereditary-physiological element is not determinative.

It is, perhaps, because no one denies that environmental factors are involved at least in part in the causation of homosexuality that there has been little discussion of the causal logic of the hereditary-physiological element in explanations of homosexuality.

I stress that my purpose here is not to make the empirical case for the importance of hereditary-physiological factors. I take the importance of such factors as a given, in order to analyze their role in an explanation of homosexuality. Should future evidence demonstrate that the "pure environmentalist" minority is correct and that an explanation of homosexuality requires no physiological primary causal role (i.e., that physiology is relevant only as mediator of environment and behavior), then this discussion will have been proven to be as pointless an exercise as an explanation of the digestive system of the unicorn. There is no scientific value in an explanation of a nonexistent empirical reality. However, to the extent that the evidence does require a hereditary-physiological element in the causal explanation, it is necessary for us to understand the causal role of this element. It is an attempt at such an understanding that is the purpose of this discussion.[1]

Homosexuality can best be conceived as a series of "go"-"no go" steps, with a "go" required at every step if homosexuality is to develop. A person who lacks the physiological necessary condition (if there is such a condition) will not become a homosexual no matter what his subsequent environment. Another person, who meets the physiological necessary precondition, will not become a homosexual if he encounters environments "A" or "B" or "C," but will if he encounters environments "D" or "E" or "F" (or, perhaps, "D" and "E" and "F" or any two of these). This is the implicit view of all researchers who explain that homosexuality is not purely the result of environmental factors.

Statistically speaking, the nature of causation one of continuous "facilitators" is rather than discrete "necessary conditions." This continuous nature of facilitators makes more clear the fact that the hereditary and environmental causal requirements have, in a sense, an inverse functional relationship. In other words, one person may have a strong hereditary predisposition to homosexuality and require only a modest environmental push to become a homosexual. Another may have a low predisposition and require a strong environmental push.

Moreover, while superficially different physiological components will likely reduce to a factor common to the various components, there may well be entirely different environmental components, each capable of engendering homosexuality independently—or in independent combinations—when combined with the physiological component.

II.

An understanding of the role of the heredity-environment interaction makes it clear that familial contribution to homosexuality likely varies from low to high. In many cases the predisposition may be strong and the environmental requirement modest (so that the parental environment has little to do with the son's homosexuality). In other cases, parents or unusual experience may present a strong homosexuality-engendering environment to a son who lacks the hereditary predisposition and who, therefore, does not become homosexual. Thus, the fact that one pair of parents have a homosexual son and another does not doesn't necessarily mean that the former more strongly exhibits the familial factors that play a causal role in engendering homosexuality; the former parents may have a son with a strong physiological predisposition requiring only a modest push, while the later have a son who, lacking the predisposition, will not become homosexual even if his parental environment is one strong in those elements capable of producing homosexuality.

The Freudian, who has as patients those people who have already become homosexuals, will explain the homosexuality in terms of early familial environment. While a Freudian will never be the discoverer of a physiological necessary condition, there is nothing in such a necessary condition that contradicts the Freudian explanation. All the physiological necessary condition means to the Freudian is that there are people who encounter the "Freudian environment" who, because they lack the physiological necessary condition, never become homosexuals and never become patients. The Freudian does not claim that those encountering the environment necessarily become homosexual, but only that those who become homosexual will have encountered the environment. One who claims that nearly all nuclear physicists went to college is not claiming that nearly everyone who went to college became a nuclear physicist.

III.

It is widely believed that children raised by homosexual parents (or one homosexual parent in a single-parent household) are no more likely to become homosexual than are children raised in heterosexual families. It is not clear whether this is true: It is probably too early to tell, and the little research that has been done—like much "research" in the area of sex differences and sex preferences—tends to be tendentious and demonstrable as inadequate by a cursory logical glance.

But let us, for argument's sake, accept as true the claim that children of, and raised by, homosexuals are not disproportionately often homosexual. The implication would tend to support the Freudian causal explanation. For the view that emphasizes an hereditary element would expect biological children of homosexuals to be homosexual disproportionately often, as would a sociological view emphasizing role models.

The Freudian view, which stresses the wife's contempt for her husband (a contempt often warranted by a passive or brutal husband) and a resulting refusal of the son to accept the male role, would not predict that children of homosexuals would disproportionately often become homosexual (because, particularly in single-parent households, the necessary maternal contempt for the husband would be lacking or not continuously displayed). There may well be other explanations of homosexuality that predict that children of homosexual parents are not disproportionately often homosexual, but of the major explanation this fact, if it is a fact, tends to support the Freudian explanation.

IV.

I have no idea whether the Freudian explanation of homosexuality will ultimately be demonstrated to be correct, but I do know that recent attempts to ignore studies claiming a "Freudian family"-homosexuality correlation and to assert it away—or to invoke studies whose failure to find such a correlation can be seen at a glance to reflect a methodology far too simplistic to uncover such a correlate—are convincing only to those with a need to believe. Moreover, far too many social scientists seem to believe that studies failing to find a correlation (such as the studies that fail to find a Freudian family-homosexuality correlation) cancel out other studies that use a different methodology and find the correlation. The fallacy here is discussed below.

It is clear that there is an environmental component to the causation of homosexuality and that the Freudian explanation, alone among environmental explanations, meets the requirement of being self-contained (assuming one takes the parents as givens). Other environmental explanations, while they may identify additional necessary conditions, tend also to beg the question. The purest version of this is sociological labeling theory, which examines the ways in which an individual is identified by society as a homosexual and then develops a personal style and social network around a nucleus of this identification. Whatever its other virtues, such a theory cannot tell us why the homosexual exhibits in the first place the behavior that permits society to identify and label him.

Likewise, the explanation that posits the determinativeness of adolescent homosexual experiences leaves unanswered the question of why the adolescent experiences of homosexuals tend to be homosexual. Unless the heterosexuality or homosexuality of first adolescent experiences is determined by randomness—which hardly seems likely—some prior factor must lead homosexuals to first adolescent experiences that are homosexual. If there is such a factor, then, obviously, the adolescent experience is not the primary causal factor. Homosexual adolescent experience could conceivably be a facilitator for becoming homosexual (or, perhaps, even a necessary condition), but it is not sufficient to explain the impulse that leads an adolescent to homosexual adolescent experiences. Further evidence that such experiences are not sufficient to generate homosexuality is the fact that, while most homosexuals may have adolescent fantasies and experiences that are homosexual, most adolescents who have homosexual fantasies and experiences (for whatever reasons) do not become adult homosexuals.

Finally, a disproportionate number of homosexuals report having had a childhood aversion to rough-and-tumble play (though most adult males who report having had such an aversion do not become homosexuals). Unless one sees this aversion as entirely the result of heredity or fetal physiological accident, he must explain what preceding postnatal environmental cause is responsible for this aversion.

V.

What is most clear about the causation of homosexuality is that it cannot be caused by the factor that plays the major role in much behavior: positive social sanction. Despite frequent claims to the contrary, no known society has given status parity to general homosexuality (as opposed to specific adolescent practices and the like).

More important, even if some societies did accept homosexuality, our society does not do so (as the homosexual movement has demonstrated beyond doubt). Thus, even if one accepts the assumption that opportunity for positively sanctioned physical pleasure will always be taken, he is left to ask why such behavior is exhibited when it is negatively sanctioned.

Let us say that our society encouraged popcorn-eating and ostracized peanut-eaters. Even though there is nothing inherently better about eating popcorn than eating peanuts, we would want to know what generated the motivation to eat peanuts of the 10 percent of the population whose peanut-eating impulse is so strong as to lead that 10 percent to risk ostracism.

We would want to know this purely in order to know it. Whether a specific behavior is good or bad, whether it should be nurtured or reversed (if it can be reversed)—a question of both what would be good to do and what we should be permitted to do even if it is not good—or whether other motivations are satisfied by the question or answer, all these are as irrelevant as analogous issues are to the question of whether the earth is round or flat.

VI.

Entwined with the question of causation of homosexuality itself is the question of the causation of behavioral tendencies associated with homosexuality. These include (A) tendencies that are more or less positively sanctioned (artistic creativity, for example), (B) tendencies that are negatively sanctioned but not in and of themselves (i.e., even in the absence of negative sanction) damaging, and (C) tendencies, like depression and suicide, that are clearly pathological in and of themselves (i.e., tendencies that would be damaging even if they were not negatively sanctioned).

(A) There has been an enormous amount written about the association between homosexuality and artistic creativity. While it seems likely that such a relationship exists, rigorous study of the subject is bedeviled by difficulties in defining creativity, agreeing on who belongs in the population of creative people to serve to determine the association, and the like.

(B) Tendencies that are negatively sanctioned but not in and of themselves damaging are difficult to study because the same social impulses that lead to negative sanction engender claims that a behavioral tendency is in and of itself damaging even if a rather farfetched argument is required to support this view. (On the other hand, homosexual spokesmen will often claim that behavior that can reasonably be seen as inherently psychologically damaging—for example, extreme promiscuity even in pre-AIDS days—is a mere alternative that is labeled damaging for reasons of prejudice.)

(C) At one time, homosexual spokesmen denied that there was any psychological or behavioral tendency, other than those concerned with sex fantasy and partner, more highly correlated with homosexuality than with heterosexuality. However, the argument for this position failed because it was supported by studies (like that of Hooker[2]) that either selected homosexuals who did not exhibit disproportionate pathology or (like the work of Alan P. Bell and Martin S. Weinberg[3]) divided homosexuals into subgroups and found that pathology was disproportionate only in some subgroups. Such an approach cannot demonstrate that homosexuals in general do not exhibit disproportionate amounts of the pathological behavior. I have dealth with this and other methodological fallacies in the preceding chapter.

The conclusions of studies alleging to find greater pathology among homosexuals may be incorrect, but if they are this can be demonstrated only by replicating the study, using the same methodology used by the study, or by demonstrating fallacy or error in the study. A non-null study can never be brought into question by the results of a study using a different methodology.

Moreover, the denial that nonsexual tendencies such as depression are disproportionately associated with homosexuality never made much sense, even in its terms of the homosexual spokesman's own argument: If social ostracism has no effects on psyche or behavior, then what difference does it make if there is social ostracism? It is such effects of ostracism that renders the ostracism oppressive.

Today homosexual spokesmen usually *do* acknowledge that homosexuals do exhibit disproportionately often such clearly pathological tendencies as depression and suicide, but argue that this is owing entirely to the negative social sanction of homosexuality The implication is that, were homosexuality accepted, homosexuals would exhibit these tendencies no more often than do heterosexuals. This position argues, in other words, that homosexuality is analogous to black skin; the price for having it may be high in a society that looks down on it, but there is nothing about it that is, in and of itself (i.e., regardless of social sanction), pathological.

The evidence argues strongly against this (and in favor of that of Freudians and others that sees the pathology as pathology that is entwined with the development of homosexuality and that would be present even if there were no negative social sanction).

Weinberg and Williams,[4] in a book entirely sympathetic to the plight of the homosexual, compared rates of depressive symptoms (using other terminology, but this is what clearly was being measured) in societies with attitudes towards homosexuality varying from the tolerant to the oppressive.

We have already seen, in the preceding chapter, that this study casts the most serious doubt on the view that the pathology is owing to social sanction.

VII.

To this point we have been speaking only of the causation of homosexuality and behaviors associated with homosexuality. Nearly invariably, however, discussion of the subject turns to the issue of normality.

Now, no discussion of normality is a purely scientific discussion. Science is concerned only with empirical relationships, and "normality" has no meaning in other than a statistical sense. "Normality" concerns an area of overlap of the scientific and the normative. Indeed, one who wishes to dismiss such discussion altogether can merely argue that all conceptions of normality are ultimately circular in that they begin with some subjective assumption.

However, this approach cannot be satisfying to anyone wishing to demonstrate that one behavior is normal as opposed to another behavior that is not. The circularity argument has power only if one is willing to run all the way with it, to include necrophilia, coprophilia,[5] and all other behaviors (or, at least, all other behaviors not clearly harmful to another person), no matter how bizarre. The homosexual does not wish merely to demonstrate that homosexuality is as normal as necrophilia and coprophilia, but that homosexuality is normal and necrophilia and coprophilia are not. To do this he must grant the abnormality of the latter behaviors and, in so doing, he surrenders the circularity argument.

The homosexual may well be able to distinguish homosexuality from necrophilia and coprophilia in a way that finds the former normal and the latter two abnormal. But to do so convincingly he will have to show that homosexuality springs from benign causes and/or (depending on technical aspects of criteria for normality that are not within the scope of this discussion) that homosexuality is not associated with clearly pathological tendencies that would assert themselves even if homosexuality were given status parity with heterosexuality. He cannot do this by invoking the argument that all assessments of normality are circular.

Homosexuality caused by a physiologically determinative factor, and not associated with behavior that would be damaging even if the behavior were socially accepted, would clearly be normal (even if social ostracism generated pathological reactions to the ostracism). It would be the sexual equivalent of black skin (an analogy that homosexuals often assert while rejecting all attempts to find causation, the only route leading to an assessment of the correctness of the analogy).

Since it is unlikely that any homosexuality is caused by a physiologically *determinative* factor, the question of normality turns on the nature of the environmental component of its causation. The physiological component—assuming that it is analogous to that causing black skin and not analogous to that causing inherently damaging symptoms like blindness—is irrelevant to an assessment of normality. Those whose interest is demonstrating the normality of homosexuality, like those whose impulses are scientific, have no alternative to searching for the causes of homosexuality. Thus, the claim that "causation is irrelevant"—which has become received "knowledge" in "liberated sexual circles"—is as wrongheaded for one wishing to demonstrate the normality of homosexuality as it is for one who wishes merely to find out why people behave as they do.

NOTES

1. It is, of course, theoretically possible that one day there will be discovered a physiological marker, present just after conception (to use one "perfect" case), in those who, no matter what their subsequent environments, become homosexual. No one, however, believes that the present evidence justifies positing such a determinative factor.

2. Evelyn Hooker, "The Adjustment of The Male Overt Homosexual," in *Journal of Projective Techniques* (1957) 21:18-31.

3. Alan P. Bell and Martin S. Weinberg, *Homosexualities* (New York: Simon and Schuster, 1978).

4. Martin. S Weinberg and Colin J. Williams, *Male Homosexuals* (New York: Oxford University Press, 1974).

5. The example of necrophilia and coprophilia demonstrates the inadequacy of some of the criteria often invoked in attempts to demonstrate the normality of a behavior popularly considered abnormal: that the behavior is found cross-culturally, that it is negatively sanctioned (and this could account for associated pathological behavior), and that those who exhibit the behavior often see it as normal. All of these things are true of necrophilia and coprophilia.

5

The Theory of Patriarchy
Why Do Males Rule?

INTRODUCTION

It is arguable that the central questions requiring explanation by the behavioral and social sciences are those falling under the rubric "nature vs. nurture." To be sure, the issue is oversimplified when stated so simply; there are both physiological and environmental elements in the causation of behavior, as well as feedback through which each alters the other. Moreover, discussions of this dichotomy can often be seen to be sterile arguments about definition, rather than answers to the empirical question of what is, in fact, happening. What matters are the roles physiology, environment, and the interaction of the two play in generating *specific* behaviors.

None of this causes the nature-nurture controversy to evaporate. It merely forces us to ask the most basic of questions—what are we?—in a sufficiently clear and precise way to satisfy the most extreme operationalist. In the case of much behavior we will not be able to do this. This may be the case when physiology imparts no behavioral direction (leaving us to wonder forever whether we are missing a physiological factor) or when the evidence that will indicate the *possibile* relevance of physiology to behavior—for example the evidence of cross-cultural universals suggesting the possibility of underlying physiological substrates—has not yet been discovered.

There is, however, one class of behavior for which there is powerful evidence of the determinative role of physiology in the development of behavior and institution. There is sufficient evidence to suggest strongly that (A) the physiological differentiation of males and females underlies the differentiation of certain, specifiable male and female behaviors; (B) the differences in male and female anatomy enable the members of a society to observe the correlation of physiological differentiation and differentiated behaviors; and (C) this permits or requires the

71

institutions of the society to reflect the sexual differences of behavior that are rooted in differences between male and female physiology.

Over the past two decades I have attempted to discover whether there are universal cross-cultural, male-female differences of behavior and institution, to see whether these are best explained by positing limits and directions imposed by certain (specified) neuroendocrinological differences between the sexes, and to examine the logical and empirical connections between the physiological and the social. The resulting theory is fairly well known, and it is not my purpose here to present it in great detail. Nor is there any attempt to present the anthropological and physiological evidence supporting the theory. Doing that took a book and the reader interested in the empirical evidence might wish to consult the book in which the initial version of the theory is presented, *The Inevitability of Patriarchy.*[1]

Here I will begin by giving only the briefest of outlines of the theory and the anthropological and physiological evidence that supports it. My purpose in this article is to focus on the reasoning of the theory, particularly that which conflicts with the reasoning used by critics of the theory. This presentation is, of necessity, schematic; much greater detail is presented in the book.

I will also consider all of the criticisms of the earlier versions of the theory. I will treat the criticism generically and will not, in most cases, discuss the specific works, many of which repeated the same criticisms. Readers wishing to see a typical exchange might wish to consult the September/October 1986 issue of *Society* in which seven critics detail their criticisms and I respond to those criticisms.

THE CROSS-CULTURAL EMPIRICAL EVIDENCE

At the time I wrote *Patriarchy,* discussion of the cross-cultural evidence on sexually differentiated behavior and institutions was so muddled that generalization was virtually impossible. The term "patriarchy" was used in scores of different ways, and an exception to one behavior or role (e.g., a society in which the men do the planting) was invoked as demonstrating that no non-maternal behavior or institution was universal. Thus, it was necessary to examine the original ethnographic sources on all societies claimed as exceptions to see whether there were empirical realities to which there were no societal exceptions. There were:

1. *Patriarchy*: All of the 1500 to 5000 societies (past or present, primitive or modern) on which we have any evidence[2] have associated hierarchical dominance with males and have been ruled by hierarchies overwhelmingly controlled by males.[3]

In the United States, less than 3 percent of the mayors of cities of 25,000 or more, 3 percent of policy makers in the federal government, 2 percent of the Senate, and 7 percent of the House are female. According to a recent *Fortune* study of the relative numbers of directors and top executives at 799 major companies, men outnumbered women 3,993 to 19.[4]

A society may have a titular queen or a powerful queen serving in a hereditary position when no appropriate male is available; there were more female heads-of-state in the first two-thirds of the sixteenth century than the first two-thirds of the twentieth. Occasionally a woman will attain the highest position in a democratic society, but this is unusual in every such society; moreover, when this does occur, it is always the case that—as in Golda Meir's Israel, Indira Gandhi's India, and Margaret Thatcher's England—the vast majority of other upper hierarchical positions are held by males. A government may claim an ideological commitment to hierarchical equality, and even that this commitment has been met. But the reality is always that the claim of achieved equality is not true; in China, for example, sixty-seven of the ministries are headed by males and the other five positions are vacant. One may choose any society that has ever existed anywhere and he or she will find the same thing. There is slight variation as power lessens: the percentage of males tends to be somewhat greater in the upper houses of bicameral systems (e.g., the Senate) than in the lower houses and unicameral houses, and somewhat greater in small unicameral houses than in large unicameral houses. But in no case do such differences approach a reduction of male percentages that would cast doubt on the presence of patriarchy.

Norway, for example, which has a higher percentage of women in its unicameral house than does any other nation, places inordinate power in the hands of its municipal councils; 443 of 454 municipal council chairpersons are men. Males outnumber females at the judicial level 15-3 (Supreme Court), 63-7 (Appellate Court), and 182-25 (District/City Courts). In general, "the large disparity in the distribution of women and men in political bodies continues to apply" and, in the Parliament, "the greatest numbers of women are to be found in committees that deal with matters relating to the family, education, and social welfare" (areas with relatively low status). "The predominance of men is far greater in committees within major economic sectors such as commerce, industry, and oil."[5]

Likewise, in Sweden, where the percentages of women in the unicameral Parliament is higher than that found in any nation other than Norway, "men dominate nearly all of the policy-making bodies." Men dominate "senior positions in employer and employee organizations as well as in political and in other associations. In senior management in the private sector there is an even lower percentage." Only five of eighty-two directors of government agencies, nine of eighty-three chairpersons of agency boards, and 9 percent of judges are women. In short, "a clear pattern emerges: the higher up the hierarchy, the fewer the women. Among the appointments studied, 251 were of senior rank; only twenty-six of them were held by women."[6]

The ten countries in which women hold the highest percentage of national legislative seats are all either Communist or Scandinavian countries, in which an unusually high percentage of the real power resides in the hands of (over-whelmingly male) alternative entities (e.g., the Communist Party, the non-parliamentary entities mentioned above, etc.).[7] As we shall see, this is analogous to the situation that obtains with nonhierarchical status roles: As status increases, males are increasingly drawn to the roles. In general, the greater the status of hierarchical or (non-maternal) non-hierarchical roles, the greater the percentage of males in such roles.

All of this is as true of the most primitive as the most modern of societies (whatever one's yardstick). In *Patriarchy* I give quotations from every ethnography I have ever seen invoked—never by the ethnographer, but always by a third party who has usually clearly not consulted the ethnography he invokes—as describing an exception; the quotations always make clear that the societies are not exceptions. In the five or six societies with very little hierarchy, it is always clear that an informal male dominance is present. This suggests that the male dominance we shall discuss presently is not a residue of patriarchy (i.e., male dominance of hierarchies), but a relatively independent manifestation of a greater male tendency to react with dominance behavior to the environmental cue of a member of the other sex. Indeed, the three institutions we discuss (patriarchy, male attainment, and male dominance) seem to be independent of each other in that each would exist even in the absence of the others. Male physiology seems to be such that hierarchy, status, and member of the other sex *each* elicit dominance behavior more easily from the male, with the result being patriarchy, male attainment, and male dominance. In other words, while no doubt these three institutions tend to reinforce one another, and while overlapping physiological factors are involved in the behavior manifested in each, the three institutions are causally independent and each would exist in the absence of the others.

It should be noted that there have been a five or six tiny primitive societies (i.e., populations in the hundreds) in which virtually everyone knows everyone else, and which are comprised of relatively independent, relatively nomadic groups of a few families. In some such societies, while there is always at least a seminal hierarchy, decision-making is primarily a function of a less-formal male dominance in dyadic and familial situations. (A group of twenty or thirty adults and children does not need to create a Senate and House; informal decision-making is sufficient.)

I have addressed the universality even in primitive societies of the institutions we discuss simply because the empirical evidence permits it and demonstrates how irresistible is the social tendency for hierarchy, status, and dominance. However, this focus tends to take our attention away from the point that is central to *Patriarchy*, the inevitability of the institutions in modern society or any non-modern society that has hierarchy and status differentiation. In other words, even if it were true that there had been "egalitarian societies" that lacked hierarchy and status differentiation, this would not imply the possibility of a society that *does* have hierarchies that are not patriarchal or status differentiation in which it is not the males who attained the high-status roles. *For when there is hierarchy and status differentiation, the hierarchical positions and high-status roles are held overwhelmingly by males.* This is, as we shall see, because the very presence of the cues of hierarchy and status (and member of the other sex) elicits the behavior relevent to hierarchical, status, and dominance attainment more readily from those whose physiology is male (statistically speaking, as always).

The modern society is, by its nature, replete with hierarchy (and, therefore, the hierarchical cues and differentiated status that elicit the more easily released male behavior and the hierarchical arenas in which this behavior can be exhibited). While, in theory, there could be a primitive society of tens of thousands of people that exhibited little hierarchy, there has never been such a society. It is likely that there is a very low limit in population past which a society must invoke considerable hierarchy in order to organize itself.

As we shall see, it is precisely the male's greater tendency to respond with dominance and attainment behavior to the cues of hierarchy and status that is rooted in neuroendocrinological differences between males and females. Loosely speaking, we can conceptualize this as a neuroendocrinologically rooted greater male *competitiveness* that is elicited by hierarchy or status when there is hierarchy or status differentiation. ("Competitiveness" is a good analog for the physiologically rooted behavior we discuss because competitiveness implies not so much a tendency to manufacture competitive situations as a tendency to behave competitively when the environment presents a competitive situation that elicits the competitiveness.)

Thus, we would expect what the evidence demonstrates; no society (modern or not) with any appreciable hierarchy approaches egalitarianism as closely as do the few primitive societies just discussed. Only the very few, very small primitive societies just discussed actually do have such limited hierarchy (and these have a clearly identifiable informal male dominance); even primitive societies are nearly always clearly hierarchical and therefore clearly patriarchal.

While the modern society is *inherently* extensively hierarchical, the primitive society is not *inherently* low in hierarchy. Many primitive societies are, for various reasons, highly stratified and replete with hierarchy, and are therefore highly patriarchal. Thus, we can say only that the minimal patriarchy *possible* in a modern society is a more extensive patriarchy than is the minimal patriarchy *possible* in a primitive (or other non-modern) society that has low stratification.

However, just as the modern society is inherently more hierarchical than those non-modern societies with low stratification, so is the modern society inherently *less* patriarchal than the most hierarchical of non-modern societies. The labor needs of a modern economy render virtually impossible a modern society as patriarchal as the most patriarchal of non-modern societies.

In any case, the variation referred to here is relatively insignificant. In nearly every society there is extensive hierarchy, and in every such society males over-whelmingly control whatever hierarchy there is. In the few (primitive) societies with relatively little hierarchy, male dominance within the family serves similar functions. (When there are all-female hierarchies, these are subordinate to all-male hierarchies).

2. *Male Attainment*: The non-maternal roles given highest status—whichever these are and for whatever cultural reasons they are given high status in any given society—are associated with males. In Margaret Mead's words:

Men may cook, or weave, or dress dolls or hunt hummingbirds, but if such activities are appropriate occupations for men, then the whole society, men and women alike, votes them as important. When the same occupations are performed by women, they are regarded as less important.[8]

A modern example describes the situation that obtains in every society. If being a medical doctor is given high status (as in the United States), most doctors are male; if being an engineer is given high status and being a doctor relatively lower status (as in the Soviet Union), then most engineers are male and most doctors may be female (though the upper positions of medical hierarchies are filled by males even in such societies). Similarly, in the short period in which egalitarian laws have raised the status and income given administrators of women's collegiate athletic programs and coaches of American women's collegiate sports teams, the number of male administrators has grown from 10 to 85 percent and the number of coaches of women's teams from 10 to 50 percent.[9]

There are societies—though modern societies with their increasingly similar occupations for men and women could not be among them—in which women perform not only their maternal roles, but also non-maternal economic functions that are of far greater objective importance than are those of men, while working longer and harder outside the home than do men. Save for political and other hierarchical leadership, internal and external security, nurturance of the young and, probably, hunting, virtually every task is seen as primarily male in some societies and primarily female in others. However, in every society, the non-maternal roles given highest status—whatever they might be in any given society and however they may vary from society to society—are associated with men.

It is tempting to explain this as a residue of male political dominance, but I think that this gets things backwards. Male roles do not have high status primarily because they are male (ditchdiggers are male). Nor do high-status roles have high status primarily because they are male. High-status roles are male because they have high status, and this high status "motivates" males (for psychophysiological reasons discussed below) more strongly than it does females. An example of this is the coaching of female athletic teams just mentioned. The status of these roles is not increasing primarily because males increasingly fill them; the status is increasing for varied social and economic reasons, and this increased status attracts increasing numbers of males.

3. *Male Dominance*: The emotions of both males and females of all societies associate dominance with the male in male-female encounters and relationships. The existence of this reality is evidenced by the ethnographies of every society; by the stated aphorisms and proverbs of every society; and, in our own society, also by feminists who document (and abhor) the extensiveness of this reality and incorrectly ascribe it to primarily social and economic causes. In nearly all societies male dominance is ratified by a formal authority system that reflects male dominance. But even when this is not the case, as in our society with its chivalrous customs, both men and women have the same expectation of male dominance men and women of all other societies have. Whether a society's values laud or abhor the emotions of male dominance is a different question, one with a purely cultural answer. It is the universal existence of the emotions of male dominance, not the attitudes toward, and values concerning, the emotions, that we address here.[10]

The issue of differing male and female emotional tendencies (i.e., the differing physiologically rooted male and female hierarchies of reactions to environmental situations) is often confused with the issue of emotional demonstrativeness. This confusion leads to the false conclusion that, because (let us assume for argument's sake) women are stoic and men emotional in some societies and men stoic and women emotional in others, this somehow demonstrates the social nature of emotions. It does not. All it demonstrates is that the degree to which males will exhibit the "male hierarchy of emotions" and women will exhibit the "female hierarchy of emotions" is a function of social factors. It does not demonstrate that the different hierarchies of emotional tendencies of men and of women are anywhere reversed or that they are reversible.

One might, incidentally, argue that, within the family, the women of some or all societies have greater real power, attributable to a male abdication of familial roles,[11] a female persuasiveness, or a female ability to "get around" males. But the question relevant to universality is why both the men and women of every society have the emotional expectation of a *male* dominance that must be "gotten around."

THE NEED FOR AN EXPLANATION

In short: Examination of the ethnographic evidence forces one to conclude, as did Margaret Mead (in a review of *Patriarchy*), that:

> all the claims so glibly made about societies ruled by women are nonsense. We have no reason to believe that they ever existed. Men have always been the leaders in public affairs and the final authorities at home.

The reader who wishes to see the extent to which introductory sociology texts present demonstrably incorrect "evidence" as fact might look at the chapter on sex roles of virtually any introductory text. He or she will find that the chapter begins with the claim that, in *Sex and Temperament in Three Primitive Societies*, Margaret Mead demonstrates the nearly complete reversibility of sex roles. This despite the fact that Mead had not said any such thing, that it would not be true even if she had, that she had written a well-known letter to the *American Anthropologist* denying that she had said any such thing, that she had tried for forty years (in statements like that above) to reiterate that she had not said any such thing, and that I had pointed all this out in a letter to *Contemporary Sociology* over a decade ago.

One cannot always know which textbook writers include the reference out of ignorance, having never looked at Mead's work (cribbing from other textbooks is a widespread tradition in textbook writing), and which authors knowingly misrepresent Mead. In both cases, however, the purpose is clear: The authors are aware that their acknowledging that all societies share our basic conceptions of male and female tendencies will lead the student to (correctly) conclude that these tendencies may run deeper than the social and may set limits on the social. To avoid this, the authors claim variation for that which does not vary, and they misleadingly invoke that which does vary to imply variation in that which does not vary. (In doing this they mimic the lawyer who says, "You may have five witnesses who saw my client commit the crime, but I have ten who didn't.")[12]

THE MEANING OF THE ANTHROPOLOGICAL EVIDENCE

Perhaps anthropology's greatest gift has been its demonstration of the astonishing social variation that our species demonstrates in the societies it creates. In five hundred years, in a world made homogeneous (as our own society is becoming increasingly homogeneous at an accelerating rate) only the ethnographic records of the nineteenth and twentieth centuries will act as counterpoise to human ethnocentricity, demonstrating that things need not be the way they are at a given time in a given world.

However, this gift of anthropology is two-edged. The very extensiveness of the variation in so many institutions forces us to ask why the institutions that do not vary (in broad outline and direction) maintain themselves in the face of such astonishing familial, religious, economic, and political variation. This question is particularly pressing when applied to the universals we discuss, universals not found unexpectedly and inexplicably in a random search of institutions, but concordantly with the dominance behavior that has always been viewed everywhere—whether favorably or unfavorably—as the defining element of maleness.

With very few exceptions, cultural anthropology does not address this question. Often it attempts to simply assert away the universality. When universality *is* granted, cultural anthropology nearly invariably begins with the incorrect assumption that the universality of the institutions we discuss must be explained in economic terms, despite the fact that the universality itself renders dubious any such explanation (because the institutions are present in all of the varied economic systems of all of the varied societies). Economic analyses may be of value in explaining *variation* within the limits imposed by psychophysiological differentiation, but there is no reason to think that the economic factors are of importance in explaining the existence of those limits.[13]

The fact that an institution is universal is not, of course, enough to demonstrate that it will exist anywhere tomorrow. This point would seem too obvious to mention; however, virtually every critic of *Patriarchy* has claimed that I suggest that an institution is inevitable *because* it is universal.

It should not be necessary to say that I do not suggest this. The point I make is that when an institution has existed always and everywhere in this world of variation and change we must ask *why*. Indeed, the attempt to answer this question—to explain the universality of the institutions we discuss—is the very *purpose* of *Patriarchy*, a fact invariably neglected by critics, whose criticisms either ignore the central fact of universality or incorrectly imply that the universals are not universal.

In ignoring or denying universality the critic renders his criticism irrelevant; it is the universality—be it a function of physiology, the inherent nature of society, or mere temporary social factors that have always been present but may not be in the future—that is the empirical reality we wish to explain.

Note, incidentally, that the oft-made criticism that this reasoning would force us to suspect that slavery might be a manifestation of physiological tendencies misses the point entirely. Most societies have never had slavery and even one society lacking slavery is sufficient to prove that slavery is not inevitable. Likewise, a single society with hierarchy, but without patriarchy, would refute claims of universality and would cast the most serious doubt on the importance of physiological differentiation.

The unpleasant truth is that the social sciences have discovered precious few institutions that are universal and whose universality is explicable with direct physiological evidence, yet whose explanation is not—like those for women's giving birth or everyone's eating—so obvious as to be trivial. When a universal is uncovered, it demands explanation.

The refusal to acknowledge that there is an empirical reality to explain is perhaps the most common of the methods invoked by those who would deny the importance of physiological differentiation to the differentiation of male-female behavior and institutions. In their *Not in Our Genes*, the leading spokesmen for this view—Richard Lewontin, Steven Rose, and Leon Kamin—take this tack. Summarizing their presentation of the cross-cultural evidence, they write:

> [Cross-cultural universals] . . . appear to lie more in the eye of the beholder than in the social reality that is being observed.[14]

With reference to the behaviors and institutions I discuss, this statement is utterly untrue. If it were true, the authors would have merely to name a society lacking the institutions we discuss and that would settle the issue. They cannot do so, so they simply refuse to address the empirical reality *Patriarchy* attempts to explain and discuss at length issues that have nothing to do with *Patriarchy*. In so refusing, Lewontin, Rose, and Kamin render irrelevant their entire discussion of sex differences (most of which purports to be a refutation of *Patriarchy*).

Anne Fausto-Sterling, Stephen J. Gould, and a hundred other writers whose impulse is to deny the central empirical issue of universality also take the above approach. They invoke variation in behaviors and institutions that have nothing to do with the universally differentiated behaviors and institutions we discuss and refuse to address the universals we discuss, the only behaviors and institutions relevant to *Patriarchy*.

Other critics often attempt to deny universality by invoking societies claimed (never by the ethnographers who actually studied the societies) to lack the institutions. Every time one looks at the sources claimed for these exceptions, one finds societies so obviously not exceptions that even those who invoked them acknowledge such. Like the believer in unicorns who acknowledges that the last claimed unicorn turned out to be a horse with a party hat, but who still expects a unicorn to appear momentarily, one who wants to believe in societies without the realities we discuss will always find another pretend-exception to invoke. He will always be a step ahead as he races over the cliff.

An addendum to *Patriarchy* provides refutory quotations from every eth-nography I have ever seen suggested as representing an exception to universality. Perhaps the most reckless of those claiming exceptions is William King Whyte.

Whyte claims that his coders uncovered a number of exceptions. I have written at length on this elsewhere, but it is worthwhile here giving a few examples for the reader who is tempted to believe that a mere claim of exceptionality necessarily confers some likelihood of exceptionality.

Let us look at the two variables that would indicate exceptions if there were exceptions.

There are four societies that Whyte claims to be exceptions to the universality of male dominance. In each case I give a quotation from the *same* ethnography on which Whyte bases his claim.[15]

The Iban: "Typically, every bilek family has as its head a man who is responsible for the general management the farm." (p. 81)

The Semang: "In each family the father alone is a respected person." (p. 226)
"The head of a Semang local group is first of all the eldest, if he has any ability at all for leadership. Nevertheless it may happen—and not rarely—that another man is leader of the group." (p. 225)

The Marquesas: "Theoretically, women could hold the highest rank, but in practice few women were actual household heads." (p. 184)

The Kenuzi Nubians: "The subservient position of women was determined by the Islamic religion." (p. 133)
"Women influence their husbands, but [their husband's] decisions are decisive." (p. 89)

The other variable that could provide an exception if there were one concerns "evidence of rough equality." Whyte fails to name the nineteen societies giving such evidence. However, this causes us no problem because Whyte names two societies alleged to give *dominance*, rather than just equality, to the female (wife). Thus, Whyte acknowledges that these are the two strongest of his twenty-one alleged exceptions. If these fail, it is implausible that any of Whyte's unnamed nineteen will succeed.

The Javanese (Modjokuto): "[The father] is expected to be, above all, patient and dignified (sabar) with his wife and children: he should lead them with a gentle firm hand . . ." (p. 107)

The Bribri: "[The brother] . . . or in the default of a brother, a cousin or uncle, [has a ruling voice] in any family council or discussion." (p. 497)[16]

All of the rest of Whyte's "exceptions" concern issues concordant with *Patriarchy* (two societies with women leaders at male levels, but few of them) or irrelevant to it (infant care). Thus, we need not consider these here.

Similarly, Rae Lesser Blumberg, in her entry in *Sociological Theory: 1984*, presents a theory attempting to correlate divergence from sexual egalitarianism with economic factors. To the extent that Blumberg considers only variation that really does exist cross-culturally, her work is irrelevant to *Patriarchy*. *Patriarchy* does not comment on variation that does exist (other than to make the obvious point that when there is very little stratification, there are few cues eliciting male hierarchical and status-attainment behavior and a small arena in which these can formally manifest themselves).

However, Blumberg (pp. 25-6) comes close to implying that five societies have virtually egalitarian conceptions of male and female dominance—that, in other words, variation comes much closer to covering the range of imaginable variation than is, in fact, the case. The societies she names are: The Tasaday, !Kung, Bontoc, Iroquois, and Mbuti.

The Tasaday have been demonstrated to be a completely fraudulent society constructed for purposes of profit (see *Newsday* Nov. 18, 1986). The !Kung, in the same source cited by Blumberg (p. 75), are described as being comprised of "male-centered groups" in which men "have power and can exercise their will in relation to women" (p. 277). The Bontoc seem egalitarian in a feminist anthology, but articles in serious journals by the same author demonstrate precisely the opposite to be the case; I discuss this at length in *Society*, Sept.-Oct., 1986. In the British edition of *Patriarchy*, the reader can find citations, from the same sources invoked by Blumberg, demonstrating the clear presence of patriarchy and male dominance among the Iroquois and Mbuti.

EXPLANATORY PARSIMONY

Any explanation of universality must be simple, if by "simple" we mean parsimonious. I mention this in response to the criticism, as inevitable as it is wrongheaded, that any physiologically rooted theory is "simplistic," "reductionist," or "biologically deterministic."

An analogy makes this clear: If one wishes to explain why every society has institutions concerning food gathering and eating, he must, if his explanation is to be plausible, find a single cause that obtains in every society. To do this he need simply demonstrate that human physiology is such that human beings must eat. He need not explain why some cultures prefer two meals a day and others three, or why some cultures prefer spicy foods and others do not. No doubt is cast on the universality of institutions of eating or a physiological explanation of their existence by invocation of variation in number of meals or types of food.

Likewise, if one wishes to offer a sufficient explanation of why every society is patriarchal—be the society in question feudal, capitalist, or socialist; autocratic, communist, or democratic; primitive, pre-industrial, or modern; puritan or libertine; Christian, Buddhist, or Moslim; matrilocal or patrilocal; matilineal, patrilineal, or bilineal—then clearly plausibility demands a single cause. It makes no sense to explain patriarchy in feudal societies in terms of feudalism, in capitalist societies in terms of capitalism, etc.

Were one to attempt to explain *variation* in the forms of patriarchy, male attainment, and male dominance in physiological terms, one's explanation *would*, indeed, be simplistic—just as it would be simplistic to explain in physiological terms why Americans have ketchup on french fries while the British prefer vinegar. Likewise, physiology is irrelevant to differences between, say, American and Jivaro patriarchy. However, an explanation sufficient to identify and explain the limits to which American, Jivaro, and all other societies conform their sex-role expectations of hierarchical leadership—an explanation identifying and explaining the universal limits within which all variation takes place—requires a single factor common to, and imposing limits on, all societies. In other words, to maintain any plausibility at all, an explanation of patriarchy must be simple.

Critics charging "simplism" often couple the charge with vague assertions of the "complexity" of anthropological and biological realities and the "pervasiveness" of culture and socialization. The mechanisms and processes that generate the institutions we discuss are not so complex or pervasive that they ever fail to work in the same direction. "Complexity" and "pervasiveness" could mean anything to our discussion, and could be more than mere attempts to avoid the issue by obfuscating it, only if we were claiming to explain variation. There is no variation on the level we attempt to explain. An explanation is "simplistic" or unjustifiably "deterministic" or "reductionist"—is ignorant of relevant "complexity"—only if it claims to offer a sufficient explanation for empirical realities that it cannot explain. Our explanation does not attempt to explain any empirical reality that our explanation is not capable of explaining.

It should be noted that there is one oversimplification that does infuse *Patriarchy:* Throughout the book I grant that any variation in behavior and institution is owing to environmental factors alone. In reality, variation is also often rooted in heredity; the height difference between Balinese men and women is considerably less than between that of Watusi men and women, but this does not imply that the difference in the difference is owing to differing nutrition or values.

This oversimplification is, however, both permissible and desirable. It is permissible because, to whatever extent it proves to be an oversimplification, the argument made here is that much *stronger*. (I.e., if not only the universal direction and limits of behavior are rooted in physiology, but also is some of the variation, then the role of physiology has that much *more* importance than *Patriarchy* credits it with. The oversimplification is desirable because we know little about the relevance of hereditary physiological factors to variation in behavior and institution and attempting to include this would require more speculation than is required when we consider only universal directions and limits.)

THE INVOCATION OF IRRELEVANT VARIATION

The very extensiveness of cross-cultural variation in virtually all roles and institutions other than those we discuss here emphasizes the need to explain why the institutions we discuss here always work within the same limits and in the same direction.

Save for simply ignoring the empirical evidence, the most common critical response to the claim of universality is the invocation of variation in roles and institutions having nothing to do with the roles and institutions we discuss, variation whose existence *Patriarchy* does not deny.

We can, for example, grant (for argument's sake) that there are societies in which values are more peaceful or unaggressive than ours; in which ownership is in the hands of women (a fact that is crucial only for those who incorrectly explain patriarchy in primarily economic causal terms—an "explanation" that has great difficulty explaining why these societies are patriarchal); in which roles and tasks (other than those related to dominance or nurturance) that are associated with males in our society are associated with females. In general, we can, for argument's sake, grant cross-cultural variation in any institution that we do *not* discuss; variation in such institutions casts no doubt on the universality of the institutions we *do* discuss.

One can cast empirical doubt on the theory I present by merely naming a society with hierarchy that lacks patriarchy, male dominance, or male attainment; but one can cast such doubt only by so doing. For example, one need only name a society in which we count the numbers of men and women in upper hierarchical positions and find that there are not overwhelmingly more of the former and one has demonstrated that patriarchy is neither universal nor inevitable. But this is the only way in which one can empirically refute *Patriarchy*. The red herrings of irrelevant variation cannot accomplish this, no matter how many red herrings are reeled in.

It was primarily for the purpose of indicating the conditions under which the theory I present could be shown to be incorrect that I titled the book *The Inevitability of Patriarchy*. A "theory" that does not state how it could be tested—that does not state the conditions such that, should these conditions come to pass, it would acknowledge its incorrectness—is not a theory at all.

The second reason for my selecting this title was to emphasize that the very *purpose* of the book is to explain the universality of patriarchy, male attainment, and male dominance. As we have seen, many critics ignore this purpose and this empirical reality, or attempt to assert it away, and proceed as if there were nothing to explain.

The third reason for my giving the book this title was to stress that the universality of patriarchy, male attainment, and male dominance was not a prediction based on the physiological evidence, but an empirical observation that, along with the behavior relevant to the institutions, predicted that we would find the neuroendocrinological evidence (i.e., the mechanism we discuss below). This is important because the argument I make is often presented to scientists in the relevant fields (physiology, neuroendocrinology, etc.) as if it generalizes from the physiological evidence to the social level. The scientists, understandably knowing nothing about any of the cross-cultural evidence whose explanation is our purpose, see this as an unwarranted generalization from the physiological level. When they are told that the analysis goes in the other direction and when they hear for the first time the evidence from the behavioral and institutional levels (i.e., when they learn for the first time about the universalities), they invariably acknowledge, as they should, that this evidence greatly increases the likelihood that the universality is a manifestation of the neuroendocrinological differences they have discovered.

INADEQUATE ENVIRONMENTAL EXPLANATIONS

There are nonphysiological explanations of universality meeting the requirements of parsimony—i.e., invoking just one causal factor to explain universality—that fail for other reasons. I cannot address these in detail here (I do so in the British edition), but this does not matter; every explanation of the universality of patriarchy, male attainment, and male dominance that does not give causal primacy to neuro-endocrinological differentiation can be seen to rest on one or more of the fallacies mentioned in this section. The reader to whom this statement seems too bold is urged to assess any nonhormonal explanation in terms of the fallacies mentioned here: He will find that the explanation rests on one or more of the fallacies and that all such explanations, even if they did not commit one or more of the fallacies, would fail for the two reasons given at the end of this section.

Socialization: Explanations—of which there are many—that see the differentiated conditioning and socialization of males and females as being of primary causal importance fail because they do not explain anything, but merely reword the question; the question becomes: "Why do all societies socialize *males* towards greater dominance behavior?" To say that males are "more aggressive" because they have been socialized to be is like saying that it is men who can grow mustaches because little girls are told that facial hair is not feminine. Socialization often reflects, more than it causes, the male-female differences.

In other words, while it is no doubt true that boys and girls are socialized to associate certain traits and tendencies with males and others with females, this does not imply that the associations are *caused by* the socialization. In many cases the socialization simply reflects a physiologically rooted reality that is observed by a population of children and parents who wish to prepare these children for the reality of adult life. (E.g., females are not more nurturant primarily because they have been socialized to be. Their lower threshold for nurturance behavior is a function of their physiology. Socialization no doubt increases the sex difference in nurturance when it performs its task of teaching the specific behaviors required of nurturance, specific behaviors that vary from society to society and era to era as child-rearing methods vary. But the female's stronger tendency toward nurturance behavior is more a cause than an effect of the differentiated socialization.)

In other words, the increasingly voluminous feminist demonstrations of differentiated socialization of males and females can just as well be argued to serve only to dig deeper the grave of the feminist claim that socialization *causes* the male-female differences in tendency and behavior. The extensiveness of the differentiation of socialization can be argued to demonstrate the strength and pervasiveness of a physiological differentiation of males and females that gives direction to the socialization.

Thus, the familiar argument that if physiological factors were important there would be no socialization is without merit. Socialization instills the methods in which physiologically rooted propensities are channeled in a particular society. For example, females are not more nurturant because little girls are given dolls. Little girls tend to select (and be given) dolls because females are more nurturant. Societies conform to the female's greater nurturance and inculcate in females—through socialization—the differing specific ways in which nurturance is manifested in various societies (the specific child-rearing practices of one's specific society, for example). (Incidentally, the evidence is clear that little girls are more nurturant as a direct result of their physiological make-up. But even if it were the case that the relevant physiological factors did not develop until puberty, the point would remain: The socialization of the girl would be preparation for the reality of female physiology, albeit a physiology that is not expressed until puberty.)

Women's Maternal Role: Explanations placing causal primacy on the time and energies expended by women in their maternal role, by the worldview engendered by it, and by the socialization related to it, simply ignore the empirical evidence of hundreds of societies in which women work harder and longer outside the home at objectively more important (but lower-status) superfamilial tasks than do men. Such explanations fail to explain why, in all such societies, males dominate in hierarchical, high-status, and male-female roles. Once one must introduce some other factor—for example, physical strength—to explain why males dominate in these roles, the maternal issue evaporates and the explanation becomes one that, incorrectly, gives male physical strength causal primacy.

Male Physical Strength: Explanations positing the importance of male physical strength ignore the low or absent correlation between strength and hierarchical attainment. One could, logically but implausibly, argue that patriarchy devolved from male physical strength and that the association of maleness and attainment continues millennia after strength is no longer relevant to attainment. But even this explanation fails to account for the results of experimental studies (of primate species known to be neuroendocrinologically similar to ours) in which physically weak males placed with stronger females immediately establish dominance.

Economic Factors and the Confusion of Cause and Function: Explanations casting economic-historical factors in the starring role usually fail on grounds of parsimony. One cannot persuasively explain patriarchy in feudal societies in terms of feudalism, in capitalist societies in terms of capitalism, and in socialist societies in terms of socialism; parsimony demands giving causal priority to some single factor found in feudal and capitalist and socialist societies. More important, such explanations invariably confuse cause and function, making arguments analogous to that which sees McDonald's need to make money as the cause of the human need to eat. All economic systems will utilize (or "exploit," if one prefers) the realities of human physiology. But the very fact that no economic system anywhere has a nonpatriarchal hierarchy certainly seems to imply that the economy conforms to some factor that sets limits of possibility on the economic system.

Modernization, Modern Attitudes, and Technology: Explanations focusing on differences between nonmodern and modern, technological societies fail because they explain where there is nothing to explain. There is not a scintilla of evidence that modernization—or, indeed, *any* change in any social, economic, or technological factors—significantly reduces the realities we discuss. There has been a slight increase in the number of women at the lower levels of government, though less than one would have expected given the enormous resources of time, energy, money, and labor expended on women's behalf in the last quarter century. But the fact remains that the number of women in the House and Senate is substantially the same as obtained before the women's movement and only marginally higher than obtained a century ago. This marginal improvement, moreover, is expected when the barriers that virtually prohibited women from entering politics altogether are removed. It may be, as many claim, that the needs of modern society are vastly different from those of nonmodern society. But such needs are not of primary causal importance in determining the sexually differentiated behavior of which we speak, and there is no evidence that they can significantly change such behavior.

Modernization can dramatically affect attitudes towards these realities, but attitudes are of little causal importance to the realities. Therefore, an explanation of universality that implies that a change in attitudes (resulting from modernization) will be manifested in reduction of the institutions we discuss when societies modernize makes a suicidal prediction. With respect to our masculinity and femininity, attitudes may determine how happy we are with what we are, but it is not attitudes that primarily determine what we are. (*When* attitudes are of causal importance—as in the case of premarital sex—changes of attitude change behavior. But this is irrelevant for the institutions we discuss.)

If, of course, our society comes to lack patriarchy or male dominance, the theory presented here will, *ipso facto*, be shown to be false. This demonstrates that the theory is a scientific one—one that stakes its empirical claim. To date there is no evidence whatsoever of a decline in the institutions whose universality it is *Patriarchy*'s purpose to explain.

Redefining "Dominance": A tack particularly favored by feminist writers for dealing with the argument we consider here is a "redefinition of 'dominance' " and a finding that "male dominance," so redefined, is not universal. (See, for example, the work of Peggy Reeves Sanday.) This fails because such a redefinition identifies something other than that which we discuss, thereby forcing one making the redefinition to create a new word to stand for the reality we term "dominance." The reality remains, whatever one wishes to call it, and it is this reality, not the word chosen to stand for it, that matters. You can call a tree an "elephant," but then you must create a new word to stand for those fat, gray things with long trunks and skinny tails. The reality is that the three institutions we discuss—and the sexually differentiated behaviors relevant to them—are, whatever one wishes to call them, universal.

"Quasi-Freudian" and other Nonphysiological Psychological Explanations: There are numerous nonphysiological psychological explantions of universality. These come in many flavors and qualities. Some accept nearly all of Freud, save his assumption of the importance of physiological underpinnings of emotion and behavior; others are not at all Freudian but use models derived from other branches of psychology. Many of all types combine the psychological with the economic and with assumptions about a specific type of early family that was universal. What all these have in common is an attempt to explain universality without invoking physiology. (They have this in common by definition; similar theories that do not deny the determinative physiological basis of universality need not concern us here.)

The shame is that some of these have real value in explaining aspects of male and female behavior for which physiological factors are unimportant. Or, in other cases, they might improve their explanatory abilities by taking account of, rather than resisting, relevant constitutional differences between the sexes. Instead, they ask that we accept both their implausibly explaining the simple with the obscure and their merely asserting away all of the direct and experimental neuroendocrinological evidence.

There is, to choose just one example, a contemporary fashion for theories, first proposed long ago, that see as determinative to male behavior a male envy of the female's ability to create life. For such theories to carry any weight at all, they must see as determinative a male dominance "motivation" comparable to that which I see as the mediator between the neuroendocrinological and the behavioral. For if they see some other factor as mediator (male physical strength, for example), then the posited male envy becomes irrelevant and the claimed determinative factor is male physical strength; this leaves the theory facing the problems faced by a straightforward male-strength theory. (In other words, in this example, the envy offers an alternative explanation of why males want to dominate, but not of how they manage to do so; this is explained by male strength).

If, however, this type of theory accepts the role of male dominance motivation and sees this motivation as deriving, in all societies, from the male envy, then it differs on the motivational and social levels from the theory I present "only" in one, crucial, way: It predicts that eradication of the male envy would eradicate the male behavior and the institutions we discuss. It differs here because it differs on the causal level—this theory positing an entirely environmental explanation of why the male is more strongly motivated toward dominance, mine positing a neuroendocrinological explanation (with the two theories agreeing that "motivation" provides the "how"). But the envy explanation of universality, like all the others discussed in this section, fails for reasons we may now enumerate.

Two Problems with All Environmental Explanations of Universality: All nonphysiological explanations share two major faults: In addition to the individual fallacies associated with individual environmental explanations, each such explanation: (1) ignores the enormous amount of direct neuroendocrinological evidence provided by experimental research on animals whose endocrinological system resemble ours, and by the medical study of human beings: It would seem unlikely that the male behavior of the hormonally masculinized female rat is owing to a newfound envy of the normal female rat's ability to give birth, or to comparable Oedipal factors (just as unlikely as it would be to explain in nonphysiological terms why a partially masculinized human female whose anatomy and socialization are female, and who is considered a normal female, exhibits the behavior associated with males); and (2) ignores the fact that, even if there were no such neuro-endocrinological evidence, the cross-cultural evidence alone would strongly suggest that some behaviorally relevant physiological factor accounts for the universality of patriarchy, male attainment, and male dominance. In other words, where the anthropological evidence I present predicts the neuroendocrinological differentiation that is so well documented, environmental theories give us no reason to expect the neuroendocrinological evidence and ignore, or attempt to assert away, the evidence once it is pointed out.

DIFFERENTIATION

Physiology and the Differentiation of Male and Female Dominance Behavior

Even if there were no direct physiological evidence whatever, the cross-cultural evidence alone would strongly suggest only one parsimonious and plausible explanation of the universality of patriarchy, male attainment, and male dominance: This is the explanation positing an as-yet-undiscovered physiological causal mechanism that differentiates male and female behavioral responses to hierarchy, status, and members of the other sex.

It often happens that we know that a cause is physiological before we know what that physiological cause is. Indeed, in medicine it is nearly always the case that a physiological mechanism is discovered only after physical or behavioral effects of the mechanism point the way to discovery of the mechanism. In the social sciences, a physiological mechanism is far less often relevant, but when it is, its existence is indicated by its universal effects long before the actual physiological mechanism is discovered.

In any case, we need not merely posit without direct evidence such a physiological mechanism. There is an enormous amount of direct neuroendocrinological evidence of the mechanism responsible for the male's greater dominance tendency.

I discuss this evidence at length in *Patriarchy*. It is not possible to recapitulate it here. I hope that I am not far off in assuming that the reader is at least generally familiar with: (1) The medical-neuroendocrinological evidence demonstrating the masculinizing and feminizing physical, emotional, and behavioral effects of masculine and feminine hormonalization, and the differentiation of the Central Nervous System it generates. (2) The implications of the evidence on human hermaphroditism, which demonstrates that dominance behavior mirrors masculine or feminine hormonalization when hormonalization conflicts with anatomy and socialization, an extraordinarily difficult thing to explain in social and environmental terms.[17] (Dominance behavior should not be confused with gender identity, an entirely different property discussed below). (3) The controlled experimental study of mammals closely related to human beings (a method of investigation that everyone accepts every time he or she swallows a pill).[18]

All of these independent, but converging, lines of evidence indicate the same thing: Differences between the male and female Central Nervous/Endocrine Systems generate in males, more strongly than in females, a predisposition to select and exhibit whatever behavior is necessary in any environment to attain position in hierarchy, to attain status, and to maintain dominance in male-female relationships and encounters.

The psychophysiological differentiation of males and females would be sufficient to engender any one of the three universals of which we speak even if the other two were somehow absent. The environmental cues of hierarchy, status, and member of the other sex are all sufficient by themselves to elicit the appropriate dominance behavior from males.

It should, then, be clear that by "physiology" we do not refer merely to anatomy. Anatomy is, of course, crucial in that it enables a population to differentiate those with male neuroendocrinological systems from those with female neuroendocrinological systems. If males and female looked alike, the members of a society would have no way of attaching male expectations to males and female expectations to females. But it is the underlying neuroendocrinological differentiation, not the anatomical differentiation, that primarily accounts for the differentiation of behavioral tendency.

Using a somewhat unrigorous term, we might say that (statistically speaking, as always) males are more strongly "motivated" than are females to attain position, status, and dominance when the environmental cues of hierarchy, status, or members of the other sex are present to elicit, and provide an arena for, such behavior. In short: Male physiology is such that males "need" these things more and are therefore more easily excited by the relevant environment to do what is necessary to attain them.

It makes no difference whether one conceptualizes this stronger male "motivation" as the male's "lower threshold for the environmentally cued elicitation of dominance behavior" (the stylistically dreadful, but most accurate, term), a greater male "drive for dominance," a greater male "need of dominance," a stronger male "ego that asserts itself more readily," a more easily released male "competitiveness," or a weaker male "ego that needs shoring up by constant attainment of dominance and status."

In this, the more easily released male "motivation" is like the "sex drive." Is the "sex drive" a "drive" or a "need"? It doesn't matter; what matters is that human physiology is such that, under certain environmental conditions, people will feel sexual arousal. Likewise, it is the reality of the male-female differentiation in dominance tendency (or "competitiveness," if one prefers), and not the model used to describe that differentiation, that matters. And any model worth consideration must acknowledge the differentiation—whether it explains the differentiation in terms of physiology, environment, or some interaction of the two— because the model's ability to explain the empirical reality of the differentiation is what justifies the model's existence.

It is worth noting that "motivation" is a relational term. In the abstract, virtually everyone is motivated, to a greater or lesser extent, to obtain everything that can be desired (position, status, dominance, love, security, power, fame, wealth, etc.). It is only when choices among desired things must be made—when a hierarchy of desires must determine that which will be sacrificed for satisfaction of that which is more desirable—that "motivation" becomes a fertile concept. Thus, it is not only males whose physiology engenders a desire for hierarchical power; female physiology does this also, though to a reduced degree that reflects the lesser degree to which the physiological development associated with dominance behavior plays a part in fetal and postnatal female development. What physiological differentiation does is give males and females differing hierarchies of emotional tendencies (i.e., differing "motivations"). Female physiology, for example, gives a higher position to lessening an infant's distress. This is why a threat to the infant can elicit from the female the willingness to risk death that battle elicits from many males.

No one has any difficulty understanding all this in practice. We speak of the "aggressive businessman" and "the maternal instinct." Many people, however, seem to have difficulty picturing the psychophysiological differentiation on a more abstract level. I suspect that this is owing to an unfortunate tendency to think in terms of an hydraulic analogy that sees people as containers of drives and emotions whose release is determined by various valve settings and channel widths. An analogy that much more clearly captures the role of environment as cue and arena for the physiologically rooted tendency is the analogy of iron and the magnet. Iron does not have a "need" or a "drive" to find a magnet, but it does have— built into its very physical make-up—a tendency to respond strongly to a magnet when there is a magnet in the immediate environment. Likewise, the tendencies we discuss are best conceptualized as built-in tendencies to respond with specific emotions to specific environmental cues and stimuli (hierarchy, status, members of the other sex). The actual behavior that successfully satisfies these emotions may vary from society to society, but the emotional responses to specific enviornmental cues will not.[19] Thus, for example, the fact that a female will react to a threat to her infant with a ferocity equalling that of a male soldier in combat represents a physiologically rooted tendency that is elicited by the environmental presence of a threat to the infant. The environmental situation promising victory in combat does not elicit such ferocity from the female.

Behavioral Manifestations on the Societal Level

Physiology does not determine the specific actions necessary for dominance and attainment in any given society. The actions required for attaining dominance in a particular society are determined by the culture of that society. It need not be the case that there are any specific actions that lead to dominance in every society. It is sufficient, for explaining patriarchy in terms of physiological differentiation, that physiology engender in the male a greater tendency ("motivation," "drive," "need," "threshold," or whatever) to act in whichever ways lead to dominance in his particular society. The tendency alone will lead males to sacrifice more to learning the actions required for attainment of dominance (whatever these behaviors be in a given society), to acting in the way required for attainment of dominance, and to subordinate other satisfactions and rewards—family, intimacy, health, relaxation, vacation, and the like—in favor of attainment of position, status, and dominance. The action required for dominance or attainment in a given society or situation may be fighting, raising one's voice, kissing babies for votes, or learning specific skills. It is the male's greater tendency to select and exhibit *whatever* action is required, and not the specific action required in a given situation, that is posited here to have its roots in male physiology.

This distinction between tendency and action is analogous to the distinction between sexual arousal and sexual action. The former is clearly a physiologically rooted tendency to respond to certain environmental stimuli. The action—be it intercourse in the missionary position, intercourse in an alternate position, masturbation, etc.—is determined, at least to a great extent, by cultural norms and other environmental factors.

I do, in fact, suspect that close analysis by ethnologists and psychologists will find specific universal sexual differences of dominance actions—differences of body presentation, voice, and the like—which are causally associated with dominance behavior and which flow from physiological factors. But it is not necessary here that this be the case.[20]

On the level of society as a whole, the law of large numbers becomes determinative. The probabilistic, continuous, and quantitative reality of the male's greater dominance tendency—a level on which there are many exceptions (males who exhibit behavior usually associated with females and *vice versa*)—becomes concretized and exaggerated on the societal level in absolute, discrete, and qualitative terms. Thus, the quantitative reality of the male's greater "aggression"[21] is generalized and made absolute, becoming the norms, expectations, and values reflecting the qualitative belief that "men are aggressive" and "women are passive." (Just as habit permits the individual to avoid the anxiety of constant decision, social expectation and social role permit social intercourse and organization that would be impossible if one had to "treat everyone as an individual.")

The belief that males are more aggressive is unavoidable because it is a reflection of the population's observation that males *are* more aggressive (i.e., have a lower threshold for dominance behavior). Social values and expectations cannot be anything one might hope; they must be concordant with observation, and a society could no more fail to associate dominance behavior with males than it could fail to associate greater height with males.

This leads to prejudice, and often discrimination, occasionally for every woman and often for the woman who is an exception. It is prejudice when a statistical fact about a group is applied to a member to whom it does not apply. Discrimination is possible precisely because the statistical reality makes the exception an exception, exposed to the possibility of discrimination. The six-foot-four-inch tall girl who wishes she were shorter lives in a world of boys who are praised for being six-feet-four-inches tall. But the fact of discrimination casts no doubt on the physiological causation of the quality being discriminated against.

Thus, the discrimination (or, more precisely and far more often, the prejudice) encountered by the high-level female executive is certainly real. But it is a discrimination that is possible precisely because that which is being discriminated against is exceptional; it is exceptional because male physiology gives males—statistically speaking—a "motivational" advantage for the attainment of high position. This advantage generates social expectations and values associating hierarchical attainment with males. The physiological advantage combines with the expectations and values to create a social context in which the woman who does attain a high-level position will encounter discrimination.

Where the height of the very tall girl is virtually all owing to physiological factors, it need not be the case that the motivation of the high-level female executive has anything to do with physiology.[22] Familial and other psychological experiential factors can engender exceptionally high "motivation." Indeed, given the prejudice the high-level female executive faces, this is a virtual requirement. But the issue relevant to our analysis is the fact that the upper levels of hierarchies are overwhelmingly male. Thus, in none of the thousands of societies on which we have evidence do the nonphysiological factors affecting the woman who is an exception play a significant role in undercutting the number of males in hierarchies, so these factors need not concern us here.

There are, of course, other facilitators of dominance behavior. On occasion these are not merely facilitators, but necessary conditions; it is not only sex that explains why South Africa is not headed by a black woman. But within the group that meets the other conditions, it is maleness that is determinative. And among males within this group, it is, by and large, only those with exceedingly high dominance tendencies that will attain the high positions (the cause of these males' *exceptionally* strong dominance motivation being another question).

Fallacies of Criticisms of Physiological Reasoning

I have mentioned that the most common responses to the *anthropological* evidence of universality are: (A) The denial of this empirical reality (by ignoring it, asserting that it does not exist, or introducing "exceptions" that are in no relevant way exceptions); (B) the invocation of irrelevant variation (i.e., variation in roles and institutions having nothing to do with the empirical realities we attempt to explain—irrelevant variation that, therefore, we can grant for argument's sake); and (C) the failed attempt to find logical error in the physiologically rooted explanation of universality.

Lewontin et al., commit all of these. But most extensive is the authors' attempt to cast doubt on the determinativeness of the neuroendocrinological differences by criticizing research on a host of biological factors that *Patriarchy* does not mention. Indeed, nearly all of the authors' presentation, putatively a criticism of *Patriarchy*, is addressed to issues not mentioned in *Patriarchy*: differentiated functions of brain hemispheres, brain size, rates of disease, longevity, and the like. Since such factors play no part in the argument I present, we can, for argument's sake, grant whatever the authors like.

The authors do make two points that are relevant. The first—the denial of anthropological universality presented above—is, as we have seen, utterly incorrect. The second should have warned the authors that they were on the entirely wrong track. In making the point that women can be medical doctors (a point no one could reasonably dispute), the authors point out that in the Soviet Union the majority of family doctors are women—*but:* "Of course, there family doctoring has a lower status and lower pay than in the United States, but that is a different point."[23]

No, that is precisely the central point. Why is lower status always associated with the (nonmaternal) roles women play? The authors run away from this question because they cannot accept the only answer concordant with the evidence: High status elicits from males a greater tendency to do that which is necessary for the attainment of the status. If the status of family doctoring in the Soviet Union were to rise (for whatever reason), men would be attracted and would choose to enter medical schools in far greater numbers than they do now. In other words, the role does not have high status primarily because it is male; it is male primarily because it has high status, a high status that elicits more strongly from those with male physiologies the behavior required to attain the high status.

Sociobiology and Evolutionary Theory: The current interest in sociobiological explanations of human behavior has led many to subsume under the term "sociobiology" all explanations that see physiological factors as causally important to behavior. This is an error, one that is made most often by those looking for justification for dismissing all nonpurely social explanations.

Sociobiological theories are evolutionary theories. As such, they unavoidably encounter the difficulties of *ad hoc*-ness and testability inherent in evolutionary theories. Theories such as that presented in *Patriarchy*, which perhaps should be distinguished from sociobiological theories by terming them "sociophysiological theories" (or some less grating term), make no evolutionary assumptions whatever. They simply take human physiology as a given and proceed from there, making no attempt to explain how it got that way. This being the case, no evolutionary criticisms can be relevant to such theories. Put another way: A theory claiming that the males of all societies are, for physiological reasons, taller than the females of their respective societies need merely (A) demonstrate that this is the case, and (B) specify the physiological differences between the sexes responsible for this. Interesting as is the evolutionary question of *why* human beings evolved in this way, it does not behoove the one proposing the theory even to address the evolutionary question.

(Having said this, I would add that it is difficult to imagine higher primate species evolving in a way that failed to associate with males aggression, dominance, and other tendencies physiologically related to the protective function and the behaviors that serve it. The loss of males is unimportant for survival of group or species; a relatively few males could impregnate all of the females. The loss of a large number of females is disastrous; each female lost forever reduces a population. It may be that we have reached a point where males are now the greatest threat to women and children and where males serve primarily to protect women and children from the violence of war and crime caused by other males.

Be that as it may, the fact is that, for better or worse, the dominance tendencies that underlie these are built into males, and there is no evidence that any environmental factors or "changing needs of society" affect this in the slightest.)

I do not here mean to be critical of sociobiological theories; it is quite likely that they will contribute tremendously to our understanding of human behavior. But they do, by their nature, carry a burden of "proof" that "sociophysiological" theories do not carry.

Sexual Difference, Racial Difference, and "Territorial Imperatives": In a similar attempt to subsume all explanations emphasizing physiology under one heading and treating all as if they exhibited the weaknesses of the weakest, many critics treat explanations of sex differences as analogous to explanations of racial differences in I.Q. I am not qualified to assess explanations of the racial differences. However, all that need be pointed out here is the obvious difference in the evidential bases of the two explanations.

The racial explanations are, by and large, based on one small minority in one society. This minority has lived in a single social environment. The evidence on male and female behavior and institution is based on all of the world's societies with all of their varied social environments, each having approximately the same number of males and females. If all these varying societies had equal numbers of blacks and whites, and in every society whites scored higher on I.Q. tests, then there would be no reasonable alternative to the conclusion that physiological differences between blacks and whites were responsible for the I.Q. differences. But there is no such universal trans-societal evidence for (or against) there being racial differences in I.Q. There is for the sexual differences we discuss. (Moreover, even if it were the case that equivalent evidence for racial difference in I.Q. existed, the difference would be one of capacity, not the far more socially important "motivational" differences we find in males and females).

Likewise, the attempt to associate serious physiologically rooted theories with "explanations" of territoriality is unwarranted. The problem with theories of territoriality in human beings is that they neither specify the physiological mechanism nor coherently define the territoriality they attempt to explain. Lack of specification of mechanism is not fatal; indeed, I have argued that the anthropological evidence would lead us to posit a differentiation of the male and female physiological mechanisms relevant to dominance behavior even if we had no direct physiological evidence. The real problem with theories of human territoriality is that they are so unclear on the nature of the territoriality they wish to explain and on how to know it when you see it. That this is not a problem with the theory I present is clear from the fact that patriarchy can be identified by merely counting the numbers of men and women in hierarchies.

Between-Sex Differences, Within-Sex Differences, and Other Statistical Confusions: I would guess that nearly half of the criticisms of *Patriarchy* would not have been made had the critic simply asked himself one question: "Is the point I am making one that would be true if we were talking about the male-female difference in height"? If the answer is "yes," then the point is obviously not in conflict with the analysis I present; both describe realities that are statistical on the level of individuals, with many exceptions expected. (The seventh tallest person on record is a woman.)

We can speak of absolutes and an absence of exceptions only on the social level, where the statistical realities found on the level of individuals are resolved in absolute terms in the institutions we discuss; i.e., in every society there is a minority of women who exhibit greater dominance behavior than a minority of men, but there is no society that is not patriarchal. Failure to understand that the issue of sex differences is, on the level of individuals, a statistical one, dooms any discussion of sex differences to incoherence.

Thus, consider the oft-made point that within-sex differences are greater than between-sex differences (i.e., the range from the least to the most within a sex is greater than the difference in averages of the sexes). This point is correct, but it does not lead to the conclusion that the difference is unimportant. Even if there were such overlap in the physiological mechanisms relevant here (and it is unlikely that there is in normal males and females), this would not begin to cast doubt on the importance of the difference. The difference in height within the category of men or within the category of women is about six feet from extreme to extreme and about two feet within the normal range. The height difference between averages of the sexes is less than six inches. Yet no one would use this to deny that men are taller, that the tallest people and best basketball teams will be male, or that the height difference has a primarily hereditary-physiological causation.[24]

This should make it clear why there is, contrary to the claims of many, no implication in *Patriarchy* that physiological differences play any role in differences of dominance tendency within-sex (i.e., among men or among women). While I think it likely that physiological differences *do* play a role within-sex (and that in the future we will have measurements sufficiently fine-tuned to isolate these relatively small differences from other causal factors), it is necessary for the theory I present only that the large neuroendocrinological differences between men and women straddle a physiological threshold that is clearly crucial to dominance behavior and that neuroendocrinological differences among males are unimportant.

This is analogous to the causal importance of size to performance as a professional football interior lineman. Size is obviously important (there are no 180-pound interior linemen), but it may be that size is unimportant once a lineman weighs 250 pounds. Thus, within-group differences in size would be irrelevant within the group of those weighing over 250 pounds. (Put another way, there is a threshold of 250 pounds, past which other factors alone can explain relative ability.)

Likewise, the fact that there are, whatever the variable under discussion, many exceptions (males exhibitng behavior associated with females and *vice versa*) is expected for a reason in addition to that expected even when a factor is, like height, virtually purely physiological. Virtually all behavior, including dominance behavior, results on occasion from causal factors having nothing to do with physiology in any but a trivial way. Experiential, particularly familial, environments no doubt predispose one to greater dominance behavior (or preclude such behavior) in some cases. For some of these cases the effects are sufficiently powerful to engender the degree of dominance behavior associated with the other sex. While this will lead to some individuals being exceptions, it need not concern us here. Such factors have never come near generating a sufficient number of women exhibiting such behavior to make a nonpatriarchal society; if they had, we would not be addressing the empirical question of universality whose answer is the purpose of *Patriarchy*.

Thus, it should be clear that there is no implication that the female head-of-state must differ in any way from the male head-of-state (except in that she is an exception in being a *female* head-of-state). A six-foot-tall woman is not, with respect to height, different from a six-foot-tall man (except in that she is an exception in being a six-foot-tall *female*).

The Confusion of Behavior and Attitude: If one asks the average person whether much has changed with reference to sexual differences, one will elicit a strongly affirmative response. In some ways this response is correct; there are virtually no professions or pursuits any longer closed to women simply because they are women.

In general, there is considerably less rigidity to sex roles than was the case a century ago. But the thing that has changed most is attitudes (at least *stated* attitudes; whether people's true beliefs have changed as much is another question).

For much behavior, socially determined attitude is of great causal importance. When this is the case, a change in attitude can be manifested in an equal change in behavior. However, when attitude does not play an important causal role, a change in attitude has little effect on the reality addressed by that attitude. A century ago, sexuality was widely considered an evil, while a man was lauded by both men and women as "an aggressive businessman" and a husband who "took the lead." Today (at least before AIDS) sexuality is encouraged and "aggression" detested. Attitude is causally important to sexual activity, and so today there is a great deal more premarital sex than there was a century ago. Attitude is not causally important to the institutions we discuss and so today males continue to dominate hierarchies, etc.

The reality of dominance has not changed to any significant extent, only the attitudes towards it have. Attitudes may determine how happy we are with what we are, but they cannot, with reference to male dominance, determine what we are. What we are, with reference to the behaviors we discuss, is a function not of attitudes, or the "needs of modern society," but of (A) the differing physiologies of males and females, (B) the differing behavioral responses to the environment engendered by these differing physiologies, and (C) the social realities that are limited and given their direction by the physiological and behavioral realities.

The Confusion of Gender Identity and Sexually Differentiated Behavior: There is no confusion as widespread in the social science literature on sex differences as that concerning "gender identity." This is discussed at length in *Patriarchy*. Here I can merely state the central point: To simplify but not distort, gender identity is one's continuing self-conception as male or female. Many sociologists have claimed that gender identity has a purely social causation. I believe this to represent a woeful misunderstanding of the pioneering work of John Money, but this need not concern us here. For our purposes we can grant—for argument's sake and for argument's sake alone—that gender identity has a purely social causation.

We can grant this because it is not gender identity, but male and female *behavior*, that is associated with sexual neuroendocrinological development and that is posited here as causally crucial to the sexual differentiation of behavior responsible for the institutions we discuss.

This can be seen clearly if we consider chromosomal female fetuses hormonally masculinized in utero. When masculinization is not too extensive, the newborn's Central Nervous System is masculinized, but the anatomy is female and socialization conforms to anatomy. In other words, no one has any reason to doubt that the child is a perfectly normal girl and the parents treat her as such. We can grant, for argument's sake, that in these individuals gender *identity* is determined by socialization alone and is as female as is that of the normal female. What is relevant here is the fact that the behavior of these individuals is—statistically speaking—far more like that found in hormonally normal males than in hormonally normal females. This cannot be explained in terms of socialization, because the socialization is female. It should be stressed that the issue is not whether the tendency of these hormonally masculinized females to behave in ways associated with hormonally normal males is "good" or "bad": the point is that these females do behave in ways associated with males and that this cannot be explained without invoking the hormonalization.

It is this behavior—behavior whose neuroendocrinological origin is attested to by an enormous volume of evidence from a varied range of scientific disciplines, and not gender identity—that is ultimately responsible for the institutions we discuss. Put another way: It does not matter whether these hormonally masculinized individuals see themselves as males trapped in female bodies (i.e., have male gender identities) or as females who are "extreme tomboys" or "aggressive" or in some similar way females who behave in ways associated with males. What matters here is that the behavior is that usually exhibited more strongly by males—despite the *female* anatomy, socialization, and even gender identity. This cannot be explained without seeing the hormonalization as determinative.

This distinction can be seen clearly by looking closely at the one of John Money's subjects most often invoked by sociologists as demonstrating the social nature of sexual differentiation—a hormonally normal male who was castrated in a circumcision accident. This male was surgically (but not, until puberty, hormonally) feminized and socialized as a female. Let us, for argument's sake, agree with the sociologist's assertion that this individual's gender *identity* was that of a normal female (i.e., was the result of socialization). The point that is relevant to our discussion is the *behavior*, not the gender identity, of this individual. Money makes it clear that this individual was "often the dominant one in a girl's group" and exhibited "tomboy" behavior, tendencies that cannot be explained in terms of the socialization, which was female.[25]

I do not mean to make a lot of this one case. I mention the case only because a good number of sociologists, who realize that all the other cases discussed by Money obviously imply the importance of sexual hormonalization to behavior, treat this case as if it argues for the unimportance of hormonalization to behavior. For the reasons we have discussed, this is obviously incorrect.

The Confusion of the Independent and the Dependent Variable: "Feedback" and "Interaction": It is reasonable for observers who wish to emphasize the social elements involved in sexual differentiation of behavior and institution to stress the fact that such social elements are always involved in the development of behavior, social expectations, and institutions that reflect sexual differences. It is, likewise, reasonable for these environmentalists to stress that the social often increases the difference between males and females (as in the weight-lifting example, below).

What is unreasonable is for these observers to treat the social as an independent variable, as the causal equal of the neuroendocrinological factor. This is unreasonable because the social gets its direction and limits from the neuroendocrinological. This is why the social works in the same direction in every society. Put another way: The environmental variable is never so independent as to be capable of preventing the physiological factor from setting the limits manifested in the universals we wish to explain.

It is true that many physiologically generated tendencies are tendencies to behave in a given way in a given environment. Thus, to use Haldane's famous example, the respective physiologies of a Jersey and a Highland cow are such that the former will give more milk if the cows are in an English pasture, while the latter will give more milk if the cows are on a Scottish moor.

However, this differs from the human male-female differences we discuss in that the environment of the cows is independent of the cows' physiology; a moor is not a moor *because* Highland cows are built the way they are. In the case of humans, the cultural environment is limited by the reality of male-female differences and the population's observation of them. That is why the environment always ratifies the reality of the physiological differentiation.

Similarly, unlike the laboratory experiment, in which an "outside experimenter" can set up any expectations and values he or she likes, societies have no "outside experimenter." The expectations and values of a society are limited by the reality of what the population observes. Just as no society could have expectations associating equal height with females, so no society can have expectations associating an equal dominance tendency with females. The range of possibilities on the level of expectation and socialization is limited by constraints imposed on the neuroendocrinological and neuroendocrinological-behavioral levels. In other words, the social-environmental factors that feed back to the physiological factors are themselves limited in possibility by the directions and limits given by the physiological realities.

For example, the expectation that males are physically stronger than females is a function of a male physiology that makes males physically stronger than females. This expectation may feed back (e.g., through male weight-lifting) to increase the strength difference. But it could not be the case that the social-environmental factor that fed back was an expectation of greater *female* strength; physiology determines that it will be greater male strength that a population will observe and this will set limits of possibility on expectations and values. This is why the environmentalist emphasis on "feedback" and "interaction" cannot succeed in demonstrating the causal equality of social factors. That there is no need to posit such a causal equality is obvious from the fact that the institutions we discuss are universal; if feedback were causally equal, there would not be the universality of the institutions for us to explain. In other words, the issue of feedback begs the question: Why does feedback never undo that which the initial physiology does?

Those examples of feedback advanced by environmentalists are invariably examples in which feedback engenders a relatively insignificant effect on physiology (i.e., effects of social environment and experience on male testosterone levels, while real, are insignificant when compared to the difference between normal male and female levels). Moreover, it is not just hormone levels, but the sensitivity of the central nervous system to whatever testosterone is present that is crucial. And the male central nervous system has been sensitized *in utero*.

Finally: I assume throughout that there is no female physiological factor, complementing the dominance tendency of the male, that motivates the female to search for, and prefer, a dominant male. Male tendencies alone would be sufficient to explain that which we wish to explain. Despite current ideology, however, it may well be that there is a "wired in" female preference for a dominant male. The male primate who ranks low in an all-male hierarchy (and who happens also to be as small as a female) rises to the top when placed in an all-female hierarchy and when his testosterone level rises. While this can be explained entirely in terms of male psychophysiology, it may be that female physiology is such that it acts on the male to increase his dominance tendency. In other words, the female role in engendering the male dominance behavior might well be a volitional one. If one looks at the actual behavior (rather than the ideological proclamations) of even the feminist, one can make a strong argument for this applying to human beings as well. This sort of picture of the female playing an equal role in the "dance" has the positive effect of replacing a social perception of female passivity with an active submission that, certainly on the level of coital behavior, is more satisfactorily concordant with our experience and observation. But I stress that none of this plays a part in the theory I present.

The "Suggestibility" of Hormones: Feminists are fond of invoking Stanley Schacter's well-known finding that the behavioral effects of epinephrine can, under experimental conditions, reflect suggestion (i.e., individuals given adrenaline will feel fearful or exhilarated, depending on the behavior of others in the room).[26] This finding will not surprise readers who have felt fear at one time and romantic love at another.

As an argument against the psychological and behavioral directions given by the male hormone, this fails for reasons similar to that mentioned above. Even if we ignore the fact that fetally differentiated central nervous system sensitivity is clearly relevant in the case of testosterone, but not clearly relevant in the case of adrenaline, and even if we ignore the dubious assumption that the effects of testosterone are as malleable as those of epinephrine, we still face the central logical problem with this argument:

In Schacter's experiment it is clear where the suggested behavior came from:

the "outside experimenter," Schacter and his assistants. But who are the "outside experimenters" in every society that has ever existed? Why is it always the case that dominance is suggested to *males*? Once one must invoke some other factor (for example, male physical strength) to explain why it is always males who dominate, then the entire issue of suggestibility is rendered an irrelevant mediator and one must defend the causal determinativeness of the newly introduced factor.

Dominance Behavior in Boys and Girls: Until puberty, boys and girls have roughly equal testosterone levels. Despite this, little boys exhibit the male behavior we have discussed more than do little girls. This is often seen as somehow demonstrating that social factors are responsible for the association of the behavior with males.

In all likelihood, boys more often exhibit the male behavior because their fetal central nervous system development has more sensitized them to the effects of whatever testosterone is present. But let us assume that this is not the case and that the boys' male behavior is entirely the result of imitation of adults and socialization. It is the behavioral effects of adult male hormonalization—in which the male testosterone level greatly exceeds that of the female—that accounts for the adult behavior to which the boy is socialized. (There are many physiological events that are not manifested until puberty; the hormonalization of which we speak accounts for the fact that boys do not have facial hair, while men do.)

Female Androgens: It is, of course, true that females have (in smaller amounts) "the male hormone," just as males have "the female hormone." However, even if there were equal amounts of the hormones, "the male hormone" in males would still be acting on a central nervous system sensitized to "the male hormone." Since males have, in fact, more testosterone and since it is acting on a central nervous system more sensitive to its behaviorally relevant properties, the presence of some testosterone in the female is irrelevant to our interests.

Lip Service: Many environmentalist analyses give lip service to the role of physiological differentiation. The reader should note that it is by the analysis itself, and not a mere claim of this sort, that the acceptance or rejection of the physiological should be assessed. A work that claims that it does not deny the role of physiology—but then proceeds to treat the overrepresentation of males in positions of power as equivalent to an overrepresentation of whites—is, in fact, denying the role of physiology. A lip-service acknowledgment of the role of physiology does not immunize such a work against the contradictions inherent in a denial of the physiological.

An Aside to Neuroendocrinological and Experimental Scientists

I have invoked three converging lines of physiological evidence in the explanation of the anthropological empirical evidence: the neuroendocrinological study of normal human beings, the study of human hermaphrodites, and the experimental study of animals neuroendocrinologically similar to us. It is the latter—the controlled experimental study of animals known, from empirical experience, to be similar to us in systems under investigation, to be genetically knowable, and to be physically manageable—that concerns us here.

Those who dislike the implications of the experimental studies invariably attempt to assert these away with the claim that "people are not animals." It is telling that they do not take this path when using any of the thousands of medications whose safety is dependent on the reliability of experimental studies. The safety of such medications is, like the evidence we have discussed, predicated on the ability of experimental studies of nonhuman animals, and medical studies of human beings, to identify the effects of chemical substances on human functioning.

The most obvious relevance of an experimental finding is, of course, to the animal being studied. But very few study the rat just to find out about the rat; rats are not all that compelling. In the back of nearly every experimentalist's mind is the ultimate relevance of his finding to human beings.

Now, when generalizing from the experimental to the human level, the experimentalist is, at least in public, reticent. In part this is owing to the admirable conservatism shared by all scientists. But, more important here, this reluctance to generalize is owing to the fact that the experimentalist, as experimentalist, lacks some of the evidence required for generalization. Thus, when you ask the experimentalist who has demonstrated the importance of male hormonalization to male behavior in rats to assess the relevance of his findings to human beings, he will say something to this effect: "It is clear, from the medical-neuroendocrinological study of human beings done by others, that the effects of male hormonalization in human beings are similar to that which we have found. But if you ask what are the human behavioral and social implications of this, I cannot say. One must consider not merely the effects of hormonalization on human behavior, but also the effects of the resulting behavior on the social environment, the effects of the social environment on physiology, the feedback that echoes from the social back to the other levels, and subsequent interactions of all of these."

This is an admirable acknowledgment on the part of the experimentalist that he lacks the sort of evidence required for him to generalize (the evidence, for example, of anthropological universality). There is, of course, no reason why he should know about the universality of the behaviors and institutions we discuss.

When, however, you tell the experimentalist that in all of the thousands of societies we have studied, with all their varied social environments, dominance is associated with males and that the institutions of dominance always reflect this, he acknowledges (at least in private) that this new evidence enormously increases the likelihood that the universal institutions are manifestations of the neuroendocrinological differentiation he investigates on a nonhuman level—as, indeed, he must: The concordance of explanations at different levels is precisely what science searches for.

Prediction on the social (i.e., cross-cultural) level is impossible for the experimentalist, then, because the experimentalist doesn't know anything about the evidence provided by the social level, the evidence that must be combined with the experimental evidence if one is to make predictions on the social level. But the experimentalist should acknowledge—and the vast majority do acknowledge, at least in private—that demonstration of the cross-cultural universality and the behavior relevant to it extends our knowledge of the effects—in some sense the ultimate effects—of differentiated hormonalization to a point that the experimental evidence alone could not predict.

In other words, the experimentalist merely acknowledges what is obviously true: It is often the case that the perimeters of a given discipline or science impose limits on explanation and prediction that are overcome when we consider the evidence provided by a number of disciplines. It is often the case that a number of logically possible explanations permitted within the limits of one discipline are ruled out when the evidence of other disciplines is considered. The causal determinativeness of human physiological differentiation to the universality of patriarchy, male attainment, and male dominance cannot be predicted by evidence from the experimental level alone; but when the human medical evidence, our observation of male and female behavior, and cross-cultural universality are all considered along with this experimental evidence, the likelihood of a physiological causal determinativeness increases enormously.

However: Those who dislike the implications of all of this evidence often merely assert the irrelevance of hormonalization to the behavior of men and women. In so doing, they are, in effect, making (incorrect) predictions about what we find on the social level; they make, in effect, the claim that the institutions we discuss will not be found to be universal or that the universality can be as well explained without reference to hormonalization.

Even those who deny merely that current experimental evidence provides any relevant information and who demand ever more specific evidence merely obfuscate a truth they do not like. One can always demand finer and finer points between the correlates included in an explanation and can refuse to accept a hypothesis by demanding explanation down to the quantum level. Likewise, one can always argue that, examined to sufficiently fine structure, all empirical realities are merely correlates and that cause and effect is illusory. But one who does these things will never have any reason to believe that any statement about the world is any more likely to be true than any other; in short, one who makes such unreasonable demands will never know anything.

The purpose of this discussion was to address the relevance of the experimental evidence to the question of universality; to demonstrate that the evidence of universality extends the knowledge that would be possible if we considered only evidence from the experimental level; and to emphasize the futility of an assertion that—because there are limits on what can be known when only the experimental evidence is considered and because all scientific evidence is tentative—we can say nothing about the role of hormonal differentiation in institutional differentiation.

At the risk of redundancy and to emphasize to the neuroendocrinological scientist—who, understandably, tends to assume that those ascribing physiological causal elements to behavior are simply (and unwarrantedly) generalizing from the physiological evidence—I will end this aside by reiterating that *Patriarchy* does *not* generalize from the physiological level, but *predicts* (correctly) that a causal mechanism will be found on the physiological level. This prediction is based on the empirical evidence of universality and the impossibility of explaining, for reasons we have discussed, this universality without positing a determinative difference between males and females in the physiological factors underlying dominance and attainment behavior. As we have seen, this prediction is supported in its entirety by the neuroendocrinological evidence, evidence that nonphysiological explanations of universality fail to predict.

Issues of Plausibility, Relevance, and Common Sense

When scientific theories compete, we first jettison those theories that contain fallacies; for these we need not even examine empirical evidence because an illogical "explanation" is not an explanation. Then we discard those theories that are intolerably discordant with the empirical evidence they claim to explain. This usually leaves us with more than one theory, at least until we uncover the empirical evidence permitting a test that only one of the theories can pass.

Surviving theories are assessed on grounds more open to subjectivity, and more vulnerable to ideological exaggeration of the value of an infertile, inelegant, or implausible theory. It is not always possible to demonstrate conclusively that a theory is infertile, inelegant, or implausible. This fact is often exploited by those who deny the importance of sexual physiological differentiation. They mimic the man who, out of a need to believe that which is extraordinarily unlikely, explains a magician's tossing fifty heads in a row as his coincidentally hitting on such a streak (which is a 1-in-2^{50} possibility) and ignores the considerably more likely explanation that the magician is using a two-headed coin.

Thus, as we have seen, some "explain" patriarchy as a manifestation of a male envy of the female ability to give birth. There may be such a male envy and it may fertilely explain some things in need of explanation. But as an explanation of the universality of male dominance it is, when compared to theories that also explain dominance behavior in animals neuroendocrinologically similar to human beings, and in hormonally masculinized human females, an attempt to deny the obvious and stronger explanation in favor of the obscure and weaker explanation. Again: It is difficult to explain the male rat's behavior in terms of an envy of the female rat's ability to give birth.

The need that leads one to deny the obvious and accept the obscure can, when sufficiently powerful, encourage one to make arguments, (A) attacking the purposes of the theorist, (B) attempting to refute his theory by invoking (imagined) consequences of its acceptance, and (C) claiming that because, in the past (before current evidence was discovered), biological theories have been incorrect or misused, contemporary theories must be incorrect. I hope that the irrelevance and fallaciousness of such arguments are apparent to the reader. Here it is necessary only to reiterate that if the devil himself claims, for the most evil of purposes, that the earth is round, this does not make the earth flat; motivation and purpose have nothing whatever to do with truth.

The standard response to this statement of the obvious is that motivation and purpose lead one to infuse his theory with values. Such a criticism has power only to the extent that the critic can show how these values have distorted the theory—how, for example, the theory is supported by a value where an empirical fact is required. If the critic can do this, then he need not make a general statement about the theory being infused with values; he will be able to destroy the theory on its own terms. But if he cannot do this, then his general claim that the theory is "infused with values" is worthless; it is equivalent to the charge of "sophistry" by one who cannot actually specify any logical error or "misrepresentation" by one who cannot specify any empirical error. In short: Motivation and purpose may explain *why* a theorist made an error in his theory, but only demonstration of the error itself can cast doubt on the theory.

Similarly the feminist charge of a male bias cannot successfully challenge any theory; the feminist must be able to specify a manifestation of this bias that renders the theory worthless. If, for example, the feminist could show that bias led a male ethnographer to report a society as having patriarchy when, in fact, the society had egalitarian hierarchies, then the challenge would be successful. However, no feminist any longer claims this and, even if one did, the relevant point is that it would be untrue. Likewise, the charge that science is "male science" is impotent unless one can show where the bias is manifested in illogic or error. When the feminist fails to specify any manifestation of the alleged bias in the theory he or she is criticizing, the charge of bias is simply another example of name calling. Even if it is true that all scientists have biases that limit their view, such biases are irrelevant to their theories unless the biases generate fallacy or error.

A feminist criticism that a male bias in science, particularly social science, manifests itself in a skewed selection of what areas or subjects to study may (or may not) have validity in pointing out that the decision to study one thing is a decision not to study another. But this is not a criticism that can successfully challenge any specific theory of the empirical realities that have been selected for study. What is worth studying is, after all, a question of values. Something close to this is implied in the feminist attempt to "redefine dominance" that we have discussed. Such a redefinition might enable the feminist to address behaviors and institutions she sees as more worthy of study than that which is addressed in analyses of the behaviors and institutions usually termed "dominance." But it cannot cast doubt on the correctness of an explanation of the reality usually referred to by the word "dominance."

Even as great a thinker as John Stuart Mill could make the silliest of arguments. Mill claimed, in essence, that we can have no idea of the importance of physiology to behavior until we reverse male and female behaviors. But it is obvious that, to the extent that a behavior is physiologically rooted, such reversal is either impossible or unlikely in the extreme. To refuse to consider all relevant evidence until the male and female behavior is reversed is akin to claiming that we can have no idea whether physiology is involved in the woman's ability to bear children until men begin to give birth.

Occasionally, in what might be called "the fallacy of the glancing blow," a critic will make an argument worth considering, but will ask the argument to carry more weight than it can handle even if it is correct. For example, a methodological criticism of an experimental study might well be valid and grounds for dismissing that study. But the criticism does not damage studies that did not commit the specified error. Much less does it damage the evidence provided by other, independent, lines of inquiry. When numerous independent lines of evidence all converge on the same conclusion, the likelihood that all lines lead to an incorrect conclusion becomes vanishingly small. This is perhaps the greatest strength of the physiological explanation of patriarchy.

Incidentally, one would be hard-put to find a discussion of male-female differences that failed to state that the similarities between the sexes are greater than the differences. Assuming that this statement has any meaning at all—which is far from clear, since the criteria for comparison are invariably left unspecified—it is only trivially true. It is true in the same sense that it is true that a person and a horse are more similar than different: Both inhale and exhale the same gases, both eat and digest food, both procreate sexually and with anatomies more similar than different when compared with most of the world's species, both react to pain and fear in a similar manner, both have five senses, etc. Save for examples of cognitive styles and behaviors that people *incorrectly* believe the sexes to differ in statistically (and one would have difficulty identifying a single example), it is only ways in which the sexes differ that are of interest in the study of the sexes. The ways in which the sexes are similar are irrelevant to discussion of the sexes and belong instead to the study of people in general.

Conclusions *Not* Justified by *Patriarchy*

It is crucial that we emphasize certain conclusions *not* justified by the arguments presented in *Patriarchy*. It is crucial not merely for the obvious reason that it would be undesirable for the reader to take from the book claims this theory doesn't make, but also because experience shows that it is precisely these unjustified conclusions that energize much of the resistance to the theory presented.

Nothing that I have written to this point has concerned performance; we have been concerned only with attainment. It is far from obvious (but not necessarily untrue in all cases) that the ability to attain has anything to do with the ability to perform (though one must become a Senator before one can perform—well or badly—as a Senator). Indeed, one might even conclude (though one need not) that the very tendencies that enable males to attain positions of power result in the positions' being held by those more likely to use violence and war in the service of domestic and international dominance.

Nothing that I have written to this point has spoken of any general superiority or inferiority on the part of one sex or the other. Nor could it have. "Superiority" and "inferiority" have meaning only when the aptitude or ability being assessed is specified. We may speak of a male superiority in physical strength or female superiority in physical flexibility, but the concept of general superiority is without scientific meaning.

Nothing that I have written to this point has argued for or against any specific social or political program. Nor could it have. As the empiricists are fond of saying, often and correctly, "*Is* does not entail *ought*." No scientific explanation of how the world works can tell us how we should politically or morally act. Science knows nothing of "should." So, for example, one might agree with all that I have written and argue that this indicates the crucial importance of an equal rights amendment limiting as much as possible a male advantage in attaining positions, an advantage that may have nothing to do with performance in those positions. Or, on the other hand, one might agree with all that I have written and argue that this indicates the need, in a time when role models are so hard to come by, for our emphasizing differences between male and female tendencies and their ability to form the nuclei of strong roles and role models. On such an issue, science must be silent.

All that I have written to this point is an attempt to demonstrate the existence of an empirical reality (the universality of patriarchy, male attainment, and male dominance) and to explain this empirical reality. This is not an issue of values or political ideals, even values and political ideals held so strongly that its adherents are willing to give them priority over truths they see as inimical. For the reasons we have just discussed, no criticism invoking issues of values, politics, or consequences can cast doubt on the correctness of a theory. If such factors lead the theorist to fallacy or error, then these can be exposed. If they have not, then they are irrelevant.

It is long past the time when the mere assertion of the unimportance of physiological differentiation to the institutions we discuss is possible for anyone who serves a scientific, rather than an ideological, master. It is long past the time when invocation of variation and complexity (on either the physiological or anthropological levels) can be invoked to deny the determinativeness of physiological differentiation to the institutions. There is no variation in that which we explain requiring the invoked variation and complexity for a sufficient explanation. (This is simply another way of saying that the institutions are universal.)

The Masculinization of the World

A century ago, the Puritan impulse denied our sexual natures and it was common for people to speak of a time when social change would render irrelevant our "base sexual natures." Today no one would take seriously a claim that the social can render irrelevant our sexual natures, but many cavalierly speak of a time when institutional arrangements will not merely channel, but will render irrelevant, the male-female psychophysiological differences we discuss. In neither case does a hatred for a reality imply the possibility of the eradication of the hated reality. Values and attitudes have been reversed, but nowhere on earth is there an iota of a hint that the institutions we discuss are being eradicated or even meaningfully reduced. For better or worse, males control the hierarchies and status positions as much as they ever have. This is because values and attitudes have little to do with the expectations and behaviors we discuss.

It is understandable that contemporary values and attitudes decry the male institutions we discuss. Modernization—with its inherent extreme stratification, its need of a suprafamilial labor one sex cannot satisfy, its encouragement of small families and discouragement of the large families desired in an agricultural society, its geographical mobility (which undercuts the extended family), and its tendency to fragment the nuclear family and to increase divorce—modernization renders impossible a societal emphasis on female advantages possible—and sometimes manifested—in nonmodern societies.

In this sense, despite the many ways in which modernization also sets limits on the degree to which society can oppress women (rendering impossible the sorts of oppression of women found in the many primitive and premodern societies that, for various reasons, did not accord women's roles high status), modernization is a masculinization of the world. It is a masculinization in that it precludes the possibility of a society's giving equal or higher status to the roles only a woman can play.

Even if there were no difference between males and females relevant to attainment and dominance, modernization's replacing the possibility of a female status based on female roles with a female status based on roles the sexes are equally capable of attaining would move women from an arena in which they could not lose to one in which they had no advantage. If males have the neuroendocrinological advantage for the attainment and dominance behavior we have discussed, then modernization's reduction of the status accorded female roles changes the game from one that women cannot lose to one that they cannot win. That all this is unfortunate does not make it any less unavoidable.

To the extent that human happiness and satisfaction are a function of congruence of social expectation and possibility, modernization provides a lower limit on female satisfaction at a cost of imposing an upper limit on female satisfaction. No modern society could treat the women as badly as did the Chukchee or as well as did the Bambuti.

I realize that many women find it self-evident that women in modern society are happier and live more satisfied lives than do the women of even those nonmodern societies that treat women the best and give women's female roles highest status. They assume that happiness is more a function of choice (which is no doubt greatest in the modern society) than of social support of roles closely tied to psychophysiology.

I happen to believe that, given a degree of autonomy precluding slavery and other extreme limitations on individual choice, the happiness of the members of a society is far more a function of concordance of socialized expectation and reality than of choice; people tend to be happiest when they are doing what they feel they should be doing, and the primary nonphysiological determinant of the feeling of what one should be doing is his or her socialization. However, the question of the roots of human happiness is far outside the area we cover and is, quite likely, unanswerable.[27]

In any case, it was to be expected that contemporary women would see happiness as determined primarily by choice: These women have been socialized and educated in a modern society that requires they have this attitude. Within certain psychophysiological constraints, in all societies all people believe what they are told to believe—and do what they are told to do—most of the time, and most people believe what they are told to believe—and do what they are told to do—all of the time. When men and women were socialized to traditional roles, they assumed the superiority of *those* roles. Because modern society *inherently* emphasizes hierarchical attainment tendencies and aptitudes, the attitudes people are socialized toward will value hierarchical and status attainment—and the attitudes, like an emphais on choice, education for the labor market, and the like—over the successes facilitated by tendencies more associated with female physiology.

There have been many changes in the past three decades. Whether these changes are "important" is a function of the context in which the assessment is being made. In terms of daily life, the most important change is no doubt the opening up of all fields to women. The woman who wishes to be an executive, politician, or fire fighter is less concerned with whether half of these positions are held by females than with the possibility of her becoming one of these without encountering the prejudice and discrimination that accompanies roles seen as off-limits to women. Thus, this change and, of course, improvement in the relative income of women are clearly "important" in the context of the daily lives of women who aspire to these roles.

In the context of the universal institutions we discuss, however, no social change that has taken place, or which we have any reason to think will take place, is "important" in the sense that it gives us any reason to believe that the institutions we discuss will fail to manifest themselves in all future societies. Indeed, all changes we have observed in the United States took place long ago in many societies. There will no doubt be a female president in the coming decades—there have always been female heads-of-state—but there will not be a time when the overwhelming number of hierarchical positions are not held by males (assuming such positions retain the high status they have always had).

In any case, we have the universality of patriarchy, male attainment, and male dominance on the social level, the universal association of dominance behavior with males on the emotional-behavioral level, and an enormous amount of direct medical and indirect experimental evidence on the neuroendocrinological level. Contrary to the widespread belief that these institutions are being seriously challenged (a belief based on perception of real changes in attitudes and an incorrect belief that attitudes are of significant causal importance to these institutions), there is not a scintilla of evidence that any social or economic change at any time in any society has seriously threatened these institutions. To assert, at this late date, the unimportance of physiology to the universality we attempt to explain is possible only for those who know nothing about, or cannot face, the relevant evidence and the universality it explains.

It is telling that those who resist in this way never specify the conditions under which they would accept the explanation offered here (as I specify, in the very title of the book, the conditions under which I would surrender the explanation). It is a willingness to so specify that separates the serious from the unserious in science. But those who resist do so because they know that, if they did specify the conditions for acceptance, they would have to specify conditions that have already been met.

ADDENDUM

The Cognitive Differences Between Men and Women

NOTE: I first made the argument presented in this section in 1971. At the time there was only suggestive empirical evidence to complement the theoretical analysis I presented. In the subsequent years, considerable research, particularly that of Camilia Benbow and Julian Stanley,[28] has very strongly supported the theoretical argument I presented.

This addendum incorporates material from "Response to Ruskai," recently published in the American Journal of Physics.

Stereotypes are statistical generalizations associating specific aptitudes, abilities, tendencies, or physical attributes with specific groups. Stereotypes represent, at least at first, a population's observations (accurate or inaccurate) of the group being stereotyped.

Stereotypes must not be confused with: (A) a population's *explanation* of the causation of the association of a characteristic and the group (which may be woefully incorrect), (B) the value judgment a population places on the association (which is often negative), or (C) the social functions served by the stereotype (which are often prejudiced and discriminatory).

Thus, if a group is derided for heavy drinking, the causal explanation of the group's drinking ("They're born that way") may be entirely incorrect, the value judgment may be negative, and the social function may be prejudiced or discriminatory. But the stereotype proper—the claim that, statistically speaking, members of the group drink more than the members of other groups—is an empirical claim amenable to empirical verification or refutation. (The stereotype is not, of course, necessarily permanent. The group that consumes a disproportionate amount of alcohol may cease doing so and, after a time lag in which perception catches up to reality, the stereotype will disappear.) I will argue later in this book that virtually all stereotypes (as opposed to the causation, values judgments, and functions) are correct.[29]

The cores of the stereotypes of males and females include these characteristics:

Males: (1) A greater tendency for dominance emotions and behavior (often termed "aggression" or "competitiveness" in the stereotype) that is the only element of the stereotype that need be true for the theory presented above to be correct; and (2) a greater aptitude for logical, abstract reasoning ("thinking like a man").

Females: (1) A greater tendency for nurturance emotions and behavior that complements, but is not required for, the theory I present above to be correct; and (2) a greater aptitude for psychological perception and insight ("women's intuition").

It is widely believed that the average female and most females exhibit a greater aptitude for psychological insight ("women's intuition") than do the average male and most males. While I cannot see how any sentient being can doubt the truth of this, psychological insight is, by its nature, difficult to demonstrate in rigorous, operational terms; this is particularly so when contemporary fashion virtually precludes the research necessary to establish or refute its existence. Thus, this will play no part in the present discussion.

(I refer here to "average" and "most" because it is likely that this trait is, like virtually all others, one in which male variation is greater, i.e., males tend to populate both extremes. Thus, the fact that Freud, Proust, Flaubert, and the like were male does not cast doubt on the general female superiority here. This stereotype speaks more of women and men in general, not merely of the Jane Austins and Sigmund Freuds.)

The male's greater aptitude for logical, abstract thought and the related aptitude for spatial relations is an indisputable fact. It is only the causation that is open to question:

A score on the Scholastic Aptitude Test mathematics aptitude section that puts a girl in the ninetieth percentile of girls puts a boy in only the sixty-eighth percentile of boys. Among mathematically precocious thirteen-year-olds with equal mathematical backgrounds, a score of 700 is thirteen times as likely to be attained by a boy as by a girl. No girl has qualified for any of the twenty-seven American teams to the Mathematics Olympiad, and only a tiny percentage has qualified for the teams of other nations (through 1986).[30]

Likewise, there seems to be a virtually linear relationship between the importance of logical abstraction to an area and the percentage of those at the highest level who are men; there has never been a woman at the very highest level of mathematics, pure scientific theory, chess, or music composition (hardly a macho enterprise), while there have been many women of genius in literature and the performing arts.

I suggest that: (1) The stereotype reflects a population's observation of a greater male aptitude (statistically speaking, as always) for a certain type of logical, abstract thinking that is demonstrated on tests such as the WAIS (relevant sections) and the mathematical aptitude SAT's, certain tests of spatial relations, and certain other tests that I operationally define as the aptitude tested by these tests; (2) an extraordinarily high aptitude of the sort measure by more difficult versions of these tests—a level of aptitude attained by few men and virtually no women— is a virtual necessary condition for genius in those areas (mathematics, pure scientific theory, chess, and music composition, but not literature or the performing arts) in which there have been no women at the highest level; and (3) there is quite strong logical evidence, and some suggestive direct physiological evidence, that the greater male aptitude (which accounts for there being only males at the highest levels in these areas) is the result of the differentiation of the central nervous systems of males and females. Socialization increases this difference in the way it does differences in dominance behavior.

Eleanor Maccoby and others have raised two objections to this line of reasoning:[31]

(1) It is claimed that there are "tests of logic" and other aptitudes that are necessary conditions (or strong facilitators) for high-level mathematics on which the sexes do not differ. This criticism carries no weight because these other tests,

whatever they might measure, cannot possibly be measuring the aptitude to which I refer, the aptitude measured by the tests mentioned above. For the one thing we know is that males do far better than females (for whatever reason) on tests measuring the relevant aptitude; thus, no test on which the sexes do *not* differ could possibly be measuring the aptitude to which I refer—an aptitude in which the sexes quite clearly do differ (for whatever reason). In short: *A null finding on one test can never cancel a non-full finding on another.*

In other words: It is not the word used to name the aptitude that matters. What matters is that there is an aptitude that is exhibited far more strongly by males, that is observed in the stereotype that sees use of this aptitude as "thinking like a man," that underlies the male's greater mathematical ability, and that is a virtual necessary condition for genius in mathematics, scientific theory, music composition, and chess. The fact that there are other aptitudes on which the sexes do not differ is irrelevant.

One need not know the causal mechanism to identify the effects of that mechanism; even people who think that "males are taller because they eat more" realize that there is an empirical reality to explain. Likewise, even the causal analysis that explains (I believe incorrectly) the male-female mathematical difference in social terms entails an acknowledgment that there is an empirical reality to explain.

Moreover, an empirical reality can stongly suggest a physiological causal element even in the absence of direct evidence of the mechanism. (Indeed, as is often the case in medicine, the similarity of the empirical effects of an as-yet-undiscovered physical mechanism often justifies the search for a similar mechanism; symptoms which are like those that often accompany bacterially caused diseases justify an attempt to discover a bacteriological cause.) Likewise, when a male-female behavioral difference manifests itself throughout a wide range of cross-cultural situations, we are justified in suspecting a cause rooted in physiology.

It is important to make this point because a scientist in a specialized field will often be overly conservative in ascribing a causal role of physiology to a tendency or behavior; one is overly conservative because one assumes that the claim is nothing more than a generalization of the tentative evidence provided by the specific discipline of this scientist. For example, the endocrinologist who studies the hormones relevant to aggression will grant that there is clearly a relationship between male-female hormones and male-female tendencies, but will deny that we can even begin to say anything specific about the relationship. The scientist would be correct if the claim were based only on the specific evidence of the work he does; but other lines of evidence, when added to the tentative evidence the endocrinologist provides (for example, a sexual difference that manifests itself in all of the world's societies' varying cultures), justifies a far stronger claim than would the evidence provided just by the specialized scientist.

Other critics have argued that some tests of spatial relations fail to find that males outperform females, but even this argument fails. It fails because—even if we grant that these tests are of the same aptitude as are the tests we discuss—these other tests do not cancel the tests we discuss; they fail to explain why, on the tests we discuss, males always do better. By far the most plausible answer is that the tests we discuss are sufficiently sensitive to discriminate the sex difference, while the other tests are not. (A yardstick that measures only to the nearest six inches will find males and females equal in height; a yardstick that measures to the inch correctly finds that males are taller.) *If* the tests we discuss often failed to find a sex difference, *then* the argument I make *would* be questionable. But as long as there is one test that consistantly finds that one sex performs better than the other, no other test—whether a test of a different aptitude or an insufficiently sensitive test of the same aptitude—can cast doubt on that single test. The ability of one sex to consistently outperform the other on that test is an empirical reality that demands explanation.

Some critics have argued that the difference between males and females on the tests we discuss are small, far smaller than the differences within-sex (i.e., the difference between the scores of low-scoring males and high-scoring males or low-scoring females and high-scoring females is much greater than that between the "average male and the average female"). That this does not demonstrate the umimportance of the difference is clear if we, once again, consider the sex difference in height. The difference in height between the shortest and the tallest male, or the shortest and the tallest female, is over three feet, while the difference between the average male and average female is a mere few inches. But this mere few percent difference at the means translates into a situation in which nearly all of the tallest people are male. Likewise, a similar difference in the male-female means on the tests we discuss translates into a situation in which nearly all of the highest-level mathematicians and theoretical scientists are male. These mathematicians are, moreover, disproportionately important in the development of social expectations and the resulting stereotype. (All this assumes the same variability for males and females; if, as is usually the case, there is greater variability for males—i.e., greater proportion at the bottom and top—then there will be an even greater proportion of males at the top than the difference in means would seem to imply).

Finally, nearly all critics claim (let us assume correctly, for arguments sake) that male and female students of mathematics at, say, MIT are equally able. This casts no doubt on the points made here. The question is, "Why are there far fewer female students at that level?"

Section 3 of the chapter on the SAT's discusses the issue of male and female performance on the mathematics tests in much greater detail.

(2) It is pointed out that the sex difference of which we speak does not manifest itself until puberty. This is seen (not necessarily by Maccoby, but by others) as indicating the social causation of the sex difference (the pubertal—relative—female decline being ascribed to an internalization of values seeing mathematics as unfeminine).

It is conceivable that this is correct, but many points argue against this being the case.

A. There are many ways in which a sequential unfolding of physiological structures do not manifest themselves until puberty or later; the young boy cannot grow facial hair until puberty, but this hardly demonstrates the social causation of the adolescent boy's ability to do so.

B. The "mathematics" studied before puberty is arithmetic. It is likely that this does not call upon the aptitude required for higher level mathematics.

C. It is possible that the sex differentiation does manifest itself before puberty and that increasingly sensitive tests will demonstrate this. This possibility is indicated by the fact that many mathematicians, composers, and chess grandmasters exhibit an extraordinary aptitude long before puberty. Likewise, there is a good number of (nearly always male) precocious mathematicians who do college-level work before the age of ten. It might be that these individuals, and these individuals alone, mature more quickly physiologically than other people and are too few in number to affect the performance of their entire age populations. But nature rarely works so discreetly. It would seem more likely that finely tuned tests will show that males in general do better than females long before puberty.

D. The socialization explanation would be far more convincing if females did worse than males in tests of all kinds. In fact, females equal males on all tests not demanding the aptitude we discuss. One cannot argue that it is only these areas that are defined as masculine; this simply begs the question and forces us to ask why these areas are defined as masculine. There seems nothing *a priori* masculine about composing sonatas. In other words, if social factors account for its being males who excel at this one aptitude, and this one aptitude only, the social factor must be an astonishly specific one—one whose specificity is not easily explained.

None of this denies either that there is socialization of females away from science and mathematics or that superior female scientists and mathematicians face discrimination where male scientists do not. The point is not that there is not such socialization and discrimination, or that they are not extensive, but that their direction conforms to a reality rooted in physiological differences. Again: The female scientist is in the position of the six-foot woman who faces discouragement for that which would elicit encouragement if exhibited by a male. The association of the quality with males, the direction of the socialization, and the possibility of discrimination all flow from the reality of the psychophysiological differentiation that makes the female more of an exception than is the male. (The reverse, of course, is true of qualities associated more strongly with the female and rooted in physiology.) Thus, the female mathematician may encounter prejudice where a male of equal ability (i.e., the same percentile for the entire population) will not. This is possible precisely because the woman is a greater exception for her group than the male is for his (i.e., the woman represents a higher percentile for women than does the man for men). And this is the case because male physiology (and social expectations that increase the male-female difference) gives males a higher mathematical aptitude.

Moreover, we would expect that, because virtually all aptitudes have some environmental causal elements that complement the physiological causal elements, the encouragement of females to take mathematics will have the effect of reducing the sex difference in mathematics somewhat. It is difficult to say how much, not only because we don't know precisely the relative causal roles of physiology and environment, but also because the "environment" is not an independent variable, but is limited by the physiological. That is, values will always associate mathematical ability with males because people observe that males *are* better at mathematics and the stereotype correctly observes that "males are more logical" ("logical" in this context means "analytical," not "less emotionally demonstrative"). In other words, it would not be possible to reverse sexual expectations and to provide an expectation that could act as a counterpoise entirely canceling the expectation rooted in the inherent sex difference. (In principle, a society could balance or reverse the sex difference by, for example, refusing males all mathematical education. This scenario, however, is too fantastical to bother with here.)

To be sure, the question of the physiological roots of sexual cognitive differences is still an open question, though an open question for which a positive answer is far more likely than contemporary ideology would acknowledge. I stress that this is an open question in order to emphasize that none of this addendum need be correct for the theory of patriarchy and dominance to be entirely correct. There are arguments (though they seem to me dubiously *ad hoc* arguments) for an entirely social basis to sexual cognitive differences.

The sexual differences in dominance tendency and cognitive styles (including the female's lower threshhold for nurturance behavior) that I have discussed cover the two most often observed core tendencies represented in the popular stereotypes of male and female (though one might also grant this status to the male's lower threshold for sexual behavior responsible, for example, for the much greater power sexually explicit materials have on males). Assuming that we remember the distinctions between stereotypes and causes, value judgments, and functions mentioned above, we see that the core beliefs of the popular stereotypes of males and females are astonishingly accurate.

A Final Aside

Sexual differences of the type just discussed are often challenged by a criticism whose inadequacy is obvious at once when it is analyzed. But this criticism is invariably just asserted, with the argument supporting it merely implied. In this form it often granted a power it does not possess.

I refer to discussions of sexual differences whose existence is challenged by the claim that studies attempting to discover male-female differences in some tendency or behavior provide "evidence that is contradictory."

Now, the evidence of studies is contradictory when the studies use the same methodology and some studies claim to find that for which it searches (in this case, a sex difference) while others do not. When this happens, there is clearly a problem: Some of the studies are poorly executed; unlike populations are inadvertently compared; or the like.

This, however, is not the usual situation. The situation we discuss is that in which the evidence is claimed to be contradictory on the basis of a conflict between the conclusions of studies using different methodologies. Worse yet, those who favor a null finding will often present the study that reaches a null finding as correct while ignoring the study that finds what it searches for.

When the property or correlation searched for is easily identified, it is not possible to get away with this misrepresentation. For example, let us say we wish to determine whether men or women are taller. You measure a thousand randomly selected men and women and conclude that men are taller. I give to a thousand randomly selected men and women a test of questions on American history and, finding that the sexes do equally well, conclude that men and women are equally tall. You would, quite correctly, consider my reasoning absurd. You would point out that your methodology was able to discriminate the characteristic of interest and to measure it (at least to the extent necessary to find out which sex had more of it), while my methodology employed a measure incapable of discriminating a height difference because it had nothing to do with height.

This methodological problem is often quantitative rather than qualitative: If you use a tape measure with inch markings, you will find that males are taller than females. If you use one capable only of measuring yards (and no smaller units) you will conclude that the sexes are equally tall.

In other words, when two studies use different methodologies and one finds what it looks for while the other does not, the two do not cancel each other. The plausible assumption is that the former study was capable of discriminating the property, while the latter was not.

This is all obvious when we use the example of height and when the two methodologies are described. However, when, for example, a newspaper reports, "Study Finds No Sex Differences In Aggression," most readers will conclude that, at the very least, this contradicts claims of a sex difference in "aggression" based on other studies. For the reason we have discussed, this conclusion is incorrect. The correct conclusion is in all likelihood that the study finding the difference used a methodology sufficiently finely structured to discriminate a property that the study reaching a null finding did not.

An analogy enables one to picture this: Let us say we have a mixture of marbles and ball-bearings. You have a strainer with a mesh gauge that lets ball-bearings through, but stops the marbles. I have a strainer with a mesh gauge so large that both the marbles and the ball-bearings get through. You conclude, correctly, that marbles are bigger than ball-bearings. I conclude, incorrectly, that they are not.

Clearly, no one would make the error described when the property in question is as easily defined and identified as is height or marble size. However, when the property is more subtle, as is the case with behavioral tendencies, the error is frequently made.

Another confusion that often infuses work on behavioral tendencies concerns the issue of the definition of the property being investigated.

These properties are often defined by the test that discriminates them. Thus, "aggression" is defined as that which a test of "aggression" measures; one who scores high is more "aggressive" than one who scores low. Now this is perfectly valid and it does avoid the knotty problem of articulating a definition of the property in question. The validity comes from correlations of test scores with other variables. So, for example, high scores on the test of "aggression" would be attained by males, drill instructors, etc. (If there were no such correlations, then the test would be valueless; but it would not—for the reasons given above—cast doubt on the value of a test of "aggression" that *is* able to correlate with other variables.)

The defense of the test-operational definition just given, while valid, does often leave the understandable impression that something is missing. What is felt to be missing is, I think, a connection of the property to real people. Many researchers understand this but feel that articulation of the definition is the only way to create such a connection, and this is felt to be too difficult to achieve.

But an articulated definition is not required. One can operationally define a property and connect it to real people by demonstrating that real people agree on the property's definition to the extent that they agree on how to identify it in reality. Indeed, this is a far more meaningful demonstration of the validity of a word for a property than mere agreement on how to articulate the definition.

In other words, most people would have a very difficult time articulating and agreeing upon a definition of "aggression." But when these people were asked to rank twenty mutual friends in terms of "aggression," there would be a high rate of agreement. The same would be true of "humorousness," "sensitivity," "friendliness," etc. This is the proof that the words mean something. For if the people were asked to rank the twenty friends in terms of "fnorcality" (or any other meaningless word), they would be unable to do so: the clustering of agreed applications of a term—the correlations of property, behavior, and individual—is what gives the term meaning.

A test, then, need not operationalize its definition only on itself and other variables. A test of "aggression" should identify the individuals identified by the friends as "aggressive." If it can do this, it can correlate test results with other variables as well as show that its "aggression" is the same as the "aggression" we speak of in everyday terms.

Note, incidentally, that this analysis demonstrates the inadequacy of the attempt to dismiss I.Q. tests on the basis of the difficulty of articulating a definition of "intelligence." If you were to rank the "intelligence" of the next twenty people you meet and speak to for five minutes or more, you would find that your ranking correlated highly with the ranking of the same twenty people made by others. If you then gave the twenty people I.Q. tests, you would find that these tests correlated highly with the identifications you and the others had made previously. This demonstrates both that the I.Q. test measures the same property you call "intelligence" and destroys the attempt to deny the validity of the I.Q. test on the basis of the difficulty of articulating a definition of "intelligence"; such an attempt cannot explain how the test identifies as "intelligent" the same individuals whom people identify as "intelligent."

NOTES

1. Revised edition: London: Maurice Temple Smith, Ltd., 1977; Original edition: New York: Wm. Morrow and Sons, 1973. A completely updated edition will be published in 1992 by Open Court Press.

2. This range does not represent any disagreement about the existence of any group but only the rigidity of one's definition of "society." The more rigid the requirements for consideration as a separate "society," the lower the number.

3. Despite the mythology often taught in grade school, there has never been a "matriarchy" or an "Amazonian society." The fact that "matriarchies" exist in myth is no more proof for the existence of matriarchies than are the myths about cyclopses evidence for the real existence of cyclopses. At the turn of the century there was a fashion for theories that posited that, before males learned of their importance to conception, there was a "matriarchal stage of history." Such theories were unable to explain what factor enabled men, once they learned of their own biological importance to conception, to "take over." Since women automatically know of their own importance to birth, the male's discovery of the mechanism of conception should enable the male merely to share power equally (if knowledge of biological importance is, in fact, determinative to control). However, while there would seem to be no reason to attach any relevance of paternity to patriarchy once one is forced to invoke some other factor (to explain why men came to dominate, rather than just share, authority), it was true that one could (logically, but not plausibly) argue that knowledge of one's role in conception is a necessary condition for dominance. Once this condition is met, however, then some other factor becomes determinative. As long as there was little relevant ethnographic data, this question had to remain on a theoretical level. Matriarchal theory positing the importance of the male's role in conception was not truly doomed until the ethnographers found societies in which males did not know of their role in paternity yet which were as patriarchal as all other societies. Most important, however, is the fact that ethnographic evidence demonstrates the difficulty with all theories that "explain" matriarchy. Such theories attempt to explain where there is nothing to explain; we have no reason to believe that there ever was a nonpatriarchal society.

4. *New York Times*, July 30, 1990.

5. *Norway Information*, June, 1984, and Royal Norwegian Ministry of Foreign Affairs, *Norway Information*, Feb. 1981.

6. The Swedish Institute, *Equality Between Men and Women in Sweden*, May, 1987.

7. *Inter-Parliamentary Union*, 1989.

8. Margaret Mead, *Male and Female* (London: Penguin Books, 1970), p. 168.

9. *New York Times*, December 11, 1990.

10. "Dominance" and "deference" always refer to the interaction of males and females in a single society. It is meaningless to refer to the females of one society as being "more dominant" than the males of another.

11. The American black family is often referred to as "matriarchal." Even if it were true that the black family did represent authority on the part of the mother, the accurate term would be "female dominance" not "matriarchy" (which applies to superfamilial, hierarchical contexts). In reality, however, the black families referred to do not represent "female dominance," but an absence of the male. When the male is a part of the black family, the expectation and reality of male dominance obtain just as they do elsewhere.

12. Quotation: Margaret Mead, *Redbook* (Oct. 1973), p. 48. Mead letter: *American Anthropologist*, 39 (July-September, 1937) pp. 558-61. My letter: *Contemporary Sociology*, V8, N6 (November, 1979). *Sex and Temperament in Three Primitive Societies*: William

Morrow and Sons, 1933. The reader who wishes to satisfy himself that Mead is correct in her denial, and that *Sex and Temperament* does not justify the claim of sex-role reversibility, might look at the devastating criticisms of *Sex and Temperament* by Jessie Bernard (*American Journal of Sociology*, 50, Jan., 1943, pp. 284-91) and Richard Thurnwald (*American Anthropologist*, 38, Oct.-Dec., 1936, pp. 663-7).

13. One might argue that the closer-than-usual approach to egalitarianism of the primitive societies mentioned above can be explained economically insofar as the relative absence of hierarchy is economically determined (i.e., other tiny societies have more hierarchy, and the difference is a result of economic factors). This would explain why one tiny society has more hierarchy than another. But the more basic question of why all *non*-tiny societies have extensive hierarchy—and why all societies have male dominance—is most plausibly and parsimoniously answered in terms of size and the requirements of organization. And the central question of why hierarchy is always primarily male is, as we shall see, most plausibly and parsimoniously answered in psychophysiological terms.

14. Richard Lewontin, Steven Rose, and Leon Kamin, *Not In Our Genes* (New York, Pantheon, 1984).

15. William King Whyte, *The Status of Women in Pre-Industrial Society* (Princeton: Princeton University Press, 1978). Bibliographical information on the ethnographies cited will be found in Whyte. Page numbers refer to the page of the ethnography on which the quotation is found.

16. Whyte attributes this quote to D. Stone and A. Skinner, who found it in the work of M. Gabb. See Whyte for complete reference.

17. In some cases, exogeneous hormonalization engendered the effects. Strictly speaking, the exogeneously administered hormone (or fetal physical accident) is "environmental," but, obviously, the implication is the power of endogeneous hormones in normal individuals. The tendency of males in every society to manifest dominance behavior is not the result of fetal accidents.

18. I do not invoke ethological evidence of the study of mammalian species in their natural habitats. While such evidence is entirely concordant with, indeed supportive of, all that I write here, invocation of ethological evidence invariably involves one in endless methodological disputes about anthropomorphism. The strength of the evidence I do invoke is, I believe, so powerful that it provides a sufficient explanation of the universalities of behavior and institution we discuss even without the ethological evidence; thus we can ignore the ethological evidence and avoid the disputes.

19. As opposed to "member of the other sex," "hierarchy" and "status" are theoretical abstractions. Now there is nothing illegitimate about using such abstractions as explanatory devices. Until recently the "atom" was a theoretical construct of this sort. However, there is something unsatisfying about our not being able to specify for "hierarchy" and "status" a physical entity equivalent to "the other sex." In other words, this question remains: What is it about a "hierarchy" or "status" that registers on the brain and elicits the behavior we have discussed? A "member of the other sex" is clearly a physical entity that is visually seen (and identified by other senses as well). But how does the brain register a "hierarchy" or "status"? Perhaps a hierarchy is the resolution of dyadic competitions in which each of the two participants is the physical stimulus for the other, the hierarchy being the result of a sort of vertical tournament. Clearly, this entire question is one that is in need of further investigation. The iron-magnet analogy captures the fact that a physiologically rooted tendency is a tendency to react to specific cues and stimuli. Note that the environments presented by all societies include these necessary cues and stimuli. It is difficult to even imagine any but the most primitive, tiny society in which this is not the case.

20. While presently less extensive than the evidence associating testosterone and dominance behavior, there is increasing evidence of the role of such hormones as oxytocin and prolactin in generating maternal behavior in the female. As further work is done in this area, an analysis, analogous and complementary to that presented here, may offer a nice balance in its ability to demonstrate the physiological basis of a large part of femininity. However, none of this is necessary for the theory presented here. The physiological basis of dominance behavior is alone sufficient to explain the universality of the institutions we wish to explain.

21. The everyday word "aggression" usually subsumes the dominance and attainment behavior we discuss, while also including fighting behavior. There is no implication in the theory I present that there is any male impulse to kill or fight *per se*. Males do these things when they see them as being necessary for dominance, not because there is any innate need to do them.

22. The average height of a population can result to a significant extent from an environmental cause. For example, it seems likely that an increase in protein intake has resulted in a significant gain in height in Japan in the past fifty years. But the universal male-female difference in height can hardly be explained by a female protein deficit in each of the world's societies.

23. Lewontin et al., p. 136.

24. The reader has no doubt noticed that I use the sex-difference-in-height analogy often—perhaps too often. I do so because I have found no other analogy that so well demonstrates: (1) Exceptions are *expected* when a finding is statistical and—assuming that they are not so numerous as to nullify the regularity—they do not cast doubt on the regularity. (2) Such exceptions are expected even when the property in question is virtually purely physiologically caused (as is the sex difference in height). (3) The fact that the range *within* each of two compared groups is greater than the difference *between* the averages of the two groups casts no doubt on the importance of the difference. (4) A very high percentage of the criticisms of the reasoning I invoke would not have been made had the critic simply asked him- or herself whether the point he or she was making was also true of the sex difference in height. When it is, then, of course his criticism is without force.

I use here the analogy of height in order to make the point that *even when conditions are such that a property in virtually entirely hereditary,* we expect the realities just mentioned. Some readers might prefer to use the analogy of weight, which more closely resembles the male-female differences in the sexually differentiated characteristics we discuss in that both hereditary and environmental causal factors play causal roles. Either analogy makes the point.

25. John Money and Anke A. Ehrhardt, *Man and Woman, Boy and Girl* (Baltimore: Johns Hopkins University Press, 1972), p. 122.

26. Stanley Schacter, "The Interaction of Cognitive and Physiological Determinants of Emotional State," in P. H. Leiderman and David Shapiro, eds., *Psychobiological Approaches to Social Behavior* (Stanford, Calif.: Stanford University Press, 1964).

27. In truth, the question of whether women (or men) are happier now than they were in the past is probably unanswerable. Attempts to determine the happiness of members of a group are rendered impossible by the fact that a society's social values concerning the expression of, and acknowledgment of, the feelings of happiness and unhappiness determine responses; thus, some individuals, and the populations of some social groups, report that they are unhappy if they have a hangnail, while others claim to be happy even as they are about to die. (In speaking of the comparison of happiness in past and

present times, I exclude such factors as improved medical care, the eradication of starvation in the modern society, and the like. It is perfectly reasonable to assume that these make people happier. But here I refer to the relative happiness of people who are healthy and sufficiently affluent to sustain themselves with at least minimal comforts. Also: One could, of course, simply *define* "happiness" and "unhappiness" in terms of the subject's report, but this would tell one only how the subject (and/or the subject's group) feels about *reporting* these, and not about the actual degree of "happiness" or "unhappiness."

28. For example, "Sex Differences in Mathematical Reasoning Ability" in *Behavioral and Brain Sciences* (Vol. 11, No. 2; June, 1988, pgs. 169-232).

29. See my article "The Truth in Stereotypes," in *Chronicles*: Nov., 1986 V.10, N. 11 pp. 14-16), a revised version of which appears in this volume.

30. Camilla Persson Benbow and Julian C. Stanley, "Sex Differences in Mathematical Ability: Fact or Artifact," in *Science* (Vol. 210, 12 Dec. 80, pp. 1262-4); Camilla Persson Benbow and Julian C. Stanley, "Sex Differences in Mathematical Reasoning Ability: More Facts," *Science* (Vol. 222, No. 2 Dec. 83, pp. 1029-30); Bower, B., "The 'Math Gap': Puzzling Sex Differences," in *Science News* (6 Dec. 86); Steven Goldberg, "The S.A.T.'s: A Logical Analysis," in *The International Journal of Sociology and Social Policy* (Vol. 10, No. 2, 1990).

31. Eleanor Emmons Maccoby and Carol Nagy Jacklin, *The Psychology of Sex Differences* (Stanford, Calif.: Stanford University Press, 1974), pp. 351-52 and *Science*, November 2, 1973, pp. 469-71.

6

Black Athletic Superiority
Why Are Blacks Better Athletes?

Suppose, for argument's sake, that I am a racist. Suppose that my psychology, my economics, and my politics are predicated on an irrational hatred of Asian peoples. Finally, suppose that, in the service of my psychological, economic, and political needs, I claim that the people of Asia are shorter than the people of the United States and that they are so for genetic reasons. Would the irrationality of my needs cast doubt on the correctness of my claim?

The reader knows the answer to this question. No sentient being would make the error of claiming that, because knowledge of the genesis of the height difference between Americans and Asians might serve irrational functions and purposes, Asians are not shorter than Americans or that they are shorter primarily because they eat less. Everyone realizes that the correctness of an empirical claim is independent of motivation.

But when discussion turns to the claim that the astonishing athletic superiority of American blacks may have its roots in a genetically generated black physiology, many otherwise intelligent people are compelled to invoke arguments so muddled that serious discussion is rendered almost impossible. Such arguments usually do not even address the empirical claim they wish to refute, but merely invoke putative psychological and social dangers that would be irrelevant even were they not dubious.

The issue is not the depth or severity of the persecution of blacks in American history but the *relevance* of that persecution to the athletic superiority that is the empirical reality we wish to explain. After spending the first half of their time in this country as slaves, American blacks have spent the second half bearing the weight of the residue of slavery. But it is no more this that has made them the best athletes on earth than it is this that has made them black.

It does not require a three-volume study to establish the black dominance of athletics. Even those whose idea of a good time does not include high-school relay races on ESPN cannot but have noticed that a group comprising only 12 percent of the population provides many times that on the athletic field. Well over 80 percent of professional basketball players, nearly two-thirds of all professional football players, and the overwhelming number of better boxers are black. Moreover, it is recognized by both those who speak of discrimination and those who offer alternative explanations that even the disproportionate number of blacks is less than it would be were only athletic ability considered.

Perhaps most telling, however, is the black dominance of the 100-meter dash. This shortest of outdoor sprints has always, correctly, been considered the single athletic event for which training, while not pointless, plays the smallest role. The 100-meter dash is an anaerobic event in which reflex and basic speed, qualities relatively resistant to training, determine excellence.

A few years ago I was told that forty-eight of the fifty fastest 100-meter men in the United States were black—and that the forty-ninth had one black parent. I called an authority on track and field to see whether this unbelievable figure was, and still is, true. The authority told me that he doubted that it was: He couldn't think of *any* white in the top fifty.

Black dominance of other running events decreases more or less linearly with distance, being nearly as overwhelming for the 200 meters and decreasing through longer distances, as explosiveness becomes less of the total story. In the 200 meters, for example, Pietro Mennea, a white Italian, set a world record in 1972 that stood until recently, and in the 400 meters there have been a number of world-class white men. Nonetheless, it is not until well into the middle-distance lengths that blacks fail to provide many, many times the world-class runners that one would predict on the basis of population, opportunity, and the like. (East African blacks of a different genetic heritage and an entirely different—lean and lightly muscled—anatomy are over-represented in the marathon, but do not dominate this event to anywhere near the extent that Western blacks of West African descent dominate the sprints.)

As is the case with the 100-meter dash, at the highest level of competence the long-jump is virtually an all-black event. Virtually every record-holder in this event has been black since blacks first entered it sixty-five years ago. Interestingly, while the only person ever to high-jump eight feet (as well as the first person to high-jump seven feet) is black, blacks have been only slightly over-represented in the high jump. Perhaps the *relatively* lesser importance of the characteristics that give blacks such a lead in the sprint and long jump, and the relatively greater importance of form and training, engender a mere moderate—rather than great— black superiority in this event. But this is only a guess, and I must acknowledge that I am not at all certain why blacks do not dominate the high jump the way they do the long jump.

Now, when we encounter a black domination that is not merely overwhelming, but is virtually total, in the events long recognized as most strongly related to natural abilities, it is difficult to avoid the suspicion that a greater natural ability accounts for the black success in these events. Were the over-representation of blacks such that they "merely" contributed a substantial, disproportionate *minority* of the best athletes, then we might suspect that purely cultural considerations such as poverty and limited access to other areas explained the over-representation.[1]

But when virtually all of the successful sprinters and long jumpers, nearly all of the best of the heavier boxers, and four out of five of the professional basketball players (a figure that would likely be higher were it not for the fear that basketball would become a nearly all-black sport) are black, the explanation that denies physiology becomes dubious indeed. The degree and immediacy of black dominance in events for which training and developed endurance is of relatively little importance, and the subsequent black dominance of the major sports—which all involve the explosive speed associated with the sprint and long jump—would make us suspect physiology even if we had no idea what the physiological mechanism was.

Spud Webb, all five-foot-seven of him, differs from many other blacks of his height, not in that he can dunk a basketball, but in that he won a recent professional basketball slam-dunk contest. Even without any direct physiological evidence, it would seem unlikely that Spud Webb and the other superior black athletes, whose ability to jump (like their ability to move explosively) so contributes to their basketball prowess, learned to jump from parents who insisted that they "jump, jump, jump, or never get out of the ghetto." It would seem far more likely that such athletes were born with a potential—a potential that is demonstrably related to the physiological qualities we shall discuss—that they nurtured with dedication, hard work, and the knowledge that they did not have full access to the routes to success available to whites. Far less often are whites born with this potential.

It is a common error in sociology—one that is abetted by a need to deny the importance of physiology—to believe that we may not suspect that physiology plays a crucial role until we know the actual physiological mechanism that is at work. In fact, it is often the case that the indirect evidence of an effect manifested throughout a wide range of environmental situations strongly indicates a primarily physiological causation *even if we have no direct physiological evidence whatever.* Even the primitive who knows nothing of our physiological make-up knows that his getting hungry is not owing to a tradition begun by his ancestors or to his socialization as a child. Likewise, the medical scientist often suspects an organic cause of a symptom even before the organic cause is discovered; the similarity of the symptom to known organic effects and its presence in a wide variety of varying environments is often the incentive that leads to the discovery of the organic cause.

The indirect evidence—in this case a correlation of color and success in athletics that transcends varying environments—is very suggestive. But it is axiomatic that correlation alone cannot establish causation. The primary function of the indirect evidence is to tell us that there is something to explain, not to provide the explanation. For that, we must look not merely to the indirect evidence of a black athletic superiority that manifests itself in so wide a variety of cross-cultural milieus, but also to the direct physiological evidence.

In fact, we do have a great deal of direct evidence of a physiological mechanism, evidence that blacks come into the world with a physiology better suited than that of whites for development into athletes of the highest order.

Before examining this evidence, however, it is necessary to make clear that the claim that blacks have a physiological superiority in athletics *incorporates* two points often suggested as somehow demonstrating the incorrectness of the claim.

(1) The claim is a statistical one, as are virtually all claims of behaviorally important physiological differences between groups. If we wish to explain the observation that all of the best basketball teams are comprised of males, we need merely point out that height is an advantage in basketball and that men are taller than women. This sufficient explanation does not doubt or deny that the male-female height difference is statistical, that there is overlap in male and female height, or that some women are taller and/or better basketball players than most men. When we say that men are taller than women, we mean that the median height of men is greater and that most tall people are men.[3]

Similarly, the statistical nature of even that which is purely physiological renders expected some fine white jumpers in basketball (Rex Chapman), some black players whose attributes mirror those of whites (Charles Oakley), and the like. The fact that the nearly 90 percent of the population that is not black manages to produce one Rex Chapman no more refutes the statistical claim of black physiological superiority than does the six-foot-tall women refute the claim that men are taller than women.

(2) Environmental-cultural factors are as necessary as are physiological advantages. Physiological advantages are never sufficient to attain athletic success on a world-class level. Without such advantages success is not possible, but the same could be said for cultural encouragement, dedication, hard work, and the like. It is only the combination that makes possible the athletic success of blacks we wish to explain. If blacks have a physiological advantage, and blacks and whites are equally dedicated and hard-working, one would expect the black physiological advantage to result in black athletic dominance—which is precisely what we observe and wish to explain.

That is true even if we consider the nonphysiological elements as independent of the physiological ones and, in theory, capable of acting as counterpoise to the physiological. However, to proceed as if this were the case would be to mirror an error often made by environmentalists: treating a dependent variable as if it were independent. Blacks and whites are not, in reality, equally encouraged to enter the sprint. Coaches tend to think of blacks as being better sprinters because black physiology is—statistically speaking—better suited to the sprint. The coaches are correct, though they no doubt take the insight too far and occasionally discourage a white who would be a world-class sprinter.

Moreover, not only the society, but also the individual himself, is affected by the reality of one's basic fitness for a sport or event. One who is clearly not suited to sprinting will decide on his own not to try to become a sprinter. Here again, the environmental variable is given its direction by the physiological variable.

For the major sports (as opposed to those calling on pure running or jumping ability), the black physiological advantage is small in the abstract but huge in practice. A white trained and experienced in basketball or football may well be a better basketball or football player than will be an untrained black when each represents the same percentile of physiological potential for his respective race.

However, when the two are equally trained, devoted, and the like, the black advantage in the basic physiological requirements will carry the day. In practice, at the highest levels the differences between blacks and whites in training, hard work, devotion and the like may well be nonexistent. The difference between being a champion and an also-ran is hundredths of a second. The physiological difference between blacks and whites is easily sufficient to account for this—and for the resulting black dominance of the sports we discuss.

Moreover, there is a crucial practical reality that is obvious in statistical terms and in everyday observation, but which resists simple description in nonstatistical terms: A small difference in means for large populations often entails huge differences in the percentages of the populations found at the extremes. For example, the difference in height between men and women is only about 7 percent. In a room filled with men and women a good number of women will be taller than a good number of men. But at the highest level (say, people above six-and-a-half-feet tall) nearly all are men. Thus, the answer to the question of whether the height difference between the sexes is "important" is a function of the issue at hand. The height difference is relatively unimportant for most people in most situations, but it is crucial for the owner of a professional basketball team who has little interest in people of average height.

Now let us consider the implications of a slight black advantage in the physiological attributes relevant to basketball. Statistician John E. Reith has forcefully made the point we discuss. Let us say that the black advantage is merely such that, when the high-school gym teacher selects the hundred best of two hundred boys, seventeen blacks, rather than the twelve expected on the basis of blacks in the population, are chosen. The difference in average ability seems rather unimportant. However, as is the case with the height of males and females, this same difference of population means manifests itself in increasing percentages of blacks as we move up the curve. At the level of professional basketball, we would expect two-thirds of the players to be black *even if the only relevant difference between the races is the mean difference that accounted for the seventeen, rather than twelve, percent blacks at the level of average ability.* If there is a black-white difference in the physiological attributes relevant to basketball only the slightest bit greater than that used by Reith in his example, it would be sufficient to account for the black dominance of professional basketball that we observe.

What, then, is the relevant physiological evidence? The relevance of the evidence is as important as the evidence itself; any difference between blacks and whites will correlate with black athletic success, but the correlation is only (but strongly) suggestive unless it describes physiological factors already known to be relevant to the success. Obviously, for example, it is not black skin *per se* that plays a causal role.

It has been known for nearly two decades that athletes who excel in explosive, short-term movements have a higher proportion of "fast twitch" muscle fibers than do most, while athletes who excel at endurance have a high proportion of "slow twitch" fibers. Fast-twitch fibers have the greater contractile capacity and generate the quickest movement, the greatest straight-jumping height and the most powerful lift.

It has been demonstrated beyond dispute that black athletes have a much higher ratio of fast to slow twitch fibers than do white athletes and a much greater ability to store and utilize energy from the blood. Moreover, it has been shown that black athletes are far superior to white in the explosive jumping ability so crucial to the jump shot and a host of other requirements for basketball, the fast start in the sprint, and the powerful launch in the long jump—in short, the burst-of-motion abilities associated with a high proportion of fast-twitch muscle fibers. Anatomically, this is complemented by longer arms and legs and a lower percentage of fat.[4]

These demonstrations alone, however, would not rule out the possibility that the black physiological advantage was environmentally generated and not heredi-tary. After all, even if environment accounted for the entire racial difference in athletic ability, there would still be a physiological mediator between environment and performance that accounted for the performance. For example, if one member of each of a hundred sets of identical twins, with their identical genes, became an executive and the other became a construction worker, we would find that the construction workers had stronger muscles and were able to lift far more weight. Yet the stronger muscles and the greater lifting ability would be entirely attributable to the physiological effects of environment (the muscle-building results of construction work).

To rule out the possibility that the physiological advantage of black athletes is owing this sort of feedback from the environmental, the tests of fast-to-slow twitch ratio were made on large numbers of sedentary blacks and whites who were matched for status, income, occupation, education, activity, and the like. The findings were the same, demonstrating that the racial difference in muscle fiber types is owing primarily to heredity and not environment.

A similar conclusion is indicated by tests of a wide range of black and white babies and children. These tests invariably demonstrate an earlier and greater motor maturation for blacks and a greater black ability at the speed and jumping actions of the type we have discussed (or, in the case of infants, analogous actions). In some cases the racial differences are measurable before the age of six months.

As is always the case in science, one whose resistance to a finding is sufficiently strong can always come up with an *ad hoc* explanation more in harmony with that which he would like to believe. One could, for example, attribute the black physiological advantages to differences between the breastfeeding practices of blacks and whites. While there is no reason to suspect that these differ, to say nothing of the fact that there is no theoretical or empirical reason to believe that they would be relevant even if they did, such an explanation could maintain logical integrity at the expense of plausibility and refusal to fairly evaluate the far more relevant evidence.

Sociologist Harry Edwards, the leading spokesman for the environmental view of racial athletic differences, has stated "that race itself is of questionable scientific, biological, and genetic validity" and that "a fundamental tenet of the social sciences is that human capability is fairly evenly distributed across all populations. . . ."

While it is true that there are methodological issues for which the definition of race is tricky, and while it is true that difference between genotype and phenotype can cause problems in investigation of other areas, this is not at all the case with the issue we discuss. The basic fact that we wish to explain is the fact that the major sports are dominated by people who clearly have some African ancestry (and therefore are visually distinguishable from the nearly nine out of ten Americans who do not have an African ancestry). No methodological tactics attempting to obfuscate the landscape can obscure this fact.

It is a sad fact that Professor Edwards is correct when he says that, for a probable majority of contemporary sociologists, it is a fundamental tenet that group differences in human capabilities must be explained in entirely environmental terms. Such is the pathetic state of a contemporary sociology in which concordance with evidence is subordinated to concordance with psychological and other needs. It should not be necessary to say that *no* empirical fact should ever be given the status of tenet. Empirical claims are to be discovered, not assumed, and to be jettisoned when found *not* to be facts. If physicists were able to surrender a belief that time is absolute, a belief supported by every human intuition, it does not seem too much to ask sociologists to refrain from declaring *a priori* as fact a claim that seems dubious even on its face.

To summarize: There can be no doubt about the empirical reality of blacks' domination of sports in which explosive bursts of action are the atoms of victory. This domination and a measurable black superiority at physical abilities clearly related to success in these sports would be best explained by our positing a black genetic physiological advantage even if we had no idea concerning the nature of the physiological mechanism responsible. However, we need not merely posit this mechanism without direct phsyiological evidence; evidence of its existence and nature is abundant. This all being the case, we might ask those who deny the black physiological advantage precisely what *could* convince them of the existence and importance of such an advantage.

Those committed to an entirely environmental explanation of black athletic success rarely even address the evidence relevant to the question. Rather, they attempt to counter that evidence by invoking the (putative) uses to which the findings will be put. Specifically, they fear and claim that acknowledgment of a black athletic superiority will be used as evidence of a black intellectual inferiority. Such an *ad consequentum* argument would be irrelevant even if it made sense; the correctness of the facts, reasoning, and conclusions presented here is independent of the uses to which belief in the conclusions could be put. This is sufficient to immunize the analysis presented here against the charge that the consequences of its conclusions somehow cast doubt on the correctness of those conclusions.

But to leave the matter at this would be to grant that people would believe that because blacks are superior athletically they are inferior intellectually. To be sure, racists have said things even more moronic, but never, to the best of my knowledge, has anyone, save for the environmentalists who fear that this will happen, ever even suggested this.

The reader might, understandably, ask why, even if all that I say here is correct, we should address the question of why blacks are better athletes. It would, I think, be sufficient to answer that any question found interesting by anyone is worthy of the effort required to find the answer.

But there is a much more important reason for exposing the inadequacy of a belief that is received wisdom in sociology. Sociology is rapidly becoming nothing more than a series of ideological claims that do not merely fail to address the relevant evidence but claim the opposite of what the evidence suggests. Authors of introductory sociology textbooks seem to care more that their students believe that which (the author thinks) is good for the student than that which is true.

In any case, it is true that in the past faulty biological explanations were offered for observations of behavior better explained in purely cultural terms. No one would wish for acceptance of such theories today. But it is worth mentioning that even the worst of such theories represented an attempt to explain that which is observed. Such an attempt is science, if not always very good science. The inevitably doomed attempt to substitute discussion of putative dangers of a finding for discussion of the relevant evidence on which the finding is based is not even common sense, much less science. Fortunately, deep down, everyone knows this.

NOTES

1. This was the case with Jewish boxers and basketball players of the twenties and Irish football players and boxers of the thirties. It is worth noting that even when, fifty years ago, Paul Gallico described a Jewish affinity for basketball in terms of the "scheming mind," "flashy trickiness," and "general smartaleckness" of the Jews, he was attributing the over-representation to a *nonphysical* superiority that, I assume, he saw as being cultural in origin.

2. In analyzing the causal roles of physiology, environment, and interaction of the two in the contribution of blacks to athletics, it is not necessary to demonstrate that environment plays some part; clearly it does. When segregation precluded black participation, there was, of course, no black contribution. When limitations on black participation in other areas renders black participation in athletics one of few alternatives, there are more blacks in athletics than there otherwise would be. On the other hand, opportunity generates possibility, not actuality; Japanese-Americans have full opportunity to play professional basketball, but inherent limitation imposed by size precludes possibility's very often becoming actuality.

3. This explanation is neither necessary (other male physical advantages are sufficient to explain male basketball superiority) or complete (cultural factors play a role), but it is *sufficient* to explain the empirical reality we wish to explain.

4. Extensive discussion of the evidence of specific physiological correlates of racially differentiated athletic aptitudes is not within the scope of this chapter. Interested readers are urged to consult the work of Claude Bouchard. Reference to Bouchard's "Genetic Basis of Racial Differences," in *Canadian Journal of Sports Science* (Vol. 13, No. 12), and "Aero Power and Capacity," in *Sport and Human Genetics* (Ed. by Robert Molina and Claude Bouchard), will lead the reader to nearly all of the directly relevant studies.

5. Were we attempting to discover the correlation of black genotype or phenotype with *degrees* of blackness, then such methodological problems, while not insurmountable, would arise. It is logically possible, for example, that the black advantage is one of threshold and is not continuous, so that, say, 100 percent black ancestry confers no advantage over 50 percent, but 50 percent confers the advantage that we attempt to explain. This is irrelevant here because we are attempting to explain only the observation that, in certain sports, athletes with some black ancestry dominate a much larger group of people with no black ancestry.

7

What Good Are the SAT's?

1. THE BASIC IRONY

The true measure of the ability of Scholastic Aptitude Tests, high-school grades, and other variables (and combinations of variables) to predict college performance would be this: A college would select its students at random, all selected students would attend the college, and the correlations of the variables with performance at the college would be determined.

In reality, however, there is no "Random College."[1] Colleges select students and, to an even greater extent, students select colleges—on the basis of the colleges' perceived high-school grade and SAT requirements. The C student with 400 SAT's does not apply to the highly selective college and would not be accepted if he did.

There is a built-in irony here. To the extent that a variable is used by a college or its students in the selection process, the ability of that variable to predict performance at that college is diminished. In its purest form this would be seen at the college that accepted only students with 800 SAT's. At such a college, the students would exhibit the full range of grades in the full range of course difficulty (i.e., there would be A students and F students, students taking topology and students taking introduction to breathing). Yet, because all had the same 800 SAT scores, *there would be no correlation between SAT score and college performance.*

Now, if one assesses the value of a predictive variable on the basis of its ability to predict real-life situations and on no other criterion, one concludes that the SAT's are—for the "800 college"—worthless. This is, in fact, the dubious strategy invariably followed by those who argue against the validity of the SAT's.

Clearly, it would be bizarre to dismiss the validity of the SAT's on these grounds. For in identifying those students capable of attaining 800 scores on their SAT's, the SAT's identify the best students—those students who would be at the top of the class at "Random College." Indeed, it could well be argued that

131

the greatest virtue of the SAT's is not their predictive abilities (which are exceptional even with the difficulties engendered by the selection process), but their ability to discriminate the relative abilities of students (i.e., abilities that for some would not be manifested in good grades at the highly selective college, but would be at "Random College").

An analogy may make this all a bit more comprehensible. Clearly, weight is relevant to an ability to be a guard in the National Football League. The 170-pounder who doubts this is in for a painful surprise. But once one narrows the population to people who weigh a muscular 260 pounds or more, the relationship between size and ability decreases; it is far more likely that a 260-pounder is a better guard than a 270-pounder than that a 170-pounder is better than a 270-pounder.

Likewise, when a college reduces the range of SAT scores of the students it accepts from 500-800 to 650-800, it becomes more likely that a student with a lower SAT score will perform better at the college than will one with a higher SAT score. The student with the 650 SAT's is more likely to outperform in college the student with the 750 SAT's than is the student with the 500 SAT's. (But, most of the time, the 750 SAT student will get better grades at a given college than will either the 650 or 500 SAT student.) If the college were to reduce the range of the students it admitted to 770-800, SAT's would become virtually worthless in their ability to predict college performance.

In other words, one can always filter out—or at least greatly reduce the importance of—a causal variable, no matter how strong that variable, by selecting a group that selects its members on the basis of that variable. This is what happens at every college (the selective college more than the unselective), and this is why the correlation of SAT scores and grades at a given college always underestimates the ability of the SAT's to measure students' academic talent. Nonetheless, with all of this, even studies of students at the same college demonstrate most clearly a relationship between SAT scores and performance. (Obviously, assessments must compare students at the same college; it makes no sense to compare a B student at a highly selective college with an A student at a college that accepts anyone who applies.)

Note that throughout we have defined "college performance" in terms of college grades and have not considered the relative difficulty of the courses in which those grades are attained. As we shall see in Part 3, when one compares a group that takes clearly more difficult courses than the group with which it is compared, course difficulty must be considered if we are to reach a sensible conclusion on the relative abilities of different predictors to discriminate relative student ability.

2. THE BASIC ASYMMETRY

All that has been said to this point is as true of high-school grades as of SAT's. Moreover, the fact that selection on the basis of the predictive variable extracts a methodological price—an inherent and inevitable underestimation of the ability of the variable to measure relative ability—would pose no problem if all variables were affected equally. The predictive ability of every variable would be equally affected by the selection process. We would never know the true absolute predictive abilities of the different variables (that which would be ascertained if there were a "Random College" to study), but we *would* know the relative predictive abilities.

However, not all variables are affected equally. There is an asymmetry between SAT scores and high-school grades that leads to a greater underestimation of the SAT's ability to reflect the relative abilities of students than is the case with high-school grades. This asymmetry reflects the SAT's superior ability to discriminate student ability and the concomitant reduction, owing to selection on the basis of SAT scores, of the SAT's ability to demonstrate this superiority in terms of prediction of college performance.

Where the SAT's correctly predict that the student from the good high school with B's and 650 SAT's will perform better at "Random College" than will the student from the poor high school with A's and 500 SAT's, the high-school grade measure incorrectly predicts that the A student will perform better. It does this because, in basing its prediction on the student's A's, it fails to take into account the fact that a B at the good high school is more difficult to attain than is the A at the poor high school. The SAT's automatically compensate for this difference of high-school quality and this is reflected in the higher SAT score of the B student and the inherent, and correct, prediction that the B student at the good high school will perform better at the college.

Because selection by high-school grades does not compensate for the quality of the high school, students from poor high schools and with low SAT scores will be admitted to colleges that select on the basis of high-school grades who would not be admitted if SAT score had been the criterion for selection. Since these students have low SAT scores, the range of SAT scores will be wider than would be the case if SAT scores were used for selection. Since the range of SAT scores will be wider than it would have been had SAT scores been used for selection, the ability of the SAT's to demonstrate their ability to identify student ability will be better reflected in prediction of college performance.

In other words, when high-school grades are used for selection, the A student with 500 SAT's from the poor high school will be accepted by the selective college and the SAT range of students at the selective college will include 500; had SAT's been used for selection, this student would have been passed over in favor of the B student with 650 SAT's from the good high school, the SAT range of students at the college would be narrower, and the correlation of SAT's and college grades would be that much less; the true ability of the SAT's to identify the better student would be hidden by selection on the basis of the very ability that, correctly, leads to the selection of the better student.

We can limit the degree to which differences in the distortive effect of selection on different variables distort our assessment of predictive validity. We can assess the ability of the SAT's to predict performance at colleges where selection is based on high-school grades and the ability of high-school grades to predict performance at colleges where selection is based on SAT's. Cross-testing in this way permits us to limit the selection effect on the better predictor to that imposed by the poorer predictor. For example, in assessing the ability of SAT's to predict performance at a college that selects on the basis of high-school grades, we limit the selection effect to that imposed by high-school grades.

This does not enable us to attain "Random College" perfection because high-school grades are correlated with SAT's; few A and B students have 300 SAT's, so even when a college and students select each other on the basis of the students' having had A's and B's in high school, and not at all on the basis of the students' SAT scores, the college cuts off not only the lower segment of the range of high-school grades, but also (to a lesser extent) the lower segment of the range of SAT scores. Nonetheless, this approach does enable us to determine the better predictor. (In reality, most colleges combine criteria in their selection process, but the logic remains essentially the same, if more complicated.)

Here we see one of the valuable properties of the SAT's: If neither the selective college nor the student with an A average and two 500 SAT's at a poor high school took the student's SAT's into account, the student would apply to, and be accepted by, the selective college. Such a student would do poorly at the selective college, the SAT's would predict this, and the SAT/college performance correlation would be much higher than it is now. The reverse is not true: high-school grades do not successfully predict performance to the extent that SAT's are used for selection (i.e., high-school grades predict that the A-500 student will do *better* than, not *less* well than, the B-650 student).

I hasten to add that, throughout this article, we discuss statistical individuals. Our example of the students at the good and poor high schools *stipulates*, on the statistical empirical evidence of subsequent college performance, that attaining an A at the poor school demands less than a B at the good school and that this is reflected in the higher SAT score of the student with the lower grades at the better school; this is how we statistically *define* the "good" and "poor" high schools. In the *case of two given individuals* at two given high schools *this stipulation might be incorrect or other factors might be paramount.*

Thus, no one suggests that either colleges or high-school students take only SAT's into account. Even when selection is discounted—i.e., even when predictive criteria are compared under "Random College" conditions—the SAT's are only slightly superior to high-school grades. The best predictor of all is comprised of the SAT verbal aptitude, SAT mathematics aptitude, and high-school grades, with the SAT's being weighted slightly more heavily than high-school grades. In all likelihood, the contribution of high-school grades devolves from their ability to reflect motivation, a factor that is an important contributor to attainment of a good grade average and possibly an even more important contributor to success in the world outside college.

Moreover, there really are students for whom deprivation in childhood and adolescence can be overcome at a highly selective college, brilliant students who panic when taking a test, late bloomers, and the like. And there are special contributions that some relatively poor students can make to a highly selective college. For all these reasons, application essays (writing ability), interviews ("social intelligence"), and the like are crucial to the admission process.

However, when we speak of the SAT's we speak of millions of students, and it is only a large, statistically accurate measure that can hope to rationally match students with the colleges most likely to benefit them. The SAT's are the best such measure we have. Most people approach the statistical norm; that's what makes it the statistical norm. When we assess the rationality of the admission process in general, our stipulation is fully justified. If factors measured by the other variables (but not by the SAT's) were more important than those measured by the SAT's, then these other factors would discriminate college ability as well as or better than do the SAT's. And they don't.

3. THE CLAIM THAT THE SAT'S DISCRIMINATE AGAINST WOMEN

Nearly all of the arguments concluding that the Scholastic Aptitude Tests discriminate against women rest on this foundation: (1) males score over fifty points higher than females on SAT's (owing almost entirely to higher scores on the mathematics test); (2) females get better grades in college; (3) therefore, the SAT's fail in the task of predicting the relative college performance of males and females; and (4) admissions and scholarships based on SAT scores represent sexual discrimination.

If males and females took the *same* courses in college and females got better grades, *then* the claim of sexual discrimination would be well taken. However, the same superiority in mathematical reasoning exhibited by males on the SAT's leads males far more often to take mathematics and math-intensive physical science courses. If females were to take these courses in the same numbers as do males, their overall grade average would be significantly lower than the males'.

Thus, the argument concluding that the SAT's discriminate against females is without merit. It equates "performance" with grades while ignoring the issue of which courses the grades are obtained in. In the case of males and females the difference in course selection is tremendous. For a comparison to make any sense, it is necessary to factor in course difficulty by asking what would happen if the females took mathematics and mathematics-intensive courses at the same rate as do males or if males took non-math intensive courses at the same rate as do females.

Note that the relevant issue is not the relative scores of males and females who *do* presently take the mathematics and math-intensive courses. Even if the (fewer) women in mathematics courses are equal to the large number of men in these courses in every way, this would *not*, despite its having been argued successfully in legal cases, imply an equal aptitude for males and females in general. To argue that it would is analogous to arguing that, because the few (exactly) six-foot-tall women are as tall as the many (exactly) six-foot-tall men, women in general are as tall as as men.[2]

Nor is the relevant issue the relative grades of males and females in the non-math-intensive courses. It is clear that the females in these courses are, in fact, better students than the males in these courses. They earn higher grades and this is predictible on the basis of the higher SAT scores of the females. In other words, a higher percentage of the better female students take non-math-intensive courses. The better male students take, to a far greater extent, math-intensive courses.

The relevant questions are these: (1) What would happen if as high a percentage of women took the math courses (or if all students took the math courses)? Clearly, as we shall see, the overall grade average of the female students would plummet relative to the overall grade average of the males. (2) What would happen if *no* students took math-intensive courses? The answer here is not as clear, but, as we shall see, it is likely that the influx to the non-math-intensive courses of the students who now take math-intensive courses (students who are better even by verbal measure than those in non-math-intensive courses) would (because disproportionate numbers of these students are male) reduce, eliminate, or reverse the sex difference in grades in non-math-intensive courses.

Let us assume that the males and females who actually take a mid-level or advanced mathematics course in college have equal, and relatively high, math-SAT scores. The course will enroll many more males than females. (It must if the SAT averages are to be equal; if the same number of males and females took the course, the male SAT average would be much higher.) Now, let us require *all* students to take this course.

It seems to me so self-evident that overall grade average of males will increase (relative to that of females) that I don't know what to say to one who denies it. Math SAT score is clearly correlated with selection of, and performance in, math-intensive courses, and the math-SAT scores of males are much higher than are those of females. Moreover, the correlation of math SAT and performance would, for reasons we have discussed, be much higher if the math courses were required and there were no diminution of SAT range resulting from selection. It's true, of course, that one can't demonstrate directly the drop in female grade average that would result from our requiring the courses; the additional males and females don't now take the courses. But to deny that the higher math-SAT scores of the additional males and the lower math-SAT scores of the additional females would increase the overall grade average of males and reduce that of females requires a scenario bizarre to the point of absurdity.

To use that argument to deny that the female grades would drop if the additional females took the courses is equivalent to making this argument: "In a weight-lifting class in which students are graded on the *absolute* amount of weight they can lift, 90 percent of the students are male. The females are unusually strong for females and do as well as the males. Now what would happen if we decided that *all* students should take the weight-lifting course? It's true that tests show that the average strength of the additional males is much greater than the average strength of the additional females. But this gives us no right to assume that the additional females wouldn't lift as much weight as the additional males in the weight-lifting course if they took it. We can't now know, because the students not now taking the course don't now take the course. Could an argument be more absurd than this?

If there were a "Random College" at which all students took the same courses, we would find that the more mathematics and science courses were required, the more the male grades would be better than the female grades.

It is less clear what would happen if *no one* took mathematics and mathematics-intensive courses. However, it does seem likely that the male-female grade difference would be reduced, eliminated, or reversed (but not nearly to the degree that it would be if students who do not now take math-intensive courses were forced to do so). The SAT *verbal* average of students intending to major in the physical sciences is higher than that of students intending to major in any liberal art discipline except English (and even here the difference of means is less than twenty points). The SAT verbal mean of students intending to major in mathematics is considerably higher than the mean for students in the other liberal art disciplines. And, of course, the mathematics SAT scores of the math and physical sciences students are much higher than those of any other liberal arts students. Thus, even considering only the greater numbers of males in the math-intensive courses and the correlation of verbal SAT and grade in predicting performance in non-math-intensive courses, it would seem clear that, if the students now in mathematics and the physical sciences were to take only non-math-intensive courses, they would do better then those students now in the courses (and the male-female grade difference would, therefore, be reduced, eliminated, or reversed).

Moreover, it seems quite likely—though at this point not documented—that students presently in the non-math-intensive courses who got high math SAT's do better than students with the same verbal SAT's but lower math SAT's. To the extent that this is true, it would lead us to expect that students from the math-intensive courses would do *much* better in non-math-intensive courses than do the students now in such courses. It might well be that the *best* students in the class would be those non-math students who had very high verbal SAT's, but the mean grade of the newly entered math and physical science students would be considerably higher than that of the non-math/science students. And, since males far outnumber females among the math and physical science students, the result of all students' taking non-math-intensive courses would be to increase the male grade average, and to decrease the female grade average, in non-math-intensive courses.

No serious researcher questions the male superiority at mathematical reasoning. This sex difference is, contrary to frequent but false claims to the contrary, found in every country on which we have evidence of any sort (college entrance tests, Math Olympics qualification, etc.). The debate concerns the role of differentiated male and female Central Nervous System-endocrine system-brain development in the causation of the universal male superiority. This question—important as it is—is not immediately relevant to the issue of tests. Tests demonstrate an aptitude or ability; they do not attempt to explain the causation of that aptitude or ability.

Thus, arguments concerning the role of physiological differentiation in explaining the sex difference in mathematical performance are irrelevant to the points I have made. I have argued only that the SAT's reflect a real sex difference in performance and that the cause of this difference—even if it is purely environmental—is irrelevant here; a pound on the scale is a pound whether that represents a chunk of bone or last night's dinner.

The task of the SAT's is to assess the likely performance of students in college. *Why* the individuals who have the aptitudes or abilities to perform better have those aptitudes or abilities is not, and should not be, the concern of the SAT.

4. THREE POINTS FOR PERSPECTIVE

The meaning of the male-female difference in scores obtained on the math-SAT's can be seen in clearer perspective if we consider three points that are not always made clear.

(1) We have seen, in the "six-foot" analogy above, that even if females in advanced mathematics classes performed as well as males, this would not cast doubt on the male superiority exhibited on the SAT's; the superiority is manifested in the greater numbers of males in the courses (just as males' greater height would be manifested in the greater number of males in a class open only to people six-feet-tall).

The six-foot analogy also makes clear a somewhat more positive point that is often confused in discussions of male and female differences. To say that males are better at mathematics, more aggressive, and the like—or females are more psychologically acute, longer-lived, etc.—is to speak statistically about the males and females in general. Even when there is a sex difference—and even when this difference is rooted in sexual physiological difference—those individuals who are greater exceptions for their sex than they would be for the other sex (the mathematically talented woman, the 100-year-old man) are just as talented, long-lived, etc. as the member of the other sex with the same talent, longevity, etc. It is simply that the exceptional person would rank in a lower percentile for the other sex if he/she were a member of the other sex. In other words, the female with a mathematics SAT score in the 90th percentile of females is every bit as talented as a male whose (same) score is in the 75th percentile of males; she is just more of an exception for women than the man is for men; i.e., there are more men than women attaining this score.

In other words, the empirical reality we wish to explain (the statistical superiority of males with reference to the aptitudes tested by the math-SAT) is, like all sex differences, a statistical reality concerning the percentages of males and females at given levels above the mean. It is not a statement about the performance of a given individual. We expect to find women with 800 scores on their math SAT's as surely as we expect to find women who are six feet, five inches tall. However, we expect to find fewer such women than men. In theory we could find that, even if physiological differentiation plays an important role in the male-female difference in mathematical aptitude and the socialization that reflects it, a woman enters the very highest rank of mathematicians.[3]

Admittedly, when the point is made explicitly, it is patently obvious that a woman who runs an eleven-second hundred-meter dash is just as fast as a man who does so. But so many analyses of sex differences contain a buried fallacy equivalent to that stating that this woman does not run as fast because she is more of an exception for women than the eleven-second man is for men (i.e., there are more eleven-second men) that the point is worth making here.

(2) Whether a difference in the means of two groups with reference to an aptitude is "important" is a function of the question: "important for what?"

For example, the difference in mathematical aptitude between males and females is relatively unimportant if our interest is the ability of the average person to perform the arithmetic and mathematical tasks encountered in daily life. If this is one's interest, the relative numbers of males and females who exhibit exceptional mathematics skills are unimportant.

However, the *same* mean difference in aptitude becomes very important if we are interested in the percentages of males and females in the top percentile, those individuals most likely to make a serious contribution to mathematics and those who will serve as models for the general population. At this level, the *same* difference in mean that is unimportant in the everyday situation becomes crucial.

Those whose interest is in the abilities and requirements of most people will see as unimportant the difference of "only" fifty points between the male and female means on the math-SAT. Those whose interest is in the ability and requirements of the most talented will see as important the fact that a fifty-point difference in means results in the overwhelming number of students who score 800 being male. That a small difference in means between two groups can result in a huge difference in the relative numbers of members of the two groups that will be found at the extremes is a reality that is patently clear in the statistics, but it's one that's sometimes difficult to convey in nonstatistical terms.

(3) Two generations ago, hardly anyone, male or female, doubted—or cared— that mathematical aptitudes were associated with males. This was merely one of a number of aptitudes seen by all as more strongly associated with one sex than the other, with males and females each emphasizing those tendencies and aptitudes more associated with their respective genders. However, as it became common for women to attend college—with its greatly reduced attention to home-making and childrearing—women have come to place less value on aptitudes and behaviors associated with women and greater value on those associated with men. Those educated in recent years believe that it is "natural" that mathematical aptitude be given high value and aptitudes associated with the home low value— just as, in former times, women who saw mathematical aptitudes as more important than female aptitudes were seen by other women as "unfeminine." Within constraints set by psychophysiological factors, people tend to do what they are told and to accept the values their socialization gives them.

5. THE QUESTION OF CAUSE

Nothing I have written to this point is predicated on any one or another views of the *causes* of the empirical realities we examine. It is irrelevant, for example, whether males outperform females on the math-SAT for purely environmental reasons or for reasons related to genetic sexual differences. Again, the task of the SAT is to measure ability, not to determine whether that ability is rooted in an aptitude affected by genetic predisposition.

However, it is clear that many of the arguments denying the ability of the SAT's to identify students who will do well in college are rooted in a fear that: (A) granting the ability of the SAT's to identify the better students somehow argues that the ability of these students is physiologically rooted, and (B) that, if this ability *is* physiologically rooted, it is by its nature unchangeable.

Even if these points were correct (which they are not), they would be irrelevant. It *should* go without saying that our purpose is to discover that which is true, not to deny for irrelevant reasons that which is true. The fallaciousness of *ad consequentium* reasoning has been obvious for millennia.

But to leave matters at this would be to leave the impression that points A and B are correct. They are not.

(A) The ability of the SAT's to predict college performance tells us nothing about why those students whose success is predicted are successful. Other evidence is required to assess the *cause* of the success.

(B) It is far from clear that the physiological is more difficult to change than the environmental. Those who are born weak and lift weights can become stronger than those who are born strong and don't. The intelligent in nonliterate societies do not learn to read. The less intelligent in literate societies *do* learn to read. Even if that which the SAT's measure is in part owing to inherited physiological factors, there is reason to hope that environmental programs and policies can improve the performance of those less well endowed. If this happens, the way we will know is by the alteration of the distribution of scores on the SAT's.[4]

It is worthwhile here to address a fallacious argument that infuses much of the discussion of sex differences on the SAT, the "explanation" of sex differences in terms of the differentiated socialization of the sexes. My purpose here is not to argue that the sex difference in mathematical reasoning *does* have a significant element of genetic-physiological causation,[5] but merely that the frequently invoked claim that differentiated socialization argues against such a causation is without merit.

This claim, invoked to deny the *possible* role of physiology, has led to a wide acceptance of the analysis that "explains" the male mathematical superiority in terms of a socialization that dissuades females from pursuing mathematics, without any explanation being given of why the socialization proceeds as it does. This, like all explanations that invoke socialization without saying why the socialization proceeds as it does, is no explanation at all. It is a mere begging of the question—which becomes: *Why* does socialization associate mathematics

—or aggression, etc.—with males? The answer in the case of any given sexually differentiated aptitude, tendency, behavior, etc., *may* be purely environmental, but the mere fact that the socialization exists is no argument that this is the case and that physiology is not crucial. It is often the case that it is a sexual physiological differentiation that engenders a (statistical) sexual differentiation that is observed by the population and incorporated into the population's expectations and socialization.

For example, men are not physically stronger primarily *because* we give boys sets of weights. Indeed, *when* there is a physiologically causal factor, a population will see its behavioral manifestation and will incorporate it in their expectations and socialization. The socialization does not demonstrate that physiology plays a causal role, but no one ever claims that it does. What is often claimed is that the socialization somehow casts doubt on the possible importance of physiology. As the strength example makes clear, this is absurd.

When it is the case that sexually differentiated physiology engenders sexually differentiated aptitudes, tendencies, or behaviors (remembering that we are always speaking statistically), the differentiation of aptitude, tendency, or behavior is observed by the population and incorporated in its expectations and socialization. It is a sociological fallacy infusing much of the literature on sex differences that treats the environmental as if it were an independent variable, capable of acting as counterpoise to the physiological. In reality, the physiological sets limits of possibility on expectation and socialization.[6] In other words, there is no outside experimenter setting whatever behaviors and expectations seem desirable; the environmental is a dependent variable given its limits and direction by the reality of physiological differentiation.[7]

Moreover, *when* it is the case that sexually differentiated physiology engenders sexually differentiated aptitudes, tendencies, or behaviors, there will be the inevitable human tendency for aspiration to reflect ability. In other words, *if* it is true that physiology underlies males' greater mathematical abilities, then males will tend to enjoy mathematics more and will be more likely to take mathematics courses. Thus, *if* there is a physiological basis to the male mathematical ability, we would expect disproportionate numbers of males taking these courses *even if socialization were identical for the two sexes* (which, for reasons given in the preceding paragraphs, it could not be). Furthermore, mathematics-intensive courses primarily attract students from the upper percentiles of mathematics ability; as we have seen, a small difference in the means of two groups can represent a huge difference in the proportion of members of the two groups found at higher percentiles.

Again: I stress here that my purpose is not to argue that the sex difference in mathematical reasoning *is* rooted in sexual physiological differentiation (that issue is not within the scope of this article), but only to argue that the fact that we and our socialization associate mathematical reasoning more strongly with males is no argument against the importance of physiological differentiation.

One can, of course, make the subjective argument that admissions and scholarships should not reflect mathematical aptitude. One can make a consistent argument that admissions and scholarships should be divided equally between the sexes, be divided equally among all, be based only on need, refuse to consider questions on which one sex or the other is superior (this is what some intelligence tests do) or be prorated among disciplines (with the quality of the individual student being ignored). Such arguments do not pretend that the SAT fails in its task of identifying differences in talent, but deny that such differences should play the role in selection that they now play. They may, for example, argue that efficiency is not as socially important as a group-proportional distribution of resources that is required if groups are to *perceive* the distribution as fair.

Such a position would, like all logically coherent subjective positions, be as impervious to attack as it would be incapable of convincing anyone who did not already share its basic subjective premise. But it would have the integrity to acknowledge its subjective foundation and would not offer illogical and empirically false arguments that should not be able to fool anyone with a rigorous mind and/or a college diploma, but which are now law.

Such is not the line of reasoning now being put forth in the courts. It is now being argued that "the probability, absent discriminatory causes, that women would consistently score 60 points less on the SAT than men is nearly zero."

Such reasoning is pathetic. What has a nearly zero probability is not a male-female difference without discrimination, but a difference without *any* cause (i.e., a difference that reflects random fluctuation or "chance"). There *is* a cause, but it is not discrimination; it is the male superiority at various spatial and mathematical aptitudes that correlate with college performance.[8]

To call this "discriminatory" is to say that any test that successfully measures that which it attempts to measure is discriminatory; such a view would see a test for height that finds men taller than women as discriminatory because it finds that men are taller than women.

6. ARE THE SAT'S AN IQ TEST?

The Educational Testing Service and the College Board, having more than their share of controversial issues, vehemently deny that the SAT's are an IQ test. The validity of the SAT's, it is argued, devolves from their ability to discriminate relative academic aptitude and, within the constraints discussed in this article, to predict college performance. What is being measured are those skills and aptitudes relevant to college performance, and not "intelligence" in general. This argument is perfectly coherent, and possibly correct.

However, one can not but be impressed by the astonishing correlation of SAT scores and scores on the standard IQ tests, a correlation about as high a nontrivial correlation as one ever finds in the social sciences.

Those who argue against the validity of IQ tests will claim that the correlation demonstrates that IQ tests do not measure intelligence in general, but only those aspects of intelligence called on in an academic setting. They will deny the central claim of those who admire the IQ test, the claim that the correlation of IQ and SAT demonstrates that the single most important factor for success in an academic (or virtually any other modern) setting is "G intelligence" (a general intelligence that informs, to varying, but always significant degrees, the various abilities—verbal, mathematical, spatial, etc.—that are themselves highly intercorrelated). They will argue that there are many forms of intelligence that are not directly measured by the IQ test and that the IQ test, while it may measure the limited forms of intelligence measured by the SAT's, cannot claim to measure "intelligence." Intelligence, they will argue, is not a single entity that plays a role in virtually all mental abilities, but a term comprising a great number of often unrelated aptitudes.

This denial of the ability of the IQ test to measure "intelligence" faces two very serious, I believe fatal, problems.

(1) Nearly all of the aptitudes that can reasonably be seen as related to "intelligence" are significantly correlated. While every aptitude also has specific requirements unrelated to general intelligence, even those not directly tested (like musical ability) turn out to be highly correlated with IQ. People whose high verbal SAT's are considerably higher than their math SAT's (or *vice versa*) tend not to believe this and will often say, "I'm good at verbal tasks, but horrible at math" (or *vice versa*). The truth is that such people are almost invariably far above average in the aptitude that they believe they lack altogether, though less above average than in their greater aptitude. There may have been a few true exceptions, but, if so, they are extraordinarily rare. Alleged exceptions are, on closer inspection, nearly always found merely to have IQ's somewhat less than one would guess and somewhat less than their less-distinguished contemporaries—say, a Nobel physicist with a 130 IQ or a Nobel novelist with a 125 IQ. Surprisingly "low" IQ's of individuals of such achievement tend to lead to exaggeration of how low the IQ's are; in fact even the 125 IQ is higher than that attained by well over 90 percent of the population.

More important: If we consider, say, not the musical aptitude of the high-IQ individual, but the IQ of the musically talented individual, we will almost always find that the musically talented individual will have an IQ in the upper percentiles of the general population. This is true—to an extent ranging from considerable to extraordinarily high—in the case of excellence in almost all areas that can reasonably be seen as related to "intelligence."

(2) IQ correlates with our use of "intelligence" in everyday life. This has always seemed to me to be the most devastating argument in favor of the ability of IQ to measure "intelligence." Opponents of the IQ test invoke vaguely described aptitudes unmeasured by the IQ test, a vagueness required by the fact that, if the aptitudes were specified, it could immediately be shown that each such aptitude correlates highly with IQ, cannot reasonably be seen as anything we usually see as related to "intelligence," or does not exist. This is easily demonstrated.

If such aptitudes were significant components of "intelligence" (as the term is generally employed), then there would be significant numbers of people who are considered intelligent who do not have relatively high IQ's. There are not. Virtually anyone who is considered to be "intelligent" has an IQ in the upper

15 percent, usually in the upper ten. This being the case, it would seem that attempts to deny the validity of IQ tests on the basis of aptitudes that are either highly correlated with IQ or of dubious relevance or existence can be seen to be nothing more than semantic fancy footwork in the service of avoidance of the ideologically unpalatable. Indeed, arguments denying the validity of the IQ tests fail to explain the empirical reality requiring explanation: the correlation of IQ and success in areas requiring intelligence.

As is the case with the correlation of SAT scores and college performance (or any other two correlates), the correlation between IQ score and "intelligence" (as intuitively identified and reported) assumes a population with a fairly wide range of scores and intelligence. Just as a ten-point difference in SAT score has little predictive value, so does a five- or ten-point difference in IQ score have little predictive value. Once the importance of intelligence is filtered out, then other factors become paramount. (Once again our football analogy applies.) However, IQ ranking over a wider range of IQ scores will nearly always match people's intuitive ranking of intelligence, and those identified as particularly "intelligent" will have high IQ's. This is true of those in lower as well as in upper social and economic groups and those with little education as well as those with graduate degrees.

The fact that people agree, in the statistical sense, on who is "intelligent" demonstrates that the word has meaning and that people use it consistently. The word "fnorcal" has no meaning and this is demonstrated by the fact that attempts, on the part of people or tests, to identify those with the most "fnorcality" are doomed to a failure of random attribution. The most plausible explanation of people's ability to independently agree on who is intelligent is one that accepts a "G-intelligence" that infuses the various specific manifestations of "intelligence"; the observation of this "G-intelligence" at work enables people to observe and independently identify the "intelligent" among them.

If "intelligence" is a meaningful word, if it is consistently applied, if it correlates highly with IQ, then there would seem no legitimate reason for denying that IQ measures "intelligence" in the only meaningful sense of the word. If IQ correlates with SAT score, then there would seem little reason to doubt that much of the SAT score measures intelligence. And to the extent that SAT score correlates with college performance, there would seem no reason to doubt that intelligence is a most important factor in college success (and success in other areas of human endeavor with which success is correlated with IQ). After all, no one ever doubted any of this except some social scientists.

Moreover, we would expect—and do find—that SAT scores are more highly correlated with IQ scores than either is with college performance. This is because motivation is more important to college performance than it is to SAT or IQ performance. While intelligence and motivation are correlated—the more intelligent succeed more often and this enhances motivation, as success enhances motivation in all endeavors—differences in student motivation engender a larger discrepancy between test and college performance than between test and test— that is, between SAT and IQ.

In short: There are two legitimate views of that which is measured by IQ tests.

The first view sees the word "intelligence" as merely an umbrella term for a configuration of aptitudes, abilities, and other factors that are associated with success in a wide variety of human endeavors (academic and professional performance, new situations, and the like). This view would see nothing being gained by the use of the word "intelligence" in the name of the test and would prefer a name like "The Smith Test." This would focus on the reality that this view sees as central (the association of test result and success in the endeavors mentioned) without raising the irrelevant objections involved in the issue of "intelligence."

The second view sees the first as correct in its acceptance of the correlation of IQ test score and success in the endeavors mentioned, but sees the first view as understating the abilities of the test. The second view sees the first as failing to reflect the ability of the IQ test to reflect the fact that the test identifies those people who are recognized by those around them as "intelligent." According to this second view, the first view refuses to acknowledge that the configuration of aptitudes and abilities it identifies *is* "intelligence" and that the general population's belief that it is intelligent people who excel in the endeavors mentioned is correct.

In other words, the first view is merely that those who do well on IQ tests tend to do well in the endeavors mentioned and makes no claim about why this is the case. The second view is that those who do well on IQ tests do well in the endeavors mentioned because those who do well on the tests are intelligent and intelligence is a virtual requirement of the endeavors. The second view sees as evidence for this the fact that those who do well on IQ tests are those who people independently identify as "intelligent" and that those who are independently identified as "intelligent" are those who succeed in the endeavors that are (correctly) believed to require "intelligence." Both views reject the objection that the IQ test is meaningless because such a objection implicitly denies the ability of the test to identify those who do well in the endeavors mentioned, an ability that cannot be legitimately denied (statistically speaking, as always).

The issue of SAT and IQ need not concern those interested only in the predictive ability of the SAT's. I mention it because nearly all readers seem to find it interesting. My view is that IQ tests do measure "G intelligence," that this "G intelligence" is precisely what we all recognize when we call someone "intelligent," and that we recognize this "G intelligence" whatever the social setting.

The anthropologist quickly identifies the intelligent members of any society he studies, and these members are recognized as "intelligent" by the members of the societies, whatever the cultural nature of the particular society. This casts serious doubt on the attempt to argue that, while IQ may measure "intelligence" as the word is used in a modern, industrial society, it would fail to identify "intelligence" in cultures different from ours.

If such an argument means only that IQ tests would, for practical reasons, fail to measure an "intelligence" in other societies that is the same thing as "intelligence" in our own, then we can grant this as trivially true; obviously, to use an extreme example, a test in English and Arabic numerals will not identify "intelligence" in a society that uses an unrelated language and non-Arabic numerals.

Clearly, however, this argument is meant to claim that "intelligence" itself is different from one society to another. Ignoring the likely logical meaninglessness of the claim that "intelligence" in society A is different from "intelligence" in society B (i.e., if it's different, then it's not "intelligence," as society B uses the word), consider the fact that the claim—if meaningful—is not true. The aborigine does not call patience "intelligence" any more than we call wisdom "intelligence."

It may be that, in aborigine society, patience is more important for individual success and societal survival than is intelligence. But even if the *value* of intelligence does vary with time and culture, that does not transform intelligence into something else; it merely alters the behavior of the intelligent person and the value of this behavior. The aborigine does not confuse intelligence with patience. He merely says of one of whom it is true: "He's intelligent, but terribly impatient."

NOTES

1. There are, however, a number or colleges—primarily religious schools attended by students for whom religion, and not SAT's or grades, are the determining factor in selection by student and college—that statistically match "Random College" in all relevant ways. The empirical evidence provided by these colleges entirely supports the conclusions that this chapter reaches on primarily logical grounds. Likewise, as we shall see, the wider the range of the SAT scores of a student body, the greater the correlation of SAT scores and grades. This is precisely what we would expect if the SAT's are valid measures of college potential.

2. In a recent *New York Times* Op-Ed article, I suggested that it makes no sense for critics to blame the math-SAT for the fact that males get higher scores than do females. The SAT would be failing to do its job if it did not reflect the fact that males exhibit considerably better mathematical reasoning abilities than do females. (Why there is this sex difference—whether physiological differentiation plays a role or environment is sufficient explanation—is an issue the article did not discuss).

The chairmen of the mathematics departments of Harvard and Princeton universities wrote: "We do not see evidence of an intrinsic deficit of mathematical ability, but we see fewer women in mathematics then we would like." These men may not see the evidence, but they are looking directly at it: a smaller number of women exhibiting the mathematical aptitude required for advanced mathematics, and not an inferiority of the women who do take advanced mathematics, is precisely the point. Moreover, the observation made by the chairmen is concordant not merely with the point relevant here, but even with a physiological explanation of the better male performance.

The relative scores of the males and females who pursue Ph.D.'s (or who major) in mathematics is not relevant to the issue of the relative aptitudes of males and females, either in general or at the highest level. These would be relevant only if the male mathematics majors came from the same male percentiles as the females came from the female percentiles and the two sexes did equally well. This is, of course, not the case; the percentile vs. percentile scores of females do not equal those of males. This is precisely the empirical reality that the math SAT demonstrates.

3. It would, however, be disingenuous to claim that this is any more likely than would be a woman eight and a half feet tall. Nearly all of the very tallest people have been male and the very greatest mathematicians (say, the hundred greatest mathematicians) have all been male. This is as concordant with an explanation stressing the role of physiology as with one stressing environment. It is true, however, that the seventh tallest person on record was a woman and, therefore, even if it is true that mathematical aptitude has strong physiological roots, this would not preclude a woman's attaining the very highest ranks of mathematicians. This would, however, preclude its being more than a very small percentage of the people reaching the highest ranks of mathematics being women even if the sexes faced identical environmental situations.

4. Such programs will, even if successful, increase equality only if the contribution of the physiological is one of a threshold, past which there is no further improvement —that is, if contribution is analogous to that of vitamins, where increased dosage is valuable up to a threshold, past which additional doses offer no improvement. If the environmental program improves everyone's performance, equality will not be reduced if all are permitted to avail themselves of the environmental boost. Indeed, reality being what it is, a program that improved the performance of anyone exposed to it would likely be most utilized by the relatively wealthy and knowledgeable.

5. In fact, there is far more evidence for a hereditary physiological basis to the sex difference in mathematical reasoning than contemporary sociological ideology and pedagogy will allow. But nothing I write here is predicated on this. See *Behavioral and Brain Sciences* (Vol. 11, No. 2; June, 1988), which is devoted to Camilla Benbow's work on this question and responses to it, the work of Julian C. Stanley, and the addendum to my article in the *International Journal of Sociology and Social Policy* (Vol. 9; no. 2) and "Are Males Better at Mathematical Reasoning, and, If So, Why?" in an upcoming (1992) issue of the same journal.

6. Within the limits, some variation is, of course, possible. Thus, for example, one can find societies as different in their treatment of women as are Western and Muslim societies. But one can not find a society in which dominance behavior in hierarchies and male-female relationships is not associated with males. Physiological reality sets a limit on social variation and possibility.

7. In principle, we could eradicate even as clearly a physiologically rooted sex difference as the the sex difference in physical strength by forcing males to remain sedentary while forcing females to lift weights. But, in reality, no society's population ignores the realities it observes or imposes a socialization system so discordant with the realities its members bring to it.

Finally: It is true that there are situations in which environment alters physiology. But—if we use the example of male "aggression" to make the point—we see that this is irrelevant to sex differences for two reasons: (1) such alteration is minor compared to the innate differences (e.g., no normal environmental stimulus is capable of bringing female male-hormone levels to the male level), and (2) even if some abnormal or experimental factor were capable of so altering physiology, this would merely underline the fact that in no human society has there ever been any factor engendering in significant numbers of females male hormone levels approaching those of males or rendering females anywhere nearly as aggressive as males. Put another way: One who wishes to emphasize an environmental factor that generates the endocrinological sex differences must specify the universal environmental factor that generates a "more aggressive" *male* physiology in every society. In doing this, one reduces the physiological factor to that of mediator and encounters all of the problems encountered by environmental explanations.

8. Note that claims that the math SAT's are culture-biased in their *content* do not claim that there is no cause to the male superiority on the tests, nor do they make the "near zero probability" argument. They argue, in essence, that the questions are such that they favor males in their content, approach, etc.

The culture-bias claim, while it is not as inherently silly as the "non-zero probability" argument, fails for an empirical reason: What "culture-bias" *means* is that the content of the empirical test is such that the test tends to underestimate the ability of the group it is biased against. What "underestimate" means is that those against whom the test is biased perform better in the mathematics courses than the test predicts they will. But, in fact, this does not happen; the test predicts female performance in college mathematics as well as it predicts male.

One might argue that college mathematics courses contain the same culture bias as do the tests. I believe that such an argument fails for reasons too remote to the issues we discuss to warrant discussion. I believe that it can be shown that in nearly all academic, and most, but not all, occupational settings, the criteria for assessment of performance does not include the irrelevant, but I do not make that argument here.

Here my point is merely that—*if* the courses do reflect such bias—then the tests *should* also reflect it; if they do not, they will decrease their ability to predict performance, their very purpose.

I hasten to add that I am not justifying bias (the inclusion of factors irrelevant to performance) in academic or occupational life. Clearly such bias is wrong. But it is the bias in the colleges and occupations that is wrong, not the reflection of this in the tests. As long as this bias exists, the test that reflects it will be a better test—will be a better predictor of grades or assessments of occupational performance—than one that doesn't. For example, if tall chess players are given extra credit in rankings just because they are tall, then the test that factors in height will do its job better—will predict rankings better— than will the test that does not consider height. Acknowledging this does not render any less abhorrent the unjustified extra credit. Clearly, the rankings should discontinue the policy of giving extra credit for height. When they do, the tests, if they are to do their job as well as they had before, will also have to stop factoring in height.

Part 2

Why We View the World As We Do

8

Are Stereotypes True?

The stereotype is in disrepute. The word is often defined in purely negative terms. Some definitions construe the stereotype as necessarily possessing the negative charge that does, indeed, energize many stereotypes. Other definitions see as inseparable from the stereotype the inappropriate application of the stereotype to those members of the stereotyped group who do not exhibit the stereotyped behavior. The problem with all such usages is that they render undiscoverable a crucial empirical fact: Stereotypes have a basis in reality.

It is more fruitful to define "stereotype" without deciding its truthfulness or correctness in advance, and without including either the value judgment made by the stereotype or the implication of any cause and effect relationship. In this way we can address the correctness or incorrectness of each stereotype as an empirical question. We might define "stereotype" as "a widely held belief associating a specific temperamental or behavioral tendency with a specific group." This definition in no way denies that stereotypes usually serve functions of prejudice or power; it merely distinguishes the stereotype proper from the functions that it serves. Many beliefs about groups that are not stereotypes clearly are incorrect. "Jews have horns" and "Jews control banking" are entirely incorrect, but they are not stereotypes because they are not beliefs about temperamental or behavioral tendencies. "Jews are good at business" and "Jews are pushy" *are* stereotypes.

A stereotype is, obviously, a statistical approximation. To apply a stereotype inaccurately or inappropriately to an individual member of the stereotyped group always constitutes a serious misuse. A six-foot-tall woman is not short simply because most women are, compared to men, short. But even if one believes stereotypes are *always* misused in this or some other manner, the misuse does not cast doubt on the (statistical) correctness of the stereotype. Those who insist that *stereotype* be defined in terms of such misuse cannot avoid the central point of this essay: Stereotypes reflect a population's nearly always correct observation that certain groups exhibit certain temperamental or behavioral tendencies that set them apart from the rest of the population. Those who insist that the definition includes misuse must redirect their attention away from the stereotype *per se* and consider instead the empirical premise of the stereotype. An empirical claim can be refuted only in empirical terms; no amount of fancy definitional footwork can avoid this requirement.

In this sense, the stereotype that Scots are penurious can be refuted only by a demonstration that Scots are no more penurious than other people. The fact that some Scots (who are exceptions if the stereotype is correct) spend wildly, the fact that these (exceptional) Scots are incorrectly labeled as "stingy," the fact that Scots see penuriousness as sensible thriftiness, and the fact that the stereotype serves functions of prejudice and power—while all true—cast no doubt on the correctness of the stereotype (unless, of course, the exceptions are so numerous that they render the group statistically indistinguishable from the general population).

It is important to keep in mind the distinction between the stereotype and (a) any causal explanation of why the group exhibits disproportionately the observed behavior, (b) the value judgment placed on the observed behavior, and (c) the functions or purposes of the stereotype.

Like the stereotype itself, any causal analysis attempting to explain the association of a stereotyped group and behavior is an empirical claim. Unlike the stereotype itself, the causal explanation postulates unobservable mechanisms which often lead the members of the general population—who see much better than they think—to believe causal explanations that are woefully incorrect. It is only the observed behavior, the stereotype, that I argue to be usually correct. The "average person" may be entirely incorrect when he says that members of a minority group are "stupid" (implying a deep-seated, perhaps innate, causation) when the members of the group tend—statistically speaking—to be uneducated. But he is correct in his observation that the members of the group are at an intellectual disadvantage, though the environmental cause may well be educational discrimination. It is precisely this disadvantage that is the primary justification offered for the battle against *de facto* school discrimination. The distinction between a (correctly) observed stereotype and an (incorrect) causal explanation is easily seen in the claim that men are taller than women and that they are taller because they eat more.

Any value judgment linked to a stereotype (i.e., the designation of Jewish behavior as, for example, "pushy" or "enterprising") is a subjective claim that cannot be empirically tested. The function or purpose of the stereotype is likewise irrelevant to the correctness of the stereotype. There are, of course, empirical questions *about* valuations, functions, and purposes—concerning, for example, the conditions under which specific valuations, functions, and purposes are found and how they operate. But the valuations, functions, and purposes themselves are not empirical claims and have no bearing on the correctness of the stereotype. The stereotype of a group may, of course, differ from time to time and place to place. American Jews are hardly viewed as great farmers, while Israeli Jews may well be. Perhaps history will be such that American Jews in the future become farmers and a stereotype will develop associating farming competence with American Jews.

The distinction between a stereotype's correctness and its value judgment can be seen clearly. It is rare that a stereotyped group and its detractors disagree entirely on the association of tendency or behavior with the group; they usually disagree on valuation or causation. Jews do not deny the behavior others see as "pushy" but see this behavior as "enterprising" or (as the word was used before picking up its contemporary association with ruthlessness) "ambitious." Irish "rowdiness" and Hispanic proliferation can be seen, and are seen by the groups themselves, as representing a "zest for life" and a "virile masculinity," respectively.

It is necessary to make one final, and crucially important, theoretical point. Some stereotypes incorrectly invert correct stereotypes. "Italians are members of organized crime" and "blacks are muggers" are obviously ridiculous in all but a minuscule statistical sense. But just as obviously they are incorrect inversions of correct stereotypes that claim that "members of organized crime are disproportionately often Italian" and "muggers are disproportionately often black." The inversions are fallacious in the same way that it is fallacious to conclude from the correct observation that professional football players are big people that big people are professional football players. But in all three cases the fallacious stereotypes are rooted in a correct observation. The inversion results in gross unfairness, but the original stereotypes are empirically correct. To show that they are incorrect would require a demonstration that members of organized crime are not disproportionately often Italian, that muggers are not disproportionately often black, or that professional football players are not disproportionately often big.

I once heard Bill Russell, the great basketball player, argue that the legendary basketball ability of blacks is solely a function of environment, the ghetto environment in which basketball is one of the few routes to success. Now, perhaps, one can accept an environmental explanation of the astonishing black dominance of professional basketball. Perhaps one might even accept such an explanation of black dominance of college basketball (though only the aged remember a championship team with a white majority). But no one who has scouted high-school players, as I have, could take seriously a claim that black jumping ability is a residue of ghetto life. Clearly, such ability is related to the same physical advantage that accounts for 90–98 percent of the top sprinters being black. (For both whites and blacks, jumping and sprinting—as opposed, for example, to foul shooting and marathon running—have long been considered the least improvable and "most innate" of athletic skills.)

The fact that the stereotyped group accepts the correctness of the stereotype (though not necessarily its associated value judgment or causal explanationn) does not, of course, demonstrate the correctness of the stereotype. A demonstration of correctness must take the form of an empirical test.

In some cases the empirical mark of the stereotyped behavior is so obvious (number of children, success in the professions, drunkenness, etc.) that no one denies the correctness of the stereotype. It is this obvious correctness that provides the evidential justification for testing those stereotypes whose correctness is not instantly demonstrable. If those stereotypes whose claim is instantly testable are correct, it certainly seems reasonable to test the less obviously true stereotypes to see if they too are correct.

But I predict that each stereotype tested will be found to be empirically true. Whether such tests *should* be conducted is another matter. The social functions and consequences of stereotypes are irrelevant to their empirical correctness.

Some may fear that acknowledging the correctness of stereotypes will have deleterious effects on those who are stereotyped. If this response were correct, we would have a moral dilemma pitting truth against good. This is how the situation is seen by those—and there are many—who, for example, publicly deny certain undeniable correct sexual stereotypes, only to admit privately that the stereotypes are true (the causation of the differentiated behavior being another issue). I must say that I find this despicable (the one thing a reader has the right to demand is that you believe what you say)—but I must also acknowledge that I can imagine situations in which I would lie rather than cause suffering.

However, the issue of stereotypes is not one that raises the conflict of truth and good. The conflict of truth and good would arise only if the correctness of stereotypes were a secret finding, known only to a few, that could be withheld from the population. The fact that stereotypes are true cannot be withheld because nearly everyone already knows they are true. People differ only in their readiness to acknowledge their validity. Only the ideologically rigid deny the truth. The laughter elicited by the ethnic joke overflows the intellect and acknowledges the belief that the stereotype is true, an acknowledgment not canceled by a post-laughter declaration that "that's not funny."

The statistical validity of stereotypes is indicated by the telling fact, mentioned above, that no one denies the correctness of stereotypes whose empirical measure is most obvious (i.e., number of children, professional success, drunkenness, etc.). It is only when slightly more sophisticated measures are needed (as in the case with the Jewish behavior that is praised as "enterprising" or criticized as "pushy") that the truthfulness of stereotypes is denied.

Since everyone recognizes the correctness of stereotypes, minorities are in fact harmed, not protected, by the contemporary pretense that ethnic commonplaces are unfounded. The pretense renders it impossible to demonstrate: (a) the statistical, rather than absolute, nature of stereotypes; (b) the subjective nature of the value judgment of the stereotyped behavior; and (c) (when it is the case) the purely environmental causation of the behavior stereotyped. Moreover, the pretense that stereotypes are untrue contaminates, and renders unconvincing, the valid demonstration of the malignant uses to which they are often put; the reader becomes skeptical about an analysis that begins with lies, even if the analysis ends with truths that are independent of the lies.

Rather than asserting the incorrectness of slurs and generalizations everyone knows to be true, we are far better off demanding that those who use such language to demean specific groups examine their assumpiton that the stereotyped behavior is actually bad and to examine skeptically any causal explanation offered for the behavior pattern in question. It is self-defeating to ask people to pretend that they have not seen what they have seen. They have seen what they have seen, and they know it. Indeed, they have even recorded what they have seen. In stereotypes.

9

Is Astrology Science?

This is based on a long note that I wrote for students in my introductory sociology class. The purpose of the note was to aid the students in understanding some basic ideas in the philosophy of science. A short time after I wrote the note, the declaration "Objections to Astrology" happened to appear. I published this essay in an attempt to demonstrate that the argument made by the scientists represented a sort of bullying, on the basis of authority and numbers, that was as scientifically dubious as they claimed astrology to be. As you might guess, no matter how many times I pointed out in the essay that astrology is about as bad science as science gets (though not, as the scientists seemed to say, "nonsense"—with that word's implication of ungroundability), most people "remember" the essay as somehow arguing for astrology's scientific usefulness. With no hope that anyone will take notice, let me, one final time, emphasize that nothing in this piece argues for the scientific validity of astrology. While logically a "science," astrology has failed every attempt to demonstrate that it can describe the world any better than random guessing can.

The search for a rigorous criterion for demarcating the scientific from the metaphysical and ungroundable has been a major quest in the philosophy of science in this century. Some would even say that the discovery of an ironclad method for severing the scientific from the metaphysical is the very purpose of the philosophy of science. Nonetheless, it is now generally accepted that we can never have a perfectly rigorous demarcation criterion. Similarly, it is generally agreed that science can never have at its disposal a method for arbitrating competing scientific theories possessing the persuasive force that logic possesses in mathematics. It may be that both the demarcation criterion and the method of arbitration owe their impossibility to the fact that science, unlike mathematics, does not derive its truthfulness solely from its own internal consistency, but from an external system ("nature") as well.

None of this is of great moment for physics or astronomy. These investigations are clearly scientific by any reasonable definition of the word; they are clearly capable of making predictive statements about the empirical relationships that are testable by empirical experiment whose outcome is not determined by the theoretical considerations that generated the predictions. $E = mc^2$, for example, could be tested by an experimentalist who does not even understand the theory that generated the hypothesis.

Difficulties arise when we wish to know the value of investigations that have not demonstrated this capability. Freudian theory and classical Darwinian theory (in the aspect discussed here) are examples of theoretical systems that are, however helpful as ordering models (or, more accurately, "paradigms"), accepted without the sort of empirical evidence associated with astronomy and physics. Freudian theory, while probably not ungroundable on a theoretical level,[1] encounters such difficulty preparing hypotheses that are testable by non-Freudian procedures that it has, to this point, been virtually untestable; tests of Freudian theory tend to be either so general that the results are concordant not only with Freudian theory but with many competing theories or, when sufficiently specific to overcome this problem, so distant from the central core of Freudian theory as to leave the central core unthreatened even when providing a refutory result.

Classical Darwinian theory, in the view of many logicians, faces an even more severe problem: Its central hypothesis that the "fittest" species survive is ungroundable, and therefore "unscientific," by virtue of tautology. (The summarization of Darwinian theory as "survival of the fittest" was Herbert Spencer's, but Darwin acknowledged the accuracy of this view and preferred it to his own, "natural selection.")

The problem with Darwinian theory, according to these logicians, is the fact that "fittest" is defined in terms of survival. If dachshunds survive and dinosaurs don't, then dachshunds are declared to have been fit; if dinosaurs survive and dachshunds don't, then dinosaurs are declared to have been fit. The same problem obtains within species that does between species: those dachshunds, donkeys, and doves that survived—and passed on their genes—are claimed to have done so because they were "fit," while those dachshunds, donkeys, and doves that did not failed because they were not "fit."

This logical criticism *does* grant as "scientific"—though of course incorrect—such hypotheses as "survival of the biggest" or smallest or greenest. These claims are clearly falsifiable; the fact that we can say that they are incorrect demonstrates this. The central problem with "survival of the fittest" is that its tautological nature precludes *in principle* its being tested.

Similarly, when applied to *specific* species, such claims are clearly not only testable, but often correct. But such claims are not theories of evolutionary survival in general (as is Darwin's); they are theories that explain in terms of a *specified, nontautological* property why one or another *specified* species survived and another did not (or why some members of a specified species survived and other members of that species did not). In other words, no one questions the logical validity of a theory that dachshunds survived because they had *specified* property A, donkeys because they had *specified* property B, etc. (The same can be said for a theory that those dachshunds that possessed and passed on the gene for property A survived, while those that did not, did not.)

Many attempts to rebut the logical criticism we discuss mistakenly invoke such theories of the survival of a specific species. Such rebuttals prove that which need not be proved; no one ever claimed that there is any logical problem with theories of the survival of specific species (or members of a specific species). Such theories are unobjectionable as long as the property seen as being responsible for survival is defined independently of survival.

However, such theories do not validate Darwin because Darwin attempts to specify a property that claims to explain survival of species *in general*. Since no independent property is associated with species survival in general, so the criticism goes, Darwin had to select a "property" that was no more than a word for "those who survive." This charge is not repelled by substituting "most adaptable" or "best designed," etc., for "fittest," because these too are determined by survival. (That is, how do we determine that a species, or members of a species, is "most adaptable" or "best designed"? By the fact that it survived.)

As the reader might guess, the argument over the scientific validity of Darwinian theory has gotten increasingly convoluted over the past century. Suffice it to say here that biologists have tended to argue that it is groundable and scientifically valid, while logicians have tended argue that it is not scientifically meaningful as the umbrella theory it is usually accepted as being. (However, even these logicians acknowledge its value as an ordering model directing the biologist to examine the requirements of survival of *specific* species.) Contemporary geneticists tend to agree that there was a problem when the issue concerned macroscopic properties, but argue that there are testable genetic hypotheses that describe species in general. Some contemporary logicians accept this as stated. Others accept it but see such hypotheses as a far cry from anything that could be called "Darwinian." Still others argue that close analysis of the genetic "property" alleged to explain the survival of species *in general* still exposes tautology.

Note, incidentally, that difficulties with the *theory* of evolution do nothing to support creationism. No serious scientist denies the *fact* that species have evolved from the simpler to the more complex, a fact denied by creationists. What is in question is only the mechanism by which this occurred.

In any case, all that need concern us here is this: The key questions determining whether the Darwinian claim meets the logical requirements of science are: (1) Is the claim one attempting to explain the survival of species in general (or members of a species in general); if the claim is attempting merely to address a given species (and if the requirement of (2) is met), then there is clearly no logical problem; and (2) Is the property specified defined nontautologically (i.e., independently of "survival"); the evidence that this requirement is met is the ability of the claim to provide a way, at least in principle, in which it can be shown to be incorrect if it is incorrect? (If it can not, then it is tautological and scientifically unacceptable; in science, if you can't lose, you can't win.)

It is well to keep all of this in mind when we consider the declaration "Objections to Astrology," which was signed by eighteen Nobel Laureates and nearly two hundred other leading scientists. This declaration, which presents in crystalized form the attitude toward astrology held by nearly all scientists, appeared in the *Humanist* (September/October 1975) along with supporting articles by Bart J. Bok, past president of the American Astronomical Society, and Lawrence E. Jerome, a writer who specializes in scientific subjects. The declaration engendered extraordinary media interest, ranging from front-page analysis in the *New York Times* to continuing coverage by the popular news magazines and television news programs.

Professor Bok and Mr. Jerome admirably present the scientific case against astrology. Stressing the magical origins of astrology, the psychological needs that can lead one to accept a view that has no intellectual merit whatever, and the virtually absolute weakness of the forces exerted by many of the celestial bodies that are seen by astrology as greatly affecting human personality, Professor Bok challenges the plausibility of astrology. Mr. Jerome attacks the statistical evidence directly, arguing that none of the (admittedly scanty) data support the claims made by astrology.

One can easily understand the anger and disgust that manifests itself in the scientific response to astrology. I share this anger and disgust; nothing I write in this essay denies that astrology is a perversion of the scientific spirit and an abnegation of psychological and intellectual responsibility. In this essay, however, I suggest that, however ill-conceived astrology might be, it does raise some exceedingly difficult questions about the logic by which we accept some scientific claims and reject others, and that the arguments against astrology invoked by the scientists are far too exclusive to be satisfactory. Such arguments force the scientist to reject that which he would not wish to reject (the speculations of early physics, for example).

"Objections to Astrology" and the articles that support it stress the magical roots of astrology. One might respond to this by making the obvious point that the sources or history of an attempt to explain empirical reality are logically irrelevant to the correctness or incorrectness of the explanation;[2] the correctness or incorrectness of an explanation must be assessed on the basis of logical consistency, concordance with known empirical realities, plausibility, and ability to predict. I assume, however, that the authors stressed the magical roots of astrology in order to emphasize that astrological explanation invokes magical terms, entities, and premises as tautological and ungroundable explanatory wild cards that pretend to explain when they merely restate the question in obfuscated form.

The authors are certainly right in emphasizing this aspect of astrology, but in doing so they are, I think, both inadvertently leaving the incorrect impression that the hard sciences were born in their present state of virtually positivistic empiricism and inadvertently invoking criteria that would have forced us to dismiss physics and the other hard sciences in their early stages. In their early stages all sciences are replete with metaphysical entities that are necessary for the development of a science to the point where it can jettison the metaphysical entities. I do not mean to imply that astrology will so develop. The probablity that a heavily metaphysical protoscience will develop into a science is about the same as that of a mutation's survival; I do not doubt that astrology will, even when assessed by criteria less unfairly demanding than those of the scientists, prove either totally incapable of prediction or incapable of prediction not more plausibly explained by other sciences. I do, however, wish to suggest that, while it is certainly legitimate to criticize the astronomical premises of astrology in astronomical terms, astrology and astronomy are basically disanalogous, in that they examine different areas of empirical reality. After all, even if astrology is total nonsense or totally incorrect, it will not tell us any less about human personality (its claimed area of empirical knowledge) than does astronomy.

Astrology should be compared with depth psychology; and it is not at all clear that depth psychology, or early physics for that matter, would have satisfied the criteria for science implicitly demanded by the scientists. I do not think that anyone can yet suggest a set of criteria that would lead one to accept early physics and modern depth psychology on the one hand, while dismissing astrology and tautological explanatory systems that did not develop into sciences on the other (if these are all incapable of prediction of correlation). But I would suggest that we would be better off assessing astrology in terms of its ability to predict correlations between horoscope and personality than dismissing it on the basis of demands that even the early hard sciences could not have satisfied.

Similarly, I am a bit wary of the argument that dismisses astrology on the basis of the "fact" that the celestial forces that are perceived in astrology as causal (to human personality) are insignificant. This argument seems to me to assume its conclusion (that celestial forces are virtually irrelevant to human personality) by assuming that astrology is incapable of prediction of a surprising correlation of horoscope and personality, *a prediction that would be sufficient to justify our positing the significance of the celestial forces.* If (and I reiterate that it is only an if) astrology were capable of making a great number of impressive predictions of correlations (between personality characteristics and highly complex, relatively unconnected celestial cycles), then, I assume, the scientists would tentatively entertain the idea that there might be celestial physical forces—at present undescribable—that were causally important to the effects predicted only by the astrologer. To be sure, these forces would be metaphysically defined until their physical properties were discovered; but we would have good reason to suspect their existence, good reason to devote ourselves to their discovery, and good reason to develop theoretical explanations that would contain metaphysical entities (the as yet indescribable forces). If this approach were not allowed, there would be no physics; physics would not have been allowed to posit the atom until the atom was seen; and the atom would never have been seen if the positing of it (and of a supra-atomic empirical experiment) had not told us how to look. In short, a science develops through an infancy of taxonomic investigation and a childhood of discovery of correlation and metaphysical speculation and, only then, to an adulthood of true explanatory success.

The question that we should ask a young science claiming the capacity to become adult is not whether its explanatory system is completely unmetaphysical and consistent but whether it is capable of making predictions that are not predicted by the more mature sciences. I, too, feel certain that astrology will prove incapable of making such predictions, of demonstrating the presence of such correlations. But our refusing, on the basis of our present knowledge and theory, to make the test that could refute (or support) the claimed correlations is not easily distinguishable from the actions of those claimed to have refused to look through Galileo's telescope because their current knowledge and theory "demonstrated" that Jupiter had no moons. Refutation will take only a test; but the test is necessary for refutation (or support).

Perhaps my emphasis on correlations, and the fact that the public looks to astrology for the sorts of information that constitute the area of empirical reality studied by psychology rather than that studied by astronomy, casts some light on the frightening acceptance of astrology by the American public. All of the criticisms of astrology as an explanatory system may be correct, but the people who accept astrology do not care about its explanatory value, only its ability to predict the correlation of celestial event and personality. This, in and of itself, is not to be ridiculed.

If an astrologer could read the horoscopes of ten of my friends and could then describe with a good deal of specificity the personalities of each, you may rest assured that I would, and should, take astrology quite seriously indeed. I would continue to consider astrology absurd as explanation, but I would be forced to acknowledge that its ability to predict correlation of celestial events and personality traits would be an empirical fact and that, even if the correlations merely reflected mutual relationship and not intimate causal connection, astrology would be capable of tapping into connections of which the other sciences were ignorant. Moreover, if astrology demonstrated further success of this type, I would, I think, come to view astrology's explanatory entities less as totally absurd, and more as terribly crude speculations that could be expected to generate valuable explanatory capabilities once they, and the empirical realities they attempted to explain, were analyzed to finer and finer structure.

One cannot dismiss an attempt at explanation that is capable of prediction on the grounds that the capability simply represents a tapping into correlations having nothing to do with the claimed causal factors (unless, of course, one has a more plausible explanation for the correlations). For no science could withstand such an attack. Some philosophers would argue that *all there is* is correlation and that the ability to predict correlation is what science is. Other philosophers would assess the relative merits of two explanatory systems with equal records of predictive success in terms of elegance, parsimony, or plausibility, concepts that often seem to lead any two such philosophers to disagree on which of two theories with equal predictive success is more elegant, parsimonious, or plausible.

Perhaps even those readers who agree with all that I have written to this point are thinking that this may all be true, but that astrology is not, in fact, capable of prediction of correlation of horoscope and personality. I, too, think that this is the case. But I cannot, for the reasons given above, assume that this is the case simply because astrology's attempts at explanation are absurd. Nor can I dismiss astrology simply because I intuitively feel that it is irrational and silly; smarter men than I have had this feeling when first confronted by the work of Einstein. I can dismiss astrology only if I can demonstrate that it fails the basic test of a science by being incapable of predictions that are not predicted and more plausibly explained by the other sciences. If astrology fails the test of prediction of correlation, then we need not even consider its explanations; for, like the explanation of the digestive process of the unicorn, it offers an explanation when there is no empirical reality to explain.

It is certainly true that it is not easy, in practice, to test astrology, because astrologers have demonstrated what might gently be called dexterity, or, less gently, cowardice. If the validity of a scientific explanation were a logical function of the scientific courage or honesty of the proponents of a science, then we could dismiss astrology forthwith. But validity is not a function of human qualities, and the claims of a scoundrel cannot be dismissed on the grounds that the claimant is a scoundrel. It is astrology, not the astrologer, that must be tested.

Astrology can be tested because, whatever the actual attempts of the astrologer to escape into tautology and obfuscation when under attack, astrology itself, however incorrect its hypotheses may be, is not untestable in principle. Astrology makes the claim that Capricorns tend to be stubborn (or perfectionistic or whatever Capricorns are supposed to be), and therefore it implies that Capricorns are stubborn (or whatever) more often than are Geminis. These are qualities that can be translated into operational terms—either test results ("stubbornness" is defined as making a high score on a test that is defined as measuring stubbornness) or observational reports ("stubbornness" is the quality independently observed by observers who term the subject "stubborn"). Thus, astrology is testable in that its predictions of correlations of personality characteristics and celestial events can be tested; it is therefore a "science"—though, in all likelihood it is a science whose hypotheses are almost all incorrect.

To put this all in a slightly different way: The words used by the astrologer to describe an individual ("stubborn," "perfectionistic," and so on) clearly do have meaning. Were we to give ten people a list of adjectives and ask them to independently choose the two adjectives whose meaning is most like "stubborn" (or "perfectionistic"), they would, to a degree of great statistical significance, select the same adjectives. This demonstrates that the word has meaning. Moreover, if the ten people had a hundred acquaintances in common and we asked each of the ten people to independently select the five acquaintances who were the most "stubborn," we would find a high degree of agreement. This demonstrates not only that the word has meaning but also that it has an operational attachment to empirical reality.

Now, neither the fact that the words used by the astrologer have meaning nor the fact that the words describe nature does anything much to support astrology; these facts merely show that astrology meets certain rudimentary, necessary conditions of any enterprise claiming to be a science.

The real test of astrology is a test not merely of whether the words have meaning or whether they describe some people and not others, but of whether the people they describe are in fact born more often under some celestial conditions than under others. We all know that some people are more stubborn, perfectionistic, or whatever than others; what astrology must demonstrate is that people who are born under certain celestial conditions are more likely to be "stubborn," "perfectionistic," or whatever than are people born under other celestial conditions.

I do not want to make light of the scientific problems involved in any questions of human personality and emotion. That such qualities have meaning above the subjective interpretation of the observer is indicated by the fact that when such qualities are defined operationally ("hostility" is the quality reported by observers as "hostility"), independent observers will similarly describe a given individual. This is what we all do when we describe an individual's personality. But it must still be granted that there are problems here that are not present when the quality in question is height. There is an enormous amount of literature on this question. Here, however, the question can be avoided because we can assume that the astrologer believes that the qualities he finds correlated with a given horoscope have some meaning other than that they are qualities describing the horoscope; for if he defines a quality as nothing more than a description of a horoscope ("hostility is a quality of an individual whose horoscope shows him to be hostile"), then clearly he is giving us nothing more than a tautological description of a horoscope.

It is easy to construct a test of astrology that allows for as much complexity as the astrologer desires. We can accept the common astrological argument that the sun sign alone is not sufficient for prediction and that more information is necessary. However, we must demand that at some point the astrologer acknowledge that he has sufficient information for prediction. If the astrologer argues that even horoscopes that are as complete as he can make them are insufficient for prediction, if he at no point ends his scurrying retreat into "complexity," then he is not even making a scientific claim, much less a correct scientific claim.

Professor Bok leaves discussion of the central question of correlation and prediction to Mr. Jerome. In his brief discussion, Jerome does indicate that there is no evidence in favor of astrology. However, it seems to me that the test discussed by Mr. Jerome, and all other tests of astrology that I have seen, demand a predictive capability such that, even if astrology had an impressive ability to predict correlation of horoscope and personality, it would fail the tests.

Jerome describes a test that attempts to correlate horoscope and occupation. It does make sense to argue that astrology claims that personality traits are correlated with horoscope and that particular occupations demand particular personality traits. Astrology should therefore be able to demonstrate that horoscope is correlated with occupation (that is, Virgos—or whoever—are logical; philosophers are logical; therefore, disproportionate numbers of philosophers should be Virgos). However, while this makes sense, it is not a severe test of astrology's primary claim of being able to identify personality characteristics by horoscope. One could argue that the correlation of horoscope and personality traits does exist, but that personality traits are not correlated with occupation.

The following analogy should make this clear. The psychiatrist would predict, correctly, that we shall find a correlation between being beaten as a child and (measurable by report) hostile tendencies in adulthood. We might reasonably expect that victims of child-beating would be disproportionately represented among drill instructors and debt collectors. But if we found that this were not the case, we would not, and should not, assume that the psychiatrist was wrong about the correlation of being beaten and having hostile feelings; we would assume that we were wrong in our assumption that hostile feelings are significantly related to the choice of occupation.

Let us go out of our way to be fair to the astrologers. Let us ask ten leading astrologers to provide us with a list of fifty adjectives of the type that represent the personal qualities that they find to be associated with specific horoscopes. Then let us give the birth-time and birthplace of five thousand individuals to the astrologers and ask them to prepare the horoscopes of these individuals. (Computers render this a simple task.)

I realize that the astronomer will object to even the physical description of celestial events of the horoscopes; the astrologer uses measurements that do not allow for the procession of the equinoxes that have taken place in the past three thousand years, or for other factors that are crucial to measurement. I ignore this problem with astrology because the crucial test of astrology is the test of correlation of celestial events (accurately or inaccurately represented) and personality traits. I suspect that a sufficiently clever astrologer could make the argument, implausible in the extreme, but not illogical, that correlated astronomical changes have resulted in the maintenance of correlation of celestial events and personality traits. By allowing the astrologer to use whatever system of celestial events or alleged celestial events he desires, we test his basic assertion of a correlation of celestial event (or alleged celestial event) and personality traits. If he fails to demonstrate any such correlation, then we need not get involved in the question of the inaccuracy of the celestial evidence.

Next let us ask the astrologers to select the thousand charts that are least ambiguous from an astrological point of view. Then let us have the astrologers choose the five adjectives (or fewer, if they feel only two or three qualities are unambiguously represented in a particular horoscope) from the list that are most clearly, by astrological interpretation, associated with each chart. We may assume that there will be a high rate of agreement among the astrologers on the selection of adjectives for each chart; astrology may be scientifically worthless, but its worthless premises are agreed upon by astrologers. Any disagreement of interpretation and prediction among representatives of various schools of astrology would merely force us to test the predictions made by the astrologers of each school separately. If necessary, we could test the correctness of each astrologer independently.

Even if there is agreement among the astrologers, this does nothing to validate astrology. Ten people who believe that foot size is correlated with intelligence will agree that people with size seventeen feet must tend to be astonishingly smart. But they would, of course, be incorrect. What matters is not agreement among astrologers, but agreement of the claims of the astrologers and reality.

It is worth mentioning that it is possible that human beings do tend to fall into categories, each of which represents a specific configuration of personality characteristics and behavioral tendencies, and that these categories correspond to the categories described as Capricorns, Geminis, and so on. This, in and of itself, would do nothing to demonstrate the validity of astrology—though perhaps it would attest to the astrologer's observational abilities—unless it could be shown that disproportionate numbers of people who had the characteristics and tendencies described as belonging to, say, Capricorn were in fact born disproportionately often during one period of the year. For example, talkativeness and stinginess tend statistically speaking not to be found in the same people; and there is a plausible psychological explanation of this empirical reality. For argument's sake, let us assume that Capricorns are supposed to be talkative and Geminis stingy. Unless it were found that people who were talkative and people who were stingy did, in fact, tend to be born during different times of the year, the existence of personality groups would do nothing to demonstrate the validity of astrology.

Now let us ask each of the thousand individuals whose charts were selected by the astrologers as astrologically unambivalent to select from the astrologers' list the five qualities most strongly represented in himself. Let us also ask a friend of each of these individuals and a psychologist who tests the individual to select the five adjectives from the list that are most applicable to the individual. Then let us discard all adjectives that are not on the individual's, his friend's, or the psychologist's lists. This is all necessary because personal qualities are not as unarguably objective as, say, height; and it is necessary to do what we can to avoid the difficulties inherent in an individual's propensity for rationalization, on the one hand, and the inability of a friend or psychologist to discover deeper and more hidden qualities, on the other.

Our solution is not perfect. There are difficulties inherent in the fact that personal qualities are not impersonally measurable in the way height is. I think, however, that most people would agree that it is reasonable to treat the qualities chosen by the individual and his friend and the psychologist as relatively objective measures against which the astrological predictions of correlation of horoscope and personal qualities must be tested. If the astrologer will not accept this measure, he must give us some other measure that is independent of astrological definition to test his predictions against. If he cannot do this, then he is admitting that his words are devoid of scientific meaning. Whether one concludes that this means that the astrologer's words are devoid of *all* meaning will be determined by the strength of one's positivistic tendencies.

In all likelihood, astrology will fail a test like this and will produce no better predictions of personality traits than random guessing would. If this were the case, we would be correct to dismiss astrology. If, on the other hand, astrology were capable of impressive prediction, then we would, whatever astrology's explanatory shortcomings, be forced to take astrology seriously.

But what if astrology should prove itself capable of a few predictions of correlations not otherwise predictable? It is highly unlikely that this will be the case, but it is not inconceivable. For example, it is not totally inconceivable that the environmental temperature around the pregnant mother during a critical stage of her fetus's development affects the biochemistry of the fetus (mediated through the biochemistry of the mother) in a way that affects the propensity of the person into which the fetus develops to respond to his environment in certain ways (that is, to have certain "personality traits"). I am certainly not arguing that this is the case, but only that there would be nothing magical about this being the case and that, if this *were* the case, astrology would be capable of prediction of correlation of birthdate and personality (though, of course, the causal factors would have virtually nothing to do with the stars).

Indeed, there would be nothing in this that would even be particularly discordant with the endocrinological evidence as it is now interpreted. We know (from the study of mental illness, drugs, human hermaphrodites, and so on) that biochemistry affects personality and that environment can alter biochemistry even to the extent of affecting the fetus's biochemistry through the mother. Of course, for astrology to tap into correlations of these sorts of environmental factors, one of the factors would have to exhibit a rough month-to-month variation (as does the temperature of the environment). There is no evidence that astrology can do this, but impressive prediction of correlation would imply that it could.[3]

It would take a certain genius in nonobservation for any "discipline" to hang around for three thousand years without tapping into, and incorporating, any observation whatsoever. If astrology has tapped into a few such correlations that are unexplained by other sciences, it remains absurd, but it is not clear how we can dismiss it as an absurdity without encountering the philosophical problems discussed above.

Some people might wonder why I have written all this when it is clear that my contempt for astrology knows no bounds. One reason is my hope that the nature of these questions is sufficiently interesting to motivate people to read Quine, Russell, Wittgenstein, and the others who have illuminated this area.

But there is also another reason. I find I have an ambivalent reaction to the declaration of the scientists, and I hope that the scientists themselves felt the ambivalence even as they were, quite rightly, signing the declaration. Even as the scientist is moved to defend rationality, there should, I think, be a small part of his mind that remembers that—while he is no doubt right that astrology will be shown to be incapable of prediction, and while for every speculator who turned out to be an Einstein, there have been a million who turned out to be quacks—still there have been declarations by great scientists that are now of interest only because they remind us that we are all capable of the lack of intellectual empathy, the lack of imagination, and the lack of courage that are found in their purest forms in the astrologer.

But the reader is not, I am sure, surprised at my ambivalence. Libras are always ambivalent.

POSTSCRIPT: THE PRACTICAL QUESTION

The practical question generated by the considerations discussed here is not whether we should accept astrology as valid. Clearly, there is not a scintilla of evidence of any kind in favor of astrology, and there is an enormous amount of indirect theoretical evidence against astrology (that is, the astronomical evidence that casts great doubt on the possibility that distant stars exert the sorts of influence astrology implies they exert). The practical question is whether astrology deserves the right to be tested for the direct empirical evidence, either for or against astrology, that we presently lack (the direct evidence that astrology can or cannot make surprising predictions of correlations of horoscope and personality). If we so test astrology and it fails, we need not get involved in the question of astrology as explanation; we will have shown that there was no empirical reality to explain.

While all would agree that we do not need as much evidence to justify testing a hypothesis as we do to accept it, we would also all agree that we are not required to test every hypothesis, no matter how ludicrous, simply because someone somewhere believes the hypothesis to be correct. What, then, suggests whether a hypothesis is so ludicrous that we need not even allow it an opportunity to prove itself?

I do not believe that there is any elegant answer to this question. One's answer to this question will be partially a reflection of one's personal attitudes. I would rather feel ridiculous for having bothered to test ten ludicrous hypotheses than to be guilty of dismissing as ludicrous a single hypothesis that was, in fact, correct. One's answer will also be, in part, a reflection of the expenditure of time, effort, and money necessary to test the hypothesis. And when one takes these factors into account, one will be forced to think in "degrees of ludicrousness" in order to compare a hypothesis's ludicrousness with the dangers of an authoritarian refusal to give it its opportunity to prove itself and with the amount of serious research that would have to be sacrificed in order to test the ludicrous hypothesis.

If a severe test of astrology required a major expenditure, we would not, and should not, consider it; but a test of the sort I have suggested could be performed easily and inexpensively. Moreover, I would suggest, at the risk of losing a few readers who have agreed with me up to this point, that—if by "astrology" we mean predicted correlations of horoscope and personality and not the hopeless theoretical explanation of the alleged correlations—the fact that millions of people claim to have made the observations reflected in the alleged correlations is, in itself, sufficient reason to attach to astrology a low enough degree of ludicrousness that we should be willing to put it to the (inexpensive) test.

I do not doubt that these millions of people are incorrect and that no such correlations exist, but it is worth stressing that these people agree on *observations*, not necessarily astrology's theoretical explanations. An implausible "explanation" does not gain an iota of plausibility simply because millions believe it. But an implausible observation does gain the credibility required to justify test when it is claimed by millions, even if the observations are of "flying saucers."

I am not making the argument that the fact that millions of people believe astrological observations requires our putting astrology to the test for the practical reason that we must dissuade them from their irrationality. I think that such an argument is correct and that the cause of rationality would be well served by putting astrology to the test even if astrology represented the highest degree of ludicrousness. Here I am suggesting that the mere fact that millions of people claim to observe a correlation of horoscope and personality reduces the degree of ludicrousness from the highest level to mere "absurdly ludicrous," and this justifies a test when the test can be easily and inexpensively performed. An observational claim does, when believed by millions, gain the minimal plausibility required to justify our putting such claims to the test when the test is inexpensive and easily done.

POST-POSTSCRIPT

No doubt a number of readers have had the same experience I've had. People who believe in astrology have, at parties, correctly guessed my sun sign and rising sign far more often than random guessing, the equivocating mention of a number of signs, or other astrological tomfoolery could explain. Moreover, I must, if I am honest with the astrologer, admit that, granting the difficulties of all psychological self-assessment, it seems to me that the salient characteristics associated by astrologers with my actual sun sign and rising sign are salient characteristics of my personality. As much as I would like it to be the case, I do not think that this can be explained by the shotgun approach that astrology takes. The characteristics to which I refer are the first ones associated with the signs in any book of astrology.

This used to bother me. It did seem to be evidence *for* astrology—very slight evidence, but one out of one is as good as any science can do; and when the one case is oneself, the evidence does have a persuasive hold that one would not feel if the evidence were for twenty other subjects.

The answer, however, should have been obvious. Of every thousand people with sun sign X and rising sign Y, there will be n number of people whose salient qualities are those associated with sun sign X and rising sign Y. These people will, like myself, find themselves accurately described by their sun and rising signs and will find that people at parties can guess their signs; all this indicates is that the one who guessed was both observant and knowledgeable about astrology (that is, this person knows what salient characteristics are associated with sun sign X and rising sign Y). This does nothing to indicate the correctness of astrology —*that* would take a demonstration that a greater proportion of people with sun sign X and rising sign Y had the salient characteristics associated with X and Y than did people with the other 143 combinations of sun sign and rising sign.

In other words, it is not surprising that *some* Libras with Taurus rising exhibit the traits astrology claims they will. Astrology would be supported only if a *higher percentage* of Libras with Taurus rising than, say, Virgos with Gemini rising exhibited those traits.

NOTES

1. See "The Logical Status of Freudian Theory," later in this volume, for an analysis of this issue.

2. The unfortunate effects of an acceptance of astrology, such as the surrender of personal responsibility, are irrelevant to the question of the correctness of astrology. If there is one thing that the history of science teaches us, it is that it is always wrong to assess the validity of an explanation in terms of the (logically irrelevant) psychological, social, or political effects of an acceptance of the explanation.

3. It is worth remembering that if astrology has inadvertently tapped into some physical correlations of the type discussed here, the correlations are more likely between personality characteristics and the date of conception (or date of a particular fetal stage) than between personality and birthdate. However, since these are correlated with the birthdate, the point is irrelevant here; a Capricorn birth is (almost always) an Aries conception.

10

Is There a Feminist Science?

Science—from that represented in the image of primitives on the beach wondering why the stones there are so smooth, to that expressed in the modern cosmologist searching for the topology of the universe—is an attempt to answer empirical questions. That which does not serve the purpose of answering questions about how things work is irrelevant to science.

The scientifically irrelevant may serve good ends or bad. It may set ethical limits on science (as in the prohibition against many types of human experimentation). Or it may be misused as a rationalization for political purposes. But ethical constraints on science, like the uses to which scientific findings are put, concern science without being a part of it. Science, like the nature it attempts to explain, doesn't know good from bad. It is rooting neither for the human being nor for the cancer cell. Such rooting is the role and the moral obligation of the human being who is the scientist.

One who claims that the earth is flat may be psychotic. Or he may have been socialized to a religion predicated on the earth's being flat. Or he may wish for a political system that rewards those who believe that the earth is flat. But none of these justify our dismissing his claim that the earth is flat. We dismiss his claim because, and only because, it does not accord with logic and empirical evidence. It fails, for example, to explain why a boat on the horizon disappears from the bottom up. To the extent that the psychological, social, and political impulses and purposes energizing a scientific explanation are relevant to the explanation, these will be manifested in fallacy or error (or a failure of the explanation to answer the question it addresses). Indeed, it is only such fallacy or error that makes the impulses and purposes relevant. If the impulses and purposes do not generate fallacy or error in the explanation, then they are irrelevant to the correctness of the explanation and can be scientifically ignored. E would have equaled mc^2 even if it had been Hitler who made the claim.

Fallacy and error can always be exposed by logic and scientific method alone. But it is *only* by logic and scientific method that these can be exposed.

As seemingly obvious as all of this is, it is ignored by a contemporary generation of "feminist scientists" who proceed as if one can invalidate the hypothesis of the scientist by attacking the scientist, his alleged purposes, and the alleged political effects of acceptance of his hypothesis.

One might think that this sort of substitution of ideology for truth, while possibly rampant in the social sciences, could not possibly threaten the physical sciences, disciplines whose areas of inquiry pretty much exclude human beings and human behavior. One would, as Margarita Levin demonstrates so stunningly in a recent *American Scholar*, be wrong.

Before proceeding with her devastating critique of specific feminist fallacies, Levin gives examples of accepted scientific findings whose putative male biases are seen by feminists as requiring "reconceptualization."

> ["Feminist scientists"] see male dominance at work in, for instance, the "master molecule" theory of DNA functioning; in the notion of forces "acting on" objects; in the description of evolution as the result of a "struggle" to survive; in the view that scarcity of resources results in "competition" between animals—in short in any theory positing what they deem destructive, violent, uni-directional, or hierarchical. . . . The idea of dominance is directly linked to the notion of scientific objectivity, which . . . is understood as "distancing oneself" from nature.

Let us ignore the fact that, as Levin points out, there is an equal number of scientific models that can be viewed as feminine: symbiosis, feedback, catalysis, mutual attraction, and the like.

Infinitely more destructive to the feminist objection is that these, like all successful scientific conceptions, are held because they are successful in explaining nature and in demonstrating their correctness by making correct predictions. In other words, *they work*.

Because it is their success that validates accepted scientific explanations, it would not matter even if it were true that (as one feminist claims) our acceptance of the concept of inertial motion is rooted in capitalism's need of the movement of money, or if it were true (as another claims) that the replacement of a Ptolemaic system by a Copernican system was a victory of the masculine over the feminine (because the Ptolemaic earth-centered system is "feminine"). Levin asks the question that in one sentence trumps all the volumes of the feminist critics: "Do they think we have a *choice* . . . ?"

We don't, of course. We believe in inertial motion because we find that, *ceteris paribus*, objects in space keep moving along at an unchanging speed and that inertial motion is our best explanation of why. We believe that the earth goes around the sun not because this is the macho way of seeing things, but because the earth *does* (speaking only a bit loosely) go around the sun.

Moreover, even if it *were* true that one scientific hypothesis would not have been made were it not for economic factors and another were it not for a need for "masculine models," this would still have nothing to do with whether the hypotheses were correct. A scientific claim that something is true—more precisely, that it approaches truth more closely than do competing claims, which is the most a scientific claim can ever hope for—is rejected or accepted on the basis of its accord with nature, its ability to predict. Where the claim came from and why it came is irrelevant to science (if not the *history* of science).

In short, the failure of "feminist science" (and "feminist models") is not that it serves psychological, political, and social impulses and purposes. The failure of "feminist science" is that it does *nothing more* than this; *it does not explain anything.* If it did, or if it demonstrated a logical flaw or failure of prediction in models invoking inertial motion or heliocentrism or anything else—if it were capable of doing *anything* that would cast doubt on *any* scientific conclusion—*then* it would be worth taking seriously. Failing utterly to achieve this, "feminist scientists" attempt to cast doubt on accepted scientific explanations through endless discussions of "male paradigms." Such discussions tend to be potpourris of irrelevant facts and misconceptions that have nothing to do with any empirical question; they serve only to fool the nonscientist, who sees impressive-looking scientific references and incorrectly assumes that these necessarily indicate that the one invoking them knows what he or she is talking about.

More important, even if these feminist discussions were entirely correct, they would cast no doubt on the fertility of the models or the correctness of the explanations they wish to cast doubt on; the validity of a scientific claim is a function of the correctness of its predictions, its accord with nature, not its terminology, its causes, or its consequences. If any of these generate error that affects an explanation, then the explanation will fail; if the explanation does not fail, then, *ipso facto*, these are irrelevant.

It is not merely wish and ideology that lead feminist science to such muddled thought: there is a *tradition*, embodied in semiotics, hermeneutics, and certain forms of phenomenology that feminist science is reflecting (or perverting, depending on one's assessment of the tradition). This tradition tends to deny that there is truth and to see perceived truths as merely shared cultural meanings that could, with proper redefinition, be converted to their opposites. It tends to deny underlying realities—biological, inherent in human in nature and society, and the like—that set limits on what may be perceived as truth.

Whatever the virtues of this tradition in the humanities, its fallaciousness in the sciences is, or should be, too obvious to mention. Science leaves far less room for differing views of truth: One who believes that gravity is such that when one lets go of a bowling ball it will fly away is simply incorrect and one who believes it will fall to earth is correct. This is validated by correct prediction and the painful, swollen foot that accompanies the incorrect prediction.

This is not to deny that there are different but *complementary* views of truth. A map showing American state borders and one showing American topology are incommensurate (without additional information), but they are in no way contradictory, nor do they imply the subjectivity of truth. That they both represent (different) objective truths is clear if we compare them to maps showing New York in the South or the Rockies in New York.

*   *   *

All of this is as true of social sciences as of the physical and natural sciences. But it is the former that first, most completely, and most nakedly exhibited the contemporary tendency for ideological wish to replace scientific curiosity. In a few major areas of the social sciences this tendency has gone so far that there is but the barest pretense of scientific objectivity. Truth is measured not by concordance of explanation and reality, but of one social scientist's ideology and that of another. Unlike the blind leading the blind, who are at least *trying* to follow the right path, the majority of practitioners in some of the subdisciplines of the social sciences do not in the slightest care about truth when wish is to be served. If the majority agrees on nonsense, then nonsense is truth.

Consider, for example, the fact that among all the thousands of societies on which we have any sort of evidence, there have never been any Amazonian or matriarchal societies (i.e., the hierarchies of all societies have always been dominated by males). Virtually anyone with a scintilla of scientific curiosity responds to this empirical fact by asking why.

An answer to this question that can be powerfully defended sees psychophysiological differences between the sexes as determinative to male and female behavior and to the social realities that reflect this behavior. (This answer does not, of course, apply to the different question of variation that occurs *within* the limits to which all social, systems conform. A psychophysiological explanation of why the people of all societies get hungry and eat does not claim to explain why Mexicans eat one kind of food and Chinese eat another.)

Feminist attempts to explain the universality of patriarchy, unwilling to entertain the possibility that psychophysiological factors are determinative, invariably:

(1) Are unparsimonious (patriarchy is a result of—for example—capitalism, an "explanation" that requires different causal factors to explain patriarchy in the thousands of societies—primitive, socialist, and the like—that are not capitalist).

(2) Beg the question by giving causal primacy to the socialization of boys and girls, an "explanation" that fails to ask the central question of *why* every society's socialization associate dominance behavior with *males*.

(3) Attempt to refute a claim of the universality of male dominance tendency and patriarchy by demonstrating that some *other* behavior or institution is not universally differentiated; this is akin to denying that males are taller by demonstrating that the sexes do not differ in knowledge of history.

(4) Confuse economic cause with economic function; to see economic factors as the *cause* of male dominance behavior is like seeing McDonald's need for profits as the cause of the human need to eat.

(5) Spend much of their time attacking "straw man" arguments that play no role in the explanation we discuss—for example, sociobiological expla-

nations of why males and females evolved the way they did. The issue here is not how male and female physiologies evolved, but the role of the male and female physiologies that did evolve in determining the differentiated psychologies and behaviors of males and females and the institutions that reflect these.

(6) Make the mistake of treating the social environment as an independent variable, thereby failing to explain *why* the social environment always conforms to limits set by, and takes a direction concordant with, the physiological (i.e., never does environment act as sufficient counterpoise to enable a society to avoid male domination of hierarchies). This is easy to explain if one sees the environment as given its limits and direction by the reality of the psychophysiological natures of males and females and the population's observation of the male-female differences so engendered.

Much feminist social science is not even bad reasoning about empirical questions, but empty or confused discussion that substitutes terminology for explanation. One would be hard-put to find another group that talked so much about science without ever *doing* any science. (There are, of course, many women scientists who *do* science; but these women never make the arguments made by the "feminist scientists" and admit, in private, to being more than a little embarrassed by them.)

Consider, for example, the myriad social science versions of "reconceptualization." Unable to deny that dominance behavior, as usually defined, is associated with males in every society, many feminist writers have redefined "dominance" in such a way that it no longer refers to the behavior whose universality we wish to explain. Having done this, they can then claim that male dominance is not universal.

The problem with this is that one cannot erase an empirical reality by changing its name. One may call a tree an "elephant," but one must then find another word to refer to those fat animals with skinny tails—and one cannot conclude that an "elephant" (as most people use the term) has leaves. If feminists wish to use the word "dominance" to refer to some reality other than that which we do, then they must select some other word to refer to the reality to which we refer. No semantic sleight-of-hand can legitimately be used to deny that which exists.[1]

* * *

The reader who may, understandably, believe that I exaggerate feminist incompetence here might consider this: In 1935, when Margaret Mead published her *Sex and Temperament in Three Primitive Societies*, the prevailing view was that the basic differences between masculine and feminine behavior was owing to physiological differences (though less specific terms were used and little was known about the actual neuroendocrinological differences between males and females). In attempting to correct a view that was nearly as exaggerated as the absurdly environmental explanation of sex differences that infuses the social sciences today, Mead exaggerated the degree to which one of the societies she studied (the Tchambuli) associated what we would call the masculine with women and the feminine with men.

Few social scientists bought this view. For example, Jessie Bernard, who would have very much liked to be able to accept Mead's conclusions, pointed out that, if the reader ignored the adjectives, the Tchambuli did not seem very different from other societies. "Effete" headhunters and "comradely" women feeding their children are still headhunters and women feeding their children, and it is only the adjectives provided by Professor Mead that even begin to suggest otherwise.

In response to such criticism, Mead wrote a famous letter to the *American Anthropologist* in which she pointed out:

> Nowhere do I suggest that I have found any material which disproves the existence of sex differences. . . . This study was not concerned with whether there are or are not actual and universal differences between the sexes, either quantitative or qualitative.

For fifty years Mead repeated her denial a hundred times, in response to one or another claims that she had found a society that reversed sex roles. In a review of my *The Inevitability of Patriarchy* Mead wrote:

> It is true, as Professor Goldberg points out, that all the claims so glibly made about societies ruled by women are nonsense. We have no reason to believe that they ever existed. . . . Men have always been the leaders in public affairs and the final authorities at home.

Finally, about a decade ago I published—in the American Sociological Association's journal of book reviews—perhaps the most-read journal in sociology—a letter making all of the above points.

Now, one would think that all this would be sufficient to preclude even the most ardent environmentalist's invoking Mead's study as evidence of sex-role reversibility. The truth is this:

A couple of years ago I went to Barnes and Noble and located thirty-eight introductory sociology books published in the few preceding years. Of these thirty-eight, thirty-six began their sex-roles chapters with a discussion of Mead's work on the Tchambuli and how it demonstrates the environmental nature of male and female behavior.

It is not clear which of these thirty-six represent knowing misrepresentation of the facts and which represent behavior that is as much incompetence as dishonesty (uninformed cribbing from other textbooks is near-standard procedure in introductory textbook writing). But it is clear why the textbooks misrepresent the evidence. They, like the discipline whose work they represent, have an ideological commitment to a denial of the possibility that masculine and feminine behaviors and emotions are rooted in male and female physiologies and that all societies conform their social systems to the limits and directions imposed by this reality.

My point here is not to defend my view that the evidence overwhelmingly supports the preceding explanation of sex differences. I have done that at great length elsewhere. My point here is merely that no claim can be made for Mead's having even *claimed* to have demonstrated that the Tchambuli serve to refute that explanation. Despite the fact that this is unarguably true, thirty-six of thirty-eight introductory sociology textbooks make this very claim.

*   *   *

The strongest impulse of the serious scientist is to eradicate the contradiction and ignorance that the unanswered question represents. The models that the scientist use serve this impulse. Because "feminist scientists" feel more strongly the need for a picture of reality concordant with their wishes than a need for a picture concordant with reality, they are incapable of understanding that the serious scientist, even one with a strong desire for one finding rather than another, is most strongly motivated by the need to overcome contradiction and ignorance; that is why the scientist is a scientist. Indeed, the history of science is replete with examples of scientists who are impelled by emotional impulse to find one thing, but to were forced by logic and evidence to find another. Where the ideologue is content with the inappropriate model or false explanation as long as it satisfies psychological and political desire, the serious scientist cannot live with the awful gnawing of the explanation that doesn't work.

But, for the reasons given above, it is the success of the answers to specific empirical questions, and not the difference of motivation between the the scientist and the ideologue, that is crucial to science. For science recognizes that even the most serious of scientists is, like everyone else, vulnerable to nonscientific impulses. This is why science has at its core the mechanism for exposing the relevant manifestations of such impulses.

Now, it *might* be the case that, were the majority of scientists women, the *selection* of empirical realities to be studied would be different. For argument's sake, let us assume that female scientists would have been less interested in studying hierarchical realities than are male scientists. Even if this is true, it has nothing to do with the correctness of analyses of that which *is* selected for study. The correctness of one's explanation of a given empirical reality is a function only of the logic and evidence relevant to that empirical reality, not of someone's wish that one had studied something else.

If "feminist science" develops a "feminist model" that helps us to answer some empirical question, or demonstrates the scientific inadequacy of accepted explanations, *then* it will be, as it should be, taken seriously. It will not need the adjective; it will be science. But as long as "feminist science" is nothing more than an empty failure to explain that for which we already have explanations—explanations that make successful predictions, the test that separates the adults from the children in science—it will be, correctly, dismissed from serious discussion.

To this point, "feminist science" has provided nothing more than endless, embarrassingly self-congratulatory discussion of terminology, discussion that neither can explain why traditional terminology permits explanations capable of making prediction nor can itself make any prediction. When such explanations do manage to avoid refutation by a cursory logical glance, they invoke bogus empirical evidence whose misrepresentation can be exposed by one's spending ninety seconds with the source invoked.

In any case, no one possessed by even the shadow of a scientific impulse cares in the slightest whether an interesting hypothesis is provided by a man or a woman or a goldfish. What matters is not the one who makes the claim, but the claim itself and its accord with nature; for it is the explanation of nature that is the only justification for the existence of the claim.

Those who follow another imperative while only pretending to care about discovering nature's secrets—those whose dishonesty and incompetence have muddled the process that has proven infinitely the best for discovering nature's secrets—they subordinate truth to an *a priori* image of how they would like truth to be. This is indefensible for the scientist or, indeed, for anyone who cares about finding out what is true. It replaces curiosity with narcissism and rationalizes the narcissism with a claim of humane purpose.

All this is obvious. Nonetheless, there is an astonishing number of scientists who publicly acquiesce in a position that they know should have long ago been justly laughed out of the university, while telling you in private that they know they support jejune nonsense, but that they do so in the service of the good. We used to call this lying.[2]

NOTES

1. The reader who wishes to judge for himself whether I accurately portray the performance of feminists might wish to look at *Society* (Sept.-Oct., 1986), in which seven feminist and environmentalist critics address my *The Inevitability of Patriarchy* and I respond to these critics.

2. The fact that hundreds of these sorts of feminists works are published by the presses of our leading universities *should* elicit from the serious the contempt for these presses that they deserve. But this must remain the subject of another discussion.

11

The Logical Structure of Freudian Theory
Is Freudian Theory Science?

INTRODUCTION

It has now been over eighty years since Sigmund Freud began construction of a system of theories that has been valued by some as the greatest explanation of the human mind ever created by a human mind and damned by others as tautology in the service of charlatanry. Freudian theory has been defended and attacked on virtually all possible grounds. The arguments have often tended toward a confusing conflation of various lines of reasoning, some of which are of little relevance to the question of the scientific status of Freudian theory. Specifically, one often finds a confusion of questions of (1) the logical nature of Freudian theory as it applies to the complex question of what makes a science, (2) the ability of Freudian theory, if it is scientific on a logical level, to explain empirical reality, (3) the value of Freudian therapy, and (4) the social and political effects of Freudian theory and therapy. This essay will suggest that Freudian theory satisfies the logical requirements of a science and that it is capable of empirical test far greater than that to which it has been put. (Whether it is capable of passing such a test is as yet an unanswered question.) This essay will not consider questions of therapeutic value or political effect.

The definition of science that is virtually intuitive for the scientist sees a statement, hypothesis, or theory as being scientific if it is testable in theory (what Popper would term "falsifiable" and what others would call "possessing empirical anchorage"). This definition does not require testability in practice; for while experimental test is always the ultimate goal, we may not possess the tools necessary for the test. $E = mc^2$ was scientific when it was created even though the tools for testing the hypothesis had yet to be developed. What must be entailed in a statement is a prediction about empirical reality such that if the prediction proves to be incorrect the theory will be surrendered or altered in a non *ad hoc* manner that makes it concordant with the observed reality.[1] Thus, metaphysical statements ("the Absolute is everpresent"), religious statements ("God exists"), and normative or ethical statements ("killing is wrong" or "killing is bad") are nonscientific because they are not testable by reference to a system ("nature") that is not defined by premises contained in the statements (i.e., they are not *even in theory* testable).

To be sure, the falsifiability criterion for defining science is open to a host of philosophical objections. Some philosophers argue that even the most seemingly scientific statement contains, or is rooted in, buried normative assumptions (and is therefore unfalsifiable). Others continue to believe in the possibility of an objective morality. Moreover, the difficulties that the falsifiability criterion encounters are not limited to the philosophical level. Astrological hypotheses, which most scientists understandably do not entertain, are clearly falsifiable hypothesized correlations of celestial events and personality characteristics. On the other hand, the "pleasure principle"—as usually conceived—is unfalsifiable because no behavior is acknowledged as capable of refuting the "pleasure principle" hypothesis. A similar problem faces Darwin's "survival of the fittest."[2]

Finally, the historical record and our present scientific experience make it clear that virtually every hypothesis encounters a number of "anomalies" that could be said to falsify the hypothesis and that every science proceeds through a metaphysical stage; strict adherence to falsifiability criterion would have had us dismiss every science before it could proceed to the stage where it could make falsifiable statements.[3]

Likewise, there can be disagreement about whether a particular finding corroborates a theory. For example, it is clear that there is an empirical reality (termed "transference" by psychoanalysts) in which an individual attaches to other figures expectations formed in the image of his parents (or other important people). Clearly this is an important finding. However, a prediction corroborates a theory only if the prediction is inherent in, and is in some sense explained by, the theory. If transference is to be invoked as corroboration of basic Freudian theory, rather than as "merely" an important peripheral finding, it must be explained in terms of facts that are central to Freudian theory. The theory must explain why transference is expected. An astrologer can correctly predict that sunspots will follow specific cycles, but this does nothing to corroborate astrological theory; the astrologer has not in any meaningful sense explained the regularity or shown it to be correlated with anything that is seen as causally important by astrology. Such observed correlations may be of great importance (though, of course, in the latter example it was not the astrologers who made the discovery), but the correlations do not, in and of themselves, corroborate the larger theories. Similarly, the psychoanalyst who argues that psychoanalytic theory is—whether or not it is capable of making long-term prediction—capable of making short-term prediction must not merely make correct short-term predictions; he must make correct short-term predictions that are surprising and inexplicable to one who does not invoke Freudian explanation. Anyone can predict that a patient will be angry when the psychoanalyst calls him a fool; the correctness of such a prediction does nothing to indicate the correctness of Freudian theory.

Most philosophers accept that the nature of nature, or our ignorance of the future route of nature, precludes our ever possessing a criterion for distinguishing the scientific from the nonscientific (or for selecting the better hypothesis over the worse hypothesis) that has the power to persuade the mind that logic has for the mathematician (who deals in closed systems). However, whatever the technical shortcomings of the falsifiability criterion, it *is* the criterion that scientists do use. When used with a tolerance for young theories and young sciences, it is our best defense against irrationality and a confusion of truth with wish.

Whatever the problems encountered by attempts to specify the criteria that define science, there is one problem that need not concern us. This is the frequently heard argument that the logic underlying hypotheses in the social sciences, and particularly psychoanalysis, is *in essence* different from that underlying theories in the physical sciences. Were this true then it would be true that the criteria for assessing the validity of hypotheses in the social sciences would have to be different from those used for assessing hypotheses in the physical sciences. But it is not true. The reader who wishes to see that the "different logic" argument is utterly indefensible might consult Ernest Nagle's magnificent *The Structure of Science.* To be sure, there are great differences between the social and physical sciences with respect to certain practical difficulties (self-fulfilling prophecies, difficulty of isolation of variables, possibility of experiment, control of experiment, etc.), and these are not overcome by aping of language and accoutrement of the physical sciences or by quantifying ill-defined variables. But these differences are quantitative, not qualitative; the structure of the social sciences is identical to that of the physical sciences, and the validity of explanation in the social sciences must be assessed by the same criteria used to assess explanations in the physical sciences. Man may not be rational, but a theory of behavior must be logical; indeed, one might conceive of Freudian theory as the search for the missing premises that make explanation of the irrational logical.

Logic and Freudian Theory

In an understandably angry response to an assertion by philosopher Morris Lazerowitz that the metaphysician "gives expression *only* to his unconscious fantasies,"[5] Donald C. Williams (another philosopher) has written:

> Philosophy, and notably metaphysics, is the candid effort to see the world entire, not in detail but in main outline, using all the resources of thought and perception, gutting and glutting language as need be, ruthlessly analyzing things to their finest structure in order to synthesize to their most embracing system. . . .
>
> Insofar as our ideas are not consciously incubated, they must be unconsciously so; and insofar as we are haggises of impulse and appetite, the appetite must be extremely vigorous to win out.[6]

Now, the *positivist* might agree with Professor Lazerowitz that metaphysics is empty (this irrelevant issue need not detain us here), but he would have no reason to assess metaphysical theories in terms of the unconscious fantasies of the metaphysician; indeed the positivist is likely to doubt whether the term "unconscious fantasy" can have any meaning. The Freudian, on the other hand, would agree with Williams that the *validity* of a theory is never a function of psychological factors. The Freudian would agree that the philosopher does precisely what Professor Williams says he does; the psychoanalyst would agree that it is as silly to argue that the philosopher's insatiable appetite for ordered truth discovers nothing more than a reflection of the tangled unconscious of the philosopher as it would be to make a similar argument about the scientist.[7]

However, after acknowledging that philosophical discovery, far from being a mere manifestation of the individual's fantasy life, represents the highest flight of the human intellect, the Freudian would ask why only certain people "think like philosophers" and choose to become philosophers, to devote their lives to the search for ordered truth. Why, in other words, is the appetite for a certain kind of ordered truth so "extremely vigorous" in some people and not in others? Intelligence alone is clearly not a sufficient answer because, while high intelligence is a necessary condition for doing high-level philosophy, there are many people who possess the required intelligence but who do not strongly feel the need for an all-embracing system, the need that energizes the thought and action of the practitioner of "philosophy, and notably metaphysics."

The Freudian would suggest that metaphysicians (and mathematicians, and other systems builders) tend, more than do other equally intelligent members of the society, to deal with emotion and environment by intellectualizing and categorizing and simplifying; he would further suggest that, statistically speaking, such people constitute a particularly talented subset of a category of individuals whose cognitive style is, relative to the cognitive styles of other people, characterizable as "obsessive." Were the Freudian to stop here he would have told us virtually nothing; he would have done little more than define "philosopher." However, the Freudian makes two claims that justify his assertion that he is presenting us with scientific hypotheses rather than mere definitional statements. He claims: (1) that individuals of the type described manifest *other, specifiable* cognitive propensities, personality characteristics, and behaviors more often than do other individuals and (2) that individuals of this type experienced *specifiable* childhood familial situations more frequently than did other individuals.

The psychoanalyst would, for example, make predictions concerning the fantasy life of children who will later become philosophers; in practice this will, of course, take the form of prediction of the types of content of childhood fantasies that will be reported by adult philosophers.[8] Consider the following fantasies and feelings of childhood: A child wonders whether his choosing not to listen to a particular game played by his favorite baseball team was of sufficient causal importance to account for his team's losing. The same child feels discomfort at division problems that leave an inelegant-feeling remainder. The same child takes an inordinate amount of time putting away finger paints because he, unlike the teacher who wishes merely that the fingerpaints be put on the shelf, feels that the paints should be placed in (an intuitively perceived) order (red, orange, yellow—or yellow, orange, red—but not red, yellow, orange). This child wonders whether one could freeze a piece of ice to a temperature sufficiently low that it would, when dropped in the ocean, freeze the water around it, which would freeze the water around the water, until the oceans were frozen. The same child feels intuitively that no two things could be exactly alike because different "causes" generate different effects (and all causes differ at least with respect to time/space).

Now these are hardly exceptional fantasies, and they are found to a greater or lesser extent in most children. The Freudian would, however, make the prediction that these sorts of fantasies will be far more frequently reported by individuals who become philosophers, mathematicians, and theoretical scientists, as well as by members of other groups who lack the interest (accountants) or intelligence (stockroom organizers) than by, say, actors. The Freudian would suggest that the reports of childhood fantasies of historians and novelists would differ markedly from those most frequently reported by the philosophers.

Even if this were all true it would not, in and of itself, do much to corroborate Freudian theory. All it would indicate would be the rather unsurprising fact that the adult mind reflects the same propensities found in the childhood mind; the same can be said of skin color. The fact that Freudian theory is concordant with childhood-adult similarity, like the fact that Freudian theory is concordant with a physicalist's view of the world, and with physiological explanations, merely allows it to stay in the game.

What is crucial is that the Freudian claims to predict not merely that there will be a consistency of childhood and adult mind and behavior, but that there will be correlations between childhood familial experiences/situations and type of mind; the Freudian claims not merely that such correlations will be surprising rather than obvious and trivial, but also that they will make sense only in terms of Freudian explanation and the factors that it sees as crucial.

The Freudian claims, in other words, that the group of individuals who become philosophers will report weaning experiences, toilet-training experiences, attitudes about the sufficiency of the mother's love and the father's strength, and the like that are specifiably and significantly different—quantitatively and/or qualitatively—from those reported by members of other groups. Whether the early experiences of the members of the two groups differed in reality or only in perceptions of the members is not ascertainable from report alone, but this is not of great importance (since it is the individual's view of the world that is seen by the Freudian as crucial).[9] In any case, such predictions are not merely falsifiable, but are translatable into correlational terms that could satisfy even the operationalist. If the Freudian specifies the reported childhood experiences and specifies the adult cognitive propensities, then the Freudian cannot be accused of making predictions that owe their correctness to biased selection, the charge that is so convincingly leveled at the clinical evidence that constitutes almost the entirety of the contemporary defense of Freudian theory.

In all of his explanations and predictions the Freudian, like anyone else making a prediction, invokes a *ceteris paribus* clause that enables him to ignore factors that are irrelevant to his prediction. He does this with physiological predispositions, certainly when they are hereditary and often even if they result from some fetal environmental experience. He does the same thing with social factors. Thus, the fact that a particular low-income group may have a much higher murder rate than does a high-income group does not cast doubt on any Freudian explanation of a murder committed by a member of the low-income group. The Freudian does not claim sufficiency for his explanation, but only necessity (or at least increased probability). To put this another way: The Freudian does not claim to explain why the members of the low-income group commit more murders (which demands a sociological explanation), but why those members of the low-income group who do commit murders do so when the vast majority of other members of the *same* social group do not; this can not be explained in terms of social group differences. (It is worth remembering that the dichotomizing of "social" and "psychological" is always a heuristic oversimplification. Social factors, for example a welfare system that drives the father out of the house, can play a great role in the development of personality.)

COMMENTS ON SOME SPECIFIC METHODOLOGICAL CRITICISMS OF FREUDIAN THEORY

Much of the philosophical criticism of Freudian theory argues that such theory, while perhaps not, strictly speaking, unfalsifiable, is so "open textured," so replete with escapist subclauses and ubiquitous theoretical constructs, that it is in practice untestable. For example, one can hardly deny that Freudians have on many occasions seemed to explain "opposite" effects in terms of identical causes and identical effects in terms of "opposite" causes.

However, it is well to remember that, on the level of gross observation, "same" causes *do* seem to generate "opposite" effects, and vice versa, and that science is an attempt to explain observation, gross observation at first. We *do* observe that the child of one overly aggressive father is overly aggressive, while the child of another overly aggressive father is passive ("same cause, opposite effect"); we *do* observe that one overly aggressive child has an overly aggressive father while another overly aggressive child has a passive father ("opposite cause, same effect"). Clearly it is to be hoped, and is usually the case, that a Freudian explanation would specify causes and effects far more precisely than this, but I would suggest that even an explanation this gross is not, as critics often assert, meaningless by virtue of unfalsifiability. This criticism would be valid if "overly aggressive" and "passive" subsumed all possibilities, if every father was seen as either "overly aggressive" or "passive." If this were the case, assertions of a relationship between paternal aggression/passivity and child aggression/passivity would be unfalsifiable and we would have no reason to believe that paternal aggression/passivity had anything to do with child aggression/passivity. But clearly this is not the case. Clearly, the Freudian conceives of most fathers and most children as being neither "overly aggressive" and "passive." The meanings of "overly aggressive" and "passive" are in theory operationally specifiable (as scoring very high or very low on an objective test measuring "aggressiveness" or as meeting behavioral requirements such as hitting and kicking, on the one hand, or extreme uninvolvement, on the other). These terms do not, therefore, subsume the behaviors of all individuals, *but only the behaviors of individuals at both extremes of a continuum.*

This can be seen more clearly if we consider the concept of "reaction formation," a concept that has been criticized in similar terms. Again we might point out that even gross observation does indicate that (A) people do "protest too much" and defend by denial, suggest that (B) this is an empirical observation demanding explanation, acknowledge that (C) if the concept of "reaction formation" "explained everything," it would explain nothing, and emphasize that (D) the concept *does* make risky predictions that are falsifiable and testable.

Thus, even if one did explain the alcoholism of one individual in terms of the same causes as the rigid temperance of another (with "reaction formation" included in the latter explanation), his explanation would be of a gross sort, but it would be better than nothing (which is perhaps the strongest argument Freudian theory has going for it). The prediction is made that the configuration of causal factors specified by the Freudian is highly correlated with both alcoholism and rigid temperance, but *not* with the moderate use of alcohol that is found in, say, 80 percent of the American population. Much Freudian explanation is of this type. The psychoanalyst would, knowing only that an individual's toilet training was unusually difficult, predict that the individual would have difficulty in the area of cheapness/generosity and would be unusually parsimonious or unusually extravagant. Likewise, the psychoanalyst would, knowing only that an individual had an unusually difficult time with weaning and toilet-training, predict that the individual would have difficulty in the area of dominance/submission and would see far more of reality in these terms than would one who did not have such difficulty in infancy. The psychoanalyst would, in other words, predict the area of life and type of concern that will dominate the individual's life, rather than the *direction* of concern or behavior.

To be sure, such explanations are incomplete and remain so until the direction of concern or behavior is specified. To be sure, the explanations are incomplete and remain so until the distinctions necessary for prediction of direction (cheapness or generosity) as well as area (cheapness/generosity) can be made. But even without this capacity the explanation does make risky predictions of unexpected correlations and can justifiably be termed scientifically meaningful.

It is worthwhile discussing two additional Freudian terms that are often incorrectly asserted to be unfalsifiable and guilty of other methodological sins: "overdetermination" and "latent homosexuality."

The concept of "overdetermination" is, like "reaction formation," valid only at a certain, and in practice, inevitable level of ignorance. Since every nonrandom event can (in theory) be shown to be different from every other event (if we accept our intuition that "every difference makes a difference"), and since, therefore, every such event has a different causation, the Freudian term "overdetermined" reflects our (inevitable) ignorance of the complete nature of the reality we attempt to explain. Sufficiently precise description of an action (and the thoughts in the actor's mind) would (in theory) enable us to present a cause that "entailed" the action, and only the action, we wished to explain. Thus, when we say that a painter's painting a nude is overdetermined in that it serves a number of needs, we mean that any one of the needs is sufficient to explain the artist's painting a nude. But this explanation is sufficient only because we describe in only the grossest of terms (painting a nude) the effect we wish to explain. If we were to describe the painter's thoughts and the minute details of the painting with sufficient explicitness, we would see that one, and only one, causal configuration of needs possessed the necessity and sufficiency to explain the effect. This point is so absurdly theoretical, given the reality that faces the psychoanalyst, that the psychoanalyst is well within his rights to ignore it altogether.

Similarly, the criticism that the concept of "latent homosexuality" is without value because it is a concept that is untestable is clearly a criticism that is without merit. Let us imagine a test administered to sixteen-year-old boys with no homosexual experience. Let us say that those boys who score above eighty turn out, with great statistical significance, to become adults whose sexual preference is solely homosexual. Let us say that those who score between sixty and eighty do not tend to participate in homosexual encounters but do remain unmarried and do tend to exhibit the defensive behavior that the Freudian associates with suppressed homosexual tendencies. It seems to me that this is the sort of thing the Freudian has in mind when he speaks of "latent homosexuality" and this is perfectly valid even from a purely operationalist point of view. Such a test may or may not exist, but the mere fact that we can imagine it is sufficient to demonstrate the methodological validity of the concept of "latent homosexuality."

Most of the philosophical criticism of Freudian theory is of the type we have discussed. When such criticism is meant as criticism of what Freudians do in practice, it is unexceptionable. The objections I raise in this essay refer only to the suggestion that the criticisms expose a logical or theoretical flaw in Freudian theory. Such criticisms are common. Arthur Pap found fault with the concept of unconscious feeling, Sidney Hook objects that the Freudian can not describe a child who does not have an Oedipus Complex, and Karl Popper implies that, because the Freudian will say that the man who drowns a child suffers from a repression of some element of his Oedipus complex while the man who saves the child acts out of sublimation, Freudian theory is capable of explaining everything and is therefore unfalsifiable.

Pap argues that the common concept "unconscious feeling" (as in "he unconsciously dislikes Mr. Smith, though he thinks he likes him") is meaningless because terms like "feeling" and "dislike" are by definition conscious states of awareness. He suggests that we are better off using the term "unconscious disposition"; thus, when we observe that Mr. Jones feels that he likes Mr. Smith, but acts as if he dislikes Mr. Smith, we are observing that Mr. Jones has a disposition, of which he is unaware, to act toward Mr. Smith as would one who consciously disliked (*felt* a dislike for) Mr. Smith. I would suggest that if one conceives of the unconscious as ultimately a physiological entity that, like the central nervous system, subsumes a great number of physiological entities, and if one imagines that Mr. Jones's (unconscious) disposition to act as if he dislikes Mr. Smith represents an environmentally generated physiological state that is identical to that found in one who consciously dislikes Mr. Smith (except with reference to the physiological factors relevant to conscious awareness), then the term "unconscious dislike" does have meaning.

I think that it is possible to describe a child who lacks an Oedipus Complex, and that this is what the Freudians have done in response to Sidney Hook's criticism. I would, however, suggest that Hook is quite correct in suggesting that the virtual nonexistence of individuals without Oedipus Complexes would render the concept virtually worthless as an explanation of anything were not described more specifically. (It would be like an explanation of nightmares that saw them as caused by life; one can describe a person who lacks life, and it would be true that a life is a necessary condition for a nightmare, but the explanation that said no more than that nightmares are caused by life would be somewhat unsatisfactory.) I would suggest that the Freudians would be better off by taking a different approach; they would acknowledge that virtually all people have Oedipus Complexes, but that "Oedipus Complex" is merely a convenient term that subsumes a number of factors (desire for mother, fear of father, anger towards father, and the like) whose relative strengths will affect the individual's adult thought and behavior. We do not have units for measuring these factors, but we can certainly speak of a relatively great fear of the father and a relatively weak fear of the father, we can specify the adult behavioral realities we are attempting to explain, and we can predict correlations between various combinations of these factors and adult thought and action. No one criticizes as meaningless the sociologist's statement that stratification "causes" alienation simply because all societies are stratified, because stratification cannot be counted, or because alienation is difficult to define precisely. One understands that the sociologist, in saying that stratification "causes" alienation, is simply oversimplifying the results of investigations that demonstrate that the strength, degree, and type of differentiation subsumed under the term "stratification" are correlated with such measures of alienation as suicide.

Similarly, Popper would be right to be dissatisfied with the "explanation" that did nothing more than say that one man drowned the child as a result of repression while another saved the child as a result of sublimation. But surely the Freudian would say something more; he would claim that he could, at least, differentiate the childhood factors tending to lead one person to develop a style in which repression is the primary defense from those tending to lead another person to develop a style in which sublimation is the primary defense.

So many psychoanalytic theorists have responded to the demand for falsifiability and testability by arguing that psychoanalytic theory requires "postdiction" rather than prediction, and so many psychoanalytic theorists have defined "postdiction" in so many different ways that it is necessary to address the point here.

(1) There is no problem when by "postdiction" the theorist means a predic-

tion of what a patient will report about his past. There is no logical distinction between such postdiction and prediction. This invocation of postdiction has the advantage of stressing that the psychoanalyst does not (necessarily) claim to be able to predict (for example) which four-year-olds will become adult homosexuals. (The theorist might argue that while the seeds of homosexuality have been sewn by this age, practical problems of observation preclude even statistically significant predictions of which four-year-olds will become adult homosexuals.) This theorist argues that the evidence for the correctness of his theory of homosexuality is not a test of the prediction of which four-year-olds will become homosexual, but the postdiction of what adult homosexuals will report about their childhoods. If the theorist is capable of predicting that his homosexual patients will more often report a particular configuration of childhood factors and a particular childhood familial situation (which the theorist specifies) than will his heterosexual patients, then he gives us a good reason to accept the correctness of his theory of homosexuality. (I ignore practical problems of self-fulfilling prophecy.)

(2) Some authors, however, seem to introduce the concept of postdiction in the belief that it—or some other concept that they give the name "postdiction" —somehow relieves psychoanalysis of the need of falsifiability that is required of all other sciences. Some of these argue that postdiction is made only for the particular individual being analyzed and that postdiction makes no statement about the class to which the patient belongs (in our example, the class of homosexuals). If one making this argument means that the psychoanalyst merely *describes* the development of the individual, then, to the extent that this is in fact true, it is unobjectionable; but it implies that Freudian theory, like literature, is science only in the most very general sense (see below).

One suspects, however, that the psychoanalyst—even the psychoanalyst who believes that he merely describes an individual's development—rarely in fact does so. Most of the "descriptive" statements can easily be shown to rest on a panoply of assumptions. These assumptions face the requirements of falsifiability required of all other scientific hypotheses.

(3) Most of those authors who argue that postdiction applies only to the particular individual being analyzed do not merely describe. They treat the individual as a system; in speaking of, for example, the homosexuality of X, they offer causal hypotheses explaining X's homosexuality. These hypotheses are falsifiable (they are not mere descriptive statements), but they can be falsified only by events that are incorrectly predicted or postdicted (in the sense of "1" above) that will occur or have occurred *in the life of X*. Unlike the purely descriptive approach described in (2), this approach can claim falsifiability, but only within the system comprised of one individual's life. Unlike the more orthodox approach described in (1), this approach forgoes any hypothesis of even such limited generalizability as to be capable of explaining the behavior of two people in similar terms.

An analogy may make this clear. Consider a cardiologist who treats a patient whose heart beats only fifty times a minute. The cardiologist predicts that in adolescence it beat sixty times a minute. This is clearly a falsifiable hypothesis. If the cardiologist claims that his hypotheses and explanations are appropriate only for explanation of the individual with the slow heartbeat, then his focus on the one individual system is analogous to that of the psychoanalyst who sees each patient as similarly idiosyncratic and who avoids generalization above the level of the individual system.

There is, however, a serious problem with this approach. It does, in theory, possess a falsifiability that allows it to satisfy the criteria suggested here. However, in practice the hypotheses utilized to explain the individual system can almost invariably be shown by even a cursory analysis to derive from general hypotheses about human behavior. This is most obvious in our analogy: The hypotheses proposed by the cardiologist devolve from general hypotheses about the behavior of the normal heart. Falsifiability does not, of course, limit the sources of an hypothesis—the source can be magical incantation and a resulting epiphany—but the desire to generalize is so great that, one suspects, few of even those who are committed to the view that the individual is the system really believe they are proposing only individually limited hypotheses.

(4) While the best of the psychoanalytic writers are fully aware of the theoretical approach that infuses their empirical writings, and while most of these subscribe to the clearly legitimate approach described in (1), it should be clear that the theoretical approaches described here outline what various Freudian writers do, in fact, do. This is not always the same as that which such writers think they are doing. Similarly, all of the theoretical psychoanalytic writings advancing methodological analyses that we do not discuss here (for example, those that emphasize change of function, interpetation, etc.) must satisfy the falsifiability criterion stressed here. When these writings concern methodological problems specific to psychoanalysis and when they do not attempt to override the necessity of falsifiability, they are no doubt important and worthwhile. But on occasion an author will advance such a factor in an attempt to deny the necessity of falsifiability in Freudian theory. Such attempts often try to avoid falsifiability with a vitually impenetrable complexity that defies analysis. It is worth remembering that complexity rooted in nonsense is still nonsense.

THE NECESSITY OF SEVERE EMPIRICAL TEST

Defenders of Freudian theory often respond to methodological criticisms with the claim that such theory is more art than science. Often the defenders do not seem quite clear on what they mean by this (though their purpose of excusing methodological deficiencies is quite clear). In any case, the distinction cannot provide a defense for anything that is known as a theory. Assuming that literature is the art to which the Freudians refer, I would point out that, while the criteria we invoke for assessing truth in literature is *in practice* quite different from what we invoke for assessing truth in science, literature and science are not concerned with mutually exclusive areas of reality. Both literature and science claim to tell us about the empirical world and both are in theory answerable to the same sorts of criteria. We accept the truthfulness of great literature on the basis of its "ringing true," on the basis of a feeling, because we sense that such literature gives us at least a glimpse of aspects of the reality of the human condition that are, in practice, unreachable by the more rigorous methods of science. We give feeling a strong (though still only partial) role in determining the truthfulness of literature because literature does not make the sorts of claims of rigor and practical replicability implied in the word "theory." Ultimately, Shakespeare's view of the world is a constellation of falsifiable, though untestable, hypotheses about how human beings will behave under certain conditions. Our feeling about Shakespeare's work indicates that he is doing something more than merely presenting observations of particular people (our identification indicates that he is saying something about human beings in general) and that his view is correct. Freudian writings, unlike novels and plays, are infused with endless implication of the sort of predictive capability of a theoretical science. It is this implication of an empirical testability coupled with a virtual absence of empirical corroboration that makes those uncommitted to Freudian theory so critical of the tautological tendencies of Freudian theoretical constructs. Were there a real body of empirical corroborations, most critics would, understanding the complexity of the reality that the Freudian studies, accept the necessity of the theoretical terms. Though the critic might, if he were a purist, hope for the eventual elimination of all such terms and a virtually complete dependence on empirical correlations, he would look far more favorably on Freudian theory. It is the grand claims coupled with the dearth of empirical corroboration and the surfeit of theoretical terms that infuriates the critic.

Now I realize that the Freudian believes that there is an enormous amount of corroboratory evidence provided by his clinical studies. The philosophical objection to such evidence—the objection that finds clinical evidence wanting not on theoretical grounds but on the practical grounds of the impossibility of preventing self-fulfilling prophecy, biased collection of data by the psychoanalyst, and the like—is so well documented that I need not repeat it here. I assume here that clinical evidence, valuable as it is once one accepts the basic premises of Freudian theory, is incapable of demonstrating the validity of the basic premises to the satisfaction of the non-Freudian.

To demonstrate the validity of the basic Freudian premises one must meet two criteria not met by clinical evidence: (1) The tests used as evidence must be independent of any commitment to Freudian theory; in practice this means that the tested hypotheses must be free of Freudian terminology (though, of course, Freudians are free to use such terminology in case studies and other materials from which the hypotheses are derived); and (2) clinical situations can play no role in the tests (though the hypotheses will be derived from clinical observations). My purpose is not to present designs for adequate tests; this is a task for which I am far from qualified. I might, however, present one example in order to make clear the sort of test I have in mind, a test that, if successful, would be more convincing than the (valid) postdictional tests described above.

There is a Freudian explanation of homosexual propensity. This explanation is replete with theoretical terms. In theory it would be possible to specify the physical realities that these terms subsume and to thereby jettison the terms. This possibility is seen as realizable only by the purest of physicalist-operationalists. What is desired by those who criticize Freudian theory is not an impossible eradication of such terms, but some convincing evidence that these terms are helpful in explaining some reality that is not created by the terms themselves. Now, the Freudian theories of homosexual propensity are not merely accumulations of terms such as superego, Oedipus complex, and the like; they include hypotheses about realities that do not depend on the explanatory terms. These theories see certain childhood familial situations (or certain other perceptions of childhood familial situations) as not engendering homosexual propensity. These are predicted correlations that are not in any way dependent on Freudian theory. It may well be that the analyst's keen eye is necessary for testing such correlations, but as long as the predictions preceed the findings (or as long as "predictions to the past" do not select for the findings, the common criticism of *clinical* evidence), this in no way casts doubt on the test; a blind man cannot see a patient's jaundice, but this does not cast doubt on the sighted doctor's ability to predict that the patient will exhibit further signs of cirrhosis. The analyst might observe a large number of four-year-old children and predict which will have homosexual propensities in adulthood. Or he might interview the children or the parents or both. Or he might give tests to the children or parents, tests that he believes discriminate between those factors that generate (or facilitate) homosexual propensity and those that do not. Or he might give adult homosexuals and a control group of adult heterosexuals a test asking questions about childhood familial situations (whether the patient's perceptions reflected in the answers are correct or distorted perceptions of childhood is another issue). If the analyst passes this test, if he makes better than random predictions, then he will have given us reason to accept his explanation and the explanatory terms it includes. He will have shown us that there was something to explain and that this something is most plausibly explained in Freudian terms and terminology. (After all, the physiologist would have no reason to predict the correlations predicted by the Freudians.)

Some Freudians respond to the request for the sort of verification discussed here by claiming that practical difficulties preclude long-term tests of the sort discussed here; these analysts argue that Freudian theory must be tested by its ability to make short-term predictions of a patient's behavior. As we have seen, this approach is legitimate *only if the success of the predictions is surprising to, and inexplicable by, the non-Freudian.*

I do not doubt that long-term tests will be enormously difficult or that they will demand theoretical intelligence coupled with great experimental aptitudes, a rare combination. Nor do I doubt that there will be disagreement about whether a successfully predicted correlation corroborates a theory. (A test in which analysts successfully predicted which four-year-olds would be homosexuals in adulthood "merely" on the basis of observation might be challenged as demonstrating only that analysts are good at recognizing traits associated with homosexual propensity early and that this does not corroborate the explanatory theory; anyone can predict with better than random results which seventeen-year-olds will be homosexual in adulthood.) But these are the sorts of disagreements that improve a science. What is needed now are the basic tests that give the non-Freudian reason to think that the Freudian explanations may be necessary. Virtually all Freudian explanations predict similar correlations between childhood experiences, perceptions, and stages, as well as adult cognitive propensities and behaviors. All are testable in theory and most are, given sufficient intelligence and ability, testable in practice.[10]

If anyone should understand the philosophical reluctance to accept the Freudian's clinical evidence, it is the Freudian. Every day the Freudian sees the human capacity for biased selection of evidence as he tries to help the neurotic who forces reality into a preconceived framework. Every day the Freudian sees how belief can be self-fulfilling; the neurotic who believes people to be hostile elicits hostility from those around him. Just as the Freudian asks the neurotic to justify his preconceptions by demonstrating that they are concordant with reality, so does the critic ask the Freudian to justify his assertions about reality. The Freudian, and many philosophers, *feel* that much of Freudian theory is correct, just as the physicist and the astrologer feel that their theories are correct. For the believer emotion is an infinitely stronger source of belief than logic and evidence can ever hope to be, but it is logic and evidence that are needed to convince the nonbeliever. It is true, as Eliseo Vivas has said, that "one can't kill Freud with methodological tommy guns," but it is equally true that Freud can no longer be defended by speculative hypotheses alone, no matter what the imaginative force of the hypotheses.

On the other hand, it is also true that philosophers have shown toward Freudian theory an ungenerosity that is difficult to explain only in terms of philosophic skepticism. It should not surprise us that the philosopher, whose quest is a world ever more ordered, ever more elegantly constructed, would experience nausea when confronted with a view that sees the human world as haggis. What is surprising is that so few philosophers are bothered by the inconsistency of their formally rejecting Freudian theory while informally discussing human thought and behavior in terms that make it quite clear that they find the Freudian approach the most fertile method for dealing with a range of behaviors that we could not otherwise even begin to explain. Whatever the logical difficulties with concepts such as motivation, unconscious, and the like, even most philosophers find that it is impossible to begin to understand behavior—particularly the aberrational behavior that most concerned Freud—without at least a partial acceptance of Freud, an acceptance that rigorous adherence to their criteria for accepting evidence would not permit. No doubt this is in part owing to the fact that we have accepted many Freudian ideas so completely that we think of them as common sense. On the other hand, it would be less than human for the philosopher not to question the validity of (valid) Freudian explanations of exhibitionism, phobic behavior, and the like, when he so often sees a psychiatrist giving phallic explanations of why some people eat more carrots at a time when the price of carrots is falling rapidly.

NOTES

1. What qualifies as a "non-*ad hoc* alteration of a hypothesis or theory" is a difficult question if one insists on a clean line demarking the *ad hoc* from the non-*ad hoc*. Suffice it to say here that a non-*ad hoc* alteration opens up a class of new predictions rather than merely avoiding specific anomolies in increasingly impausible ways.

2. See my chapter on astrology for a fuller discussion of "survival of the fittest."

3. An "anomoly" is a finding that refutes a hypothesis one likes; a "refutation" is a finding that refutes an hypothesis one dislikes.

4. New York: Harcourt, Brace, and World, 1961, pp. 447–546. The interested reader will certainly want to consult Nagle's discussion of Freudian theory in the Hook volume mentioned below.

5. Emphasis in original. Morris Lazerowitz, "The Relevance of Psychoanalysis to Philosophy" in *Psychoanalysis, Scientific Method, and Philosophy,* Sidney Hook, ed. (New York: New York University Press, 1959), p. 134.

6. Williams, Donald C., "Philosophy and Psychoanalysis," in Hook, pp. 163 and 165.

7. The Freudian might or might not see metaphysical theory as empty, but this would be determined by his positivist leanings and would be in no way necessitated by Freudian theory.

8. I ignore here the enormous practical difficulties of self-fulfilling prophecy, selection to please the psychoanalyst, and the like. These are of practical importance to the testing of Freudian hypotheses, but they are of little theoretical importance.

9. For example, it is conceivable that the mothers of infants who find weaning a traumatizing experience do not differ from mothers of infants who do not. It may be that the infants in the former group have a physiologically rooted greater need for nurturance and that it is this that accounts for the trauma. It would, however, seem more plausible that there was at least some real difference between the mothers.

10. Subsequent to the completion of this essay came the welcome publication of Seymour Fisher and Roger Greenberg's *The Scientific Credibility of Freud's Theories and Therapy* (New York: Basic Books, 1985). While, as the authors themselves stress, much of the research reported in this compendium is open to the criticisms discussed in this essay, the book represents a marvelous beginning and points the way toward more satisfactory tests of Freudian theory. Among the few other relatively large scale attempts to consider the scientific validity of Freudian theory is R. Sears's "Survey of Objective Studies in Psychoanalytic Concepts," in *Social Science Research Council Bulletin,* 1943, 51.

12

Is There a Correct Use of Language?

People with more than a passing interest in words fall into two groups, pre-scriptivist and descriptivist. The prescriptivist believes that there is an ideal of correctness in the use of words—shifting and temporally based as it ultimately may be. The descriptivist finds the concept of "correctness" elitist at best and, more often, incomprehensible.

The one inviolable rule of descriptivism is this: There are no correct defini-tions, meanings, or usages other than those used by people-in-general; any at-tempt to substitute a definition, meaning, or usage for that used by people-in-general is invalid. Where the prescriptive subordinates popular usage to correct usage, the desciptivist denies to correctness *and all other criteria* parity with use by people-in-general.

Now consider what happens when you ask a descriptivist how he defines "dictionary" in his descriptivist dictionary.

The descriptivist might, as his inviolable rule says he must, accept the defini-tion of "dictionary" used by people-in-general. If he does this, he will define "dic-tionary" as people-in-general really do, as giving correct definitions, correctness being determined by a literary elite.[1] The descriptivist must accept the view of people-in-general that there is a correct usage—in this case correct definitions—because his inviolable rule requires that he accept the view of people-in-general. In granting that there is a correct usage, the descriptivist grants what his inviola-ble rule, his basic premise, denies.

The descriptivist might, on the other hand, reject the definition used by peo-ple-in-general and substitute the definition of "dictionary" implied by his violable rule, the definition that *denies* that there is a "correct" usage other than that used by people-in-general. But if he does this, he does the one thing that his inviolable rule prohibits: He substitutes a "correct" definition whose existence his basic premise denies for the only definition that his basic premise—his inviolable rule—grants as legitimate, the definition used by people-in-general.

The descriptivist cannot argue that people-in-general are incorrect in defin-

193

ing a "dictionary" as giving correct usage because "incorrect" (or "wrong") has no meaning in the descriptivist universe (except, perhaps, to describe a misrepresentation of the usage of people-in-general, which is just what the descriptivist does if he alters the definition of "dictionary" used by people-in-general; people-in-general cannot, according to the descriptivist premise, be incorrect).

Whether the descriptivist accepts the definition of "dictionary" used by people-in-general or rejects the definition used by people-in-general, the descriptivist's descriptivism is exposed as rotten at its core. Note that the contradiction is not merely an oddity relevant only to a single definition. The problem of defining "dictionary" is but a focused view of a contradiction that infuses all of descriptivism and that can be stated without reference to a definition of "dictionary." The general contradiction is that descriptivism is founded on an axiom that accepts "A" (popular usage) and rejects "B" (any other authority or criterion for correctness) even when acceptance of "A" commits descriptivism to an acceptance of "B," which is rejected by the axiom ("A") that requires its acceptance.

There are problems with descriptivism that many will find even more serious than the failure of logical structure. Descriptivism would have us almost immediately follow the lead of people-in-general, even when doing so would eradicate a distinction that increases precision. So, for example, as soon as people begin to ignore the distinction between "continuous" (how a faucet runs) and "continual" (how a faucet drips), the distinction dissolves for the descriptivist. The prescriptivist, on the other hand, believes that, when a distinction increases precision, as does the distinction between "continuous" and "continual," there is every reason to maintain it well past the point where people-in-general have begun to ignore it.

There does, no doubt, often come a time when only the etymologist remembers the distinction, and by that point even the prescriptivist has come to favor ignoring the distinction. But while a significant minority maintains the distinction, so that its fate remains in question, the prescriptivist favors maintaining it. Indeed, it is primarily this that makes the prescriptivist a prescriptivist.

Now it might seem, and often is the case, that the prescriptivist is the conservative yearning for stability, while the descriptivist is the radical who sees the hands of the people as the only proper repository for power, linguistic or otherwise. But this is not always the case. Some of us find the most dependable defense against the tendentiousness of *all* groups, the literary elite included, to be a precision of language that exposes muddled thought.

The difference between the prescriptivist who is an elitist and the prescriptivist who trusts not even the literary elite can be seen in the defense each supplies for his prescriptivisim. While both are interested primarily in precision and the other virtues of correct usage, the elitist tends to accept for its own sake the value of speaking and writing like—indeed being like—the literary elite that provides his correct definitions and usages.

The nonelitist proscriptivist, on the other hand, cares only about the precision and other virtues. Moved only by valid argument, he rejects the assessment made by the literary elite when the assessment is supported only by self-appeal.

Analogously, he (if not his editors) is likely to ignore the illogical rule stating that the quotation marks at the end of the preceding paragaph should come after the period. Likewise, the prescriptivist of this stripe rarely has much interest in pronunciation because mispronunciation rarely interferes with the rigor, precision, and communication that are his interests.

The distinction between the two types of prescriptivists can be seen in their differing attitudes towards the alleged distinction between "less" and fewer." The traditionalist prescriptivist does not question the value of the claim that "less" must be used with the continuous (a stream of water) and "fewer" with the discrete (drops of water).[2]

Superficially, the distinction between "less" and "fewer" seems analogous to that between "continuous" and "continual." But note the crucial difference between the two pairs. The distinction between "continuous" and "continually" increases precision by providing information not otherwise provided: "The leak is continuous" is different from "the leak is continual."

In the case of "less" and "fewer," however, the information that determines the choice of words *must be stated* (i.e., *less water* or *fewer drops of water*). Thus, the distinction between "less" and "fewer" does not provide any new information or precision; the distinction is merely redundant. The only effect of this redundancy is to increase inelegance.

Now, the inevitable response to all this by the traditionalist prescriptivist is to argue that such "logic chopping" would maim, if not rend, the language. The problem with this criticism is that its assumption is untrue. Removing redundant distinctions like that between "less" and "fewer" would not do any harm to the language, but would merely remove a few analogous nondistinctions (like that between "amount" and "number").

The first fact I ever heard about our language remains the fact that most impresses me: No two synonyms mean exactly the same thing. The capacity for precision that this fact implies is our language's greatest strength. (No one has ever claimed for English the honor of being the most euphonious or most easily learned language.) We should not let the language shred at the edges for no reason.

There are many other aspects of English for which elegance, simplicity, and precision do not justify the jettisoning of distinction. We would not, for example, change all of the present-tense forms of "to be" to "am" ("I am," "you am," "he am," . . .) because, at the very least, euphony would be lost. In the case of "to be," in other words, there is a need met by the maintenance of distinctions, and the distinctions are not, therefore, redundant. But this cannot be said for the nondistiction between "less" and "fewer" and the few nondistinctions analogous to that between "less" and "fewer." That such distinctions are not necessary is clear from the fact that it has been hundreds of years since anyone has had the nerve to insist that we distinguish between "more" and "mo" when describing "water" and "drops of water."[3]

NOTES

1. Looking up correct definitions—as determined by those whom people-in-general accept as being expert in the use of words, the literary elite—*is precisely what people-in-general use a dictionary for.*

2. I must admit that I abhor the increasing use of "less people" as much as the traditionalist prescriptivist does. But my point is precisely that feelings on such matters—whether one's own feelings or those of an elite—have no persuasive power when not supported by valid argument. "Less people" sounds terrible only because of the rule that one must maintain the alleged distinction between "less" and "fewer." If, as I suggest, the distinction is not a legitimate one, then a sensibility rooted in the illegitimate distinction is illegitimate as well.

3. *Oxford English Dictionary* ("M" volume, page 557 / Micro Edition, page 182). "MO: 2. As the comparative of MANY; more in number (as distinguished from *more*, greater in amount or quantity)."

13

When Logic and Science Are Not Enough
The Question of Abortion

THE MORAL ISSUE OF ABORTION: WHY THERE IS NO SOLUTION

This is based on a note I wrote for students who were especially interested in—and had strong feelings about—the issue of abortion.

Throughout the centuries philosophers have written millions—perhaps hundreds of millions—of words on abortion. The conclusion that follows from all of these words, and all of the thought they represent, is identical to that reached by any intelligent person who reflects on the subject for fifteen minutes. *No logical or scientific analysis can ever tell us whether abortion is morally acceptable or unacceptable, because the moral status of abortion is entirely a function of the definition of the fetus (or embryo) as a "person" or "non-person."*

This fact is not altered—though it is often obscured—by the enormousness of the passions of those who adhere to one or the other of these definitions. Some feel that the fetus is a "person" and that ending its life is "murder." Others feel that it is absurd to consider the fetus to be a "person" or that ending its life is "murder."[1] The peoples of numerous cultures have felt just as deeply as either of these that it would have been ridiculous to consider the unsocialized infant to be a "person" or the parental decision to end the infant's life to be "murder." All of these find abhorrent the thought of ending the life of those they define as "persons." But these varied feelings are all irrelevant to the validity of the conflicting moral claims they engender. The genesis of a claim and the depth of feeling attached to it are always irrelevant to the truth of that claim.

Assuming for the moment that no one is willing to argue for the killing of normal, innocent persons, it is clear that if one defines the fetus as a "person," then there is nothing more to say. When the fetus is so defined, abortion is an extermination of persons that is indifferentiable from wide-scale infanticide or genocide.

It is just as clear, however, that if one defines a fetus as a "non-person," then there is likewise nothing more to say. When the fetus is so defined, abortion is a purely personal act akin to a decision to have cosmetic surgery. No defense of abortion is required (or at least no more defense than the assertion of rights on which all agree).

The issue cannot be settled on the grounds that a prohibition (one *must* not abort a fetus) takes priority over a right (one *may* abort a fetus). The supremacy of a prohibition over a right obtains only if there is agreement on definition and moral status of the act that is at issue. The central point here is that there is no such agreement.

The various attempts to override the determinativeness of definition all fail. *If* the law in a democratic society defines the fetus as a "person," *then*:

(1) A law prohibiting abortion is no more a law against "a matter of religion" than is a law against murder the same as the Commandment "Thou shalt not kill." From a legal standpoint, an act is a "matter of religion" only to the extent that it is not a "matter of law."

(2) A law that defines the fetus as a "person" and prohibits abortion is no more a law against "a matter of choice" than is a law that defines the black as a "person" and prohibits slavery a law against a "matter of choice" of the slaveholder. Likewise, a law that defines the fetus as a "person" and prohibits abortion is no more a law against "a matter of choice" than is a law that defines the infant as a "person" and prohibits infanticide. The refusal to acknowledge the *right* of society to define the fetus as a "person"—and, therefore, an entity protected by the law—would preclude the passing of laws prohibiting the slaveholder from defining the slave as a "non-person" and the mother from defining the infant as a "non-person," positions that, I assume, no one now is willing to take.[2]

It will not do for one to distinguish the slave or the infant from the fetus on the grounds that the former has been born; this begs the question because the criterion for the definition of "person" is precisely the point of disagreement.

(3) A law against abortion is not a law against a "matter of conscience." From a legal standpoint, a matter is a "matter of conscience" only to the extent that it is not a "matter of law." To argue otherwise is to justify a "legal illegality," a contradiction in terms and a position that no legal system could reasonably accept.

An act can, of course, be *moral* and illegal, but this is a different issue. Likewise, a law may incorporate acts of conscience (as it does for conscientious objectors). But if the law does not do this, it cannot accept conscience as a defense without rendering itself impotent.

(4) A law against abortion is not a legal infringement of a "woman's right to her own body," because a legal definition of the fetus as a "person" inherently denies that there is any such right. One may argue for the *morality* of invoking a right that the law does not recognize (though the argument for invocation of an illegal moral *right* that one may choose to invoke or not is far less compelling than the invocation of a moral *imperative*, an act one morally *must* perform). But to argue that one may *legally* invoke a moral right (or a moral imperative) not recognized as legal is to argue for the incoherent.

More important, on a logical level the entire issue of "a woman's right to her own body" is superfluous and obfuscatory. If the fetus is defined as a "non-person," then, again, a woman no more need defend her decision to have an abortion than she need defend a decision to have cosmetic surgery. If the fetus is defined as a "person," then no claimed non-vital right can have (or at least no one claims that it has) parity with the right of the fetus to life.

This is reflected in the fact that no one argues that the fetus is a "person" but that "a woman's right to her own body" takes priority over the right of the fetal person to live. Such an argument *would* render the invocation of "a woman's right to her own body" unsuperfluous and relevant. However, every argument that invokes a "woman's right to her own body" defines the fetus as a "non-person" and, like all arguments that begin with the definition of the fetus as a non-person, implicitly denies that abortion needs special justification in terms of "a woman's right to her own body" or in any other terms. By defining the fetus as a non-person and thereby distinguishing between the fetus and the infant in a way that it declares to be determinative, this argument guarantees its logical integrity and immunizes itself against attack on logical grounds. It accomplishes this as surely as it renders itself incapable of overcoming the argument that defines the fetus as a "person" and refuses to accept the distinction between fetus and infant. As always, the only relevant issue is the definition of the fetus.

(5) No attempt to argue that the fetus is a "person," but one without the right to survive of a person who has been born, can be successful. Given the constraints accepted by all parties to the current abortion debate, "person" *entails* "having the right to survive of all other innocent persons." In other words, any attempt to define the fetus as a person, but a person different from other persons in a way that renders its life less protected than are those of the other innocent persons, takes the position, in all respects relevant to abortion, that the fetus is not a person. "Person" and "non-person" in the context of the abortion debate are, in effect, shorthand words for "may not be aborted" and "may be aborted." Terming the latter "a person who may be aborted" simply confuses the issue, forcing us to use different terms to designate the only point that matters: the permissibility or impermissibility of aborting the fetus (a permissibility or impermissibility that is entailed in the definitions we use).

The mutilations of pregnant women and the other horrors associated with "back alley" abortions move to nausea anyone capable of being called "human." They are not, however, capable of justifying abortion when the fetus is defined as a "person." For the number of abortions performed when abortion is legal is far greater than the number of illegal abortions performed when it is not. Even if one considers illegal abortions being as justified as are legal abortions, one can hardly argue for the moral rightness of killing millions of "persons" for the sake of saving a much smaller number of persons. As always, if the fetus is defined as a "non-person," then abortion needs no special defense at all.

Human behavior is rarely a function of the legitimacy of the argument rationalizing that behavior. In the present case, it cannot be. For, despite the inevitably arbitrary nature of the definition of the fetus,[3] once one has chosen a definition, one is automatically fully committed to one of two opposing political actions.[4]

If one defines the fetus as a "person," then one may justifiably see abortion as an extermination indistinguishable from wide-scale infanticide or genocide requiring (morally, though not legally) almost any response.

Indeed, the only position on abortion that has never made sense to me is the one that sees the fetus as a "person" and then argues for polite, nonviolent attempts to resolve the issue. One who sees the fetus as a "person" must see the present levels of abortion as rapidly becoming an extermination unparalleled in human history. It seems to me that one who so defines the fetus virtually must view the bombing of an abortion clinic as being as justified as would have been the bombing of a crematorium in 1943.

To one who defines the fetus as a "non-person," this response is, of course, a brutal and heartless terrorism aimed at those who are merely invoking a right that is inherent in a (legally recognized) definition of the fetus as a non-person.

Incidentally, despite constant claims to the contrary, it is not true that the right to abortion would be a foregone conclusion if left in the hands of women. While such a view is superficially plausible, and while it no doubt is psychologically satisfying to some proponents of abortion, many surveys have found either that men more strongly favor abortion or that there is no significant sex difference in this regard. A moment's reflection will indicate that this is what one should expect; when there is disagreement over whether a woman should have an abortion, it is certainly far more common (particularly among unwed people) for the *male* partner to favor the woman's having an abortion. (It may be that, in most cases of unwanted pregnancy, the man and the woman agree on whether or not to employ abortion. But such cases are irrelevant here. Here we speak of cases in which there is disagreement. I have known young couples in which the woman wanted to have an abortion that the man did not favor. But these were far outnumbered by cases in which the reverse was true.)

Moreover, even if women did favor abortion more strongly, it is far from clear that that one would look to those most intimately involved for the answer to the question of what is morally right. At least in the case of justice, we prohibit the victim from doing the judging precisely because (among other reasons) deep involvement seems to confuse reasoning ability.

In any case, no considerations of this sort can be relevant. To the extent that the moral argument over abortion represents anything more than subjective desires, the validity of an argument is independent of the characteristics of the proponent.

There are many powerful pragmatic arguments for the legalization of abortion: the welfare of the woman who will otherwise suffer the illegal abortion or give birth to a baby she does not want; the desirability of every child's being wanted; the need to limit population; the psychological costs imposed on, and the social and economic costs imposed by, millions of unwanted (and usually poor) children; and the like. For one who defines the fetus as a "non-person," the power of arguments based on these benefits is overwhelming.[5] But for one who defines the fetus as a "person," such considerations no more justify abortion than would they justify infanticide or genocide.

*   *   *

I was fascinated, but not surprised, to find that *every* person who read this piece before publication concluded that I supported the view of abortion that he or she opposed.

Opponents of abortion felt, correctly, that my granting of definitional parity to the views of the fetus as a "person" and as a "non-person" denied the (claimed) "obviousness" of the personhood of the fetus that is the core of their argument, and that this renders their argument impotent for anyone who does not accept its definitional assumption. They felt, correctly, that if the definition is inherently arbitrary there is no imperative forcing anyone who does not already accept their definition and position to do so.

Supporters of a right to abortion felt, correctly, that more of the piece was devoted to casting doubt on their claims than those of the opponent. This is inevitable because the opponent of abortion focuses on the issue that is determinative, that of the personhood or non-personhood of the fetus (and assumes, illegitimately, that one is compelled to accept the definition of the fetus as a "person"). The supporter of the right to abortion tends to avoid the determinative issue and to introduce such ultimately irrelevant issues as social consequences and "a woman's right to her own body." The space I devote to the irrelevance of such issues merely reflects this fact.

Both the supporter and the opponent of a right to abortion believe that I see the definition of the fetus as being determinative to the moral question and then refuse to acknowledge the correctness of their respective definitions. They are correct. It is not I, however, who am responsible for the determinativeness of the definition, but the nature of logic and science (on the one hand) and moral questions (on the other).

*   *   *

I do happen to support a right to abortion—for no more defensible reasons than those underpinning others' opposition to a right to abortion. It seems to me reasonable, in the absence of an overwhelmingly compelling reason to define the fetus as a "person," for us to reap the individual and social benefits of not doing so. But to the opponent, who gives priority to the fact that, when in doubt, we usually prefer to give the benefit of the doubt to life, I cannot provide any objective reason why it is not just as reasonable to give priority to this fact.

Thus, we can see that the logic of the entire abortion question, and the reason it can never be solved, can be summarized in a paragraph:

If the fetus is defined as a "non-person," then no special justification of abortion is required. If the fetus is defined as a "person," then no defense of abortion is possible (assuming that no one is willing to justify infanticide). "A woman's right to her own body," "the desirability of every child's being wanted," the social advantages of abortion—all such arguments for abortion are unnecessary if the fetus is defined as a "non-person" and insufficiently powerful if the fetus is defined as a "person." This is easily seen if, when considering such arguments, one replaces "fetus" with "infant" or "slave" or "Jew" or "white Protestant." The proponent of a right to abortion predicates the definitional distinction between a "person" and a "non-person" on the distinction between the newborn and the fetus (or the later fetus and the earlier fetus) precisely because the proponent wishes to avoid having to defend a right of the mother to kill her infant. While it is perfectly legitimate for the proponent to make this definitional distinction (just as it is perfectly legitimate for the opponent to refuse to accept it), it is not legitimate for the proponent to deny society the *right* to define the fetus as a "person." To do so is to mimic the slaveholder who distinguishes the slave from the "person" on the grounds that he owns the slave; no society could, would, or should surrender its *right* to protect those it defines as "persons." (Whether a society *should* invoke this right in the case of the fetus and *should* define the fetus as a "person" is, of course, another question.)

One wishes that logic and science could solve this most important of all moral problems. But it is in the limited nature of logic and science that they cannot help here. A science infused with logic can determine the empirical characteristics of the fetus at given times: when conception takes place, when brain activity begins, when sentience becomes possible, when the fetus can survive if removed from the pregnant woman, when the fetus becomes an infant, and the like. But science cannot tell us whether any given property meets the (inherently arbitrary) definition of a "person." If one person believes that a being becomes a "person" at conception, a second when synaptic development begins, a third at the point of sentience, a fourth when brain activity is measurable, a fifth with the capability of independent survival, and a sixth at birth, then science can only remain silent.

As is the case with all moral questions, the answer is a human, subjective one; nature will not help us out. The question of abortion cannot be solved. It can merely be settled—by brute force or its modern equivalent, democratic vote and judicial decision.

NOTES

1. Those who distinguish the "non-person" from the "person" at some point in fetal development are analogous to the latter when discussing a fetus that has not reached that point and analogous to the former when discussing a fetus that has reached that point.

2. It is true that distinguishing the slave or the infant from the fetus on the grounds that the latter has been born does invoke a criterion that *seems* to possess a qualitative quality greater than that possessed by distinctions made at various seemingly quantitative fetal stages, a qualitative quality matched only by that which accords "personhood" at the point of conception. While no less arbitrary than other definitional criteria, and therefore no more logically persuasive than are the other criteria, the birth criterion does seem to gain some practical advantage from its making a distinction that seems to be qualitative while most others seem quantitative.

However, this would impart even the practical advantage only if the prevailing opinion of those who favor a right to abortion accepted birth as the quality distinguishing between the "person" and the "non-person." It is clear, however, that this is not the case. The opinion of even the majority of those favoring a right to abortion clearly makes the distinction, as did the Supreme Court, at the point at which the fetus could survive if removed from the pregnant woman. Thus, the majority position of even those who support a right to abortion accepts a definitional distinction that is seemingly "less qualitative" than that which makes birth the distinguishing criterion.

3. I realize that many of those who believe in "natural rights" will take exception to my terming "inherently arbitrary" the choice of definition of the fetus and the moral claims referred to in the next footnote. Here is not the place once again to debate the empiricist and natural rights views. In this essay I assume the correctness of the empiricist position.

4. To be sure, there are philosophical arguments that (A) accept the personhood of the fetus and yet see abortion as justified, and arguments that (B) deny the personhood of the fetus and yet see abortion as unjustifiable. However, such arguments are found wanting by virtually all but those very few who make them. If the issue of abortion were a scientific question, then, of course, truth would be on the side of even a minority of one. But these arguments invariably introduce an arbitrary moral claim analogous to the claim that the fetus is/isn't a "person." Just as invariably, this claim is rejected by anyone for whom acceptance would lead to a position on abortion discordant with the definition of the fetus, which all of the arguments I refer to in this footnote do (by definition). As is the case with the definition of the fetus as a "person" or "non-person," the arbitrary nature of the claim renders both it and its denial both entirely defensible and incapable of persuading anyone who does not accept it.

5. It is often, and incorrectly, claimed that a right to abortion entails the requirement that the state pay for an abortion desired by one who cannot otherwise afford an abortion. While there may be good social and economic reasons for the state to pay for an abortion, it is certainly not required that the state do so if the majority does not wish it to do so. Even a Constitutional right to abortion that takes priority over majority wishes and prohibits the state from outlawing abortion does not require that the state pay for an abortion if the majority does not wish it to do so (either because the majority finds abortion immoral or because it finds it moral but does not wish to support it financially). One has a Constitutional right to own a Rolls Royce, but this implies neither a moral nor a Constitutional imperative that the state buy one a Rolls Royce.

14

Sociology: Uncommon Sense, Common Sense, or Nonsense?

The "Common-Sense Sociology Test" is now a familiar fixture in introductory sociology courses and textbooks. From the beginning its exciting novelty instantly captured the hearts and minds of graduate students and young professors facing their first lecture halls—lecture halls filled with a student skepticism that is now only a memory. It is not difficult to see why the test is so popular a teaching device.

The purpose of the test is to demonstrate to the introductory student the misconceptions that allegedly derive from everyday observation and common sense, misconceptions that can be corrected only by an infusion of sociological knowledge. What more could one ask for when encountering students whose naïveté cannot preclude their believing that "sociology is just common sense"?

By forcing students to realize the fallibility of their intuitions and observations of social life, the test is meant to make them realize that they have found sociology just in time to enable them to avoid a life of misconception. Its pedagogical virtues are so obvious that no one seems to have noticed what everyone should have noticed immediately. The test does not merely fail to make its point, but succeeds in demonstrating that precisely the opposite point is true: The beliefs of the student, based on his observations and common sense, are basically correct.

The *actual* effect of nearly every question and answer is to engender a feeling on the part of the students that they have been given no reason to doubt their long-held belief or the intuition and observation on which it is based. The students feel (or should feel) that the wording of the questions and answers claimed correct by the test rests on statements that are dubious, misleading, or outright false; at best, the answers only *seem* to refute the important beliefs held by the students, but, in fact, they refute unimportant beliefs that the student does not hold.

In other words, to the extent that this test represents what sociology does, it indicates that sociology is worse than a restatement of common sense; it is a denial of common sense. Fortunately, sociology at its best is much more able than this, as we shall see.

The problem is not that this is a poor test that fails where a good test would succeed. The problem is much deeper. The test is based on the false premise that the sociologist's primary contribution is an observational eye far keener than that of the average person. I would suggest that, save for those sociologists gifted with the novelist's eye (who can be counted on the one finger deserved by Erving Goffman), sociologists only rarely make observations not made with far greater frequency, and with as much accuracy and subtlety, by other people. The "average person" has a far greater observational ability than he is usually credited with, and any test that attempts to demonstrate an inadequacy in the average person's observational powers is doomed either to direct failure (students answer the questions correctly) or failure that only *seems* to succeed by using misleading wording and giving incorrect answers (the test examined here).

While his observation of group behavioral realities is astonishingly accurate, the "average person's" *explanation* of the behavior he observes is often woefully contradictory and inaccurate.

A clear example of this is the stereotype. As observations stereotypes are nearly always accurate (remembering, of course, that a stereotype is a *statistical* claim about observed group behavior, not a description of any given individual). It is the average person's *explanation* of the behavior he observes that is so often hopelessly inadequate. It is by providing correct explanations of accurate observations (*i.e.,* explaining why the members of the group tend to exhibit the characteristics or behavior that is observed), not by pretending that the observations are inaccurate, that we sociologists can justify our existence.

The variety of human behavior, the limits our physiology sets on social possibility, the social structure that serves to organize human interaction and provide a template for culture, and the culture that binds and separates human beings—these all justify the study of social reality. This is self-evident from the fact that there is a social reality, and that it can, in practice, no more be understood atomistically than can the nature of the "team" be understood by studying only individual players.

It is not the observation, but rather the discovery of the causal connections explaining that which is observed, that is worthy of calling upon the genius of a Vico or a Weber or a Durkheim. It is only through such explanations that we are justified in denying the widely held view that "sociology is just common sense."

The Common-Sense Sociological Test follows. The entire test and the complete questions ("Q") and answers ("A") are given; however, the order of the questions has been altered to obviate repetition in the "comments" I have added. *According to the test,* all questions are true/false and the correct answer to every question is "false."

Q. Revolutions are more likely to occur when conditions are very bad than when previously bad conditions are rapidly improving.

A. Revolutions are actually more likely to occur when conditions have been bad but are rapidly improving. When conditions are bad and stay bad, people take their misfortune for granted, but when conditions suddenly improve people develop higher aspirations and become easily frustrated.

Comment: This is an excellent question. It is precisely the sort of question that the test promises but fails to deliver throughout. It attacks a belief that really is held by the student (the worse the conditions, the more likely is revolution), surprises him with the correct answer, and prepares him for a valuable sociological finding (rising expectations outpace improvement in condition). It is not coincidental, however, that this question and misconception have to do with a correlation (improvement and revolution) much further removed from the student's daily observation than are the subjects of most of the other questions. The more abstract the correlation in question, the more likely that the student holds an incorrect belief.

Q. Lower-class youths are more likely to commit crimes than middle-class youths.

A. Lower-class youths are not more likely than middle-class youths to commit crimes. Middle-class youths are at least as likely to engage in delinquent acts, but they are less likely to be arrested, and therefore do not show up as frequently in the court statistics.

Comment: To most beginning students, as to the general population, "crime" means "violent crime" or, at most, "violent crime and major white-collar crime." The student is hardly going to be knocked off his chair by the fact that for every mugging by a member of the lower class there is a marijuana joint smoked by a high-school student. In other words, this question could achieve its goal of surprising the student (and giving a correct answer) only by showing that middle- and lower-class youths commit equally violent crimes at equal rates. And, of course, it cannot show this because it is not true.

Q. The best way to get an accurate assessment of public opinion is to poll as many people as possible.

A. The number of people involved in a public opinion poll is largely irrelevant. What matters is that the sample should be fully representative of the population whose opinion is wanted. A properly chosen sample of two or three thousand Americans can give a highly accurate test of national opinion; a poorly chosen sample of three million, or even 30 million, could be hopelessly off target.

Comment: This answer is true only in the sense that it would be correct to say that a football player's size is unimportant to his ability because large, but uncoordinated, people are less likely to make the National Football League than are superb athletes of average size. Clearly, when we say that size is important to football ability we mean that, other things being equal, size is important.

Likewise, when we say that a large sample is better than a small sample, we mean "when members of the samples are equally representative." And, in saying this, we are correct; in this sense—the only sense in which the claim makes any sense—the larger the sample, the better.

Q. People who are regular Christian churchgoers are less likely to be prejudiced against other races than people who do not attend church.

A. Regular churchgoers are generally not less prejudiced than nonchurchgoers;

in fact, they tend to be more prejudiced.

Comment: This question and answer *seem* to address the question of the effect of religion (or at least of churchgoing) on prejudice, a question of monumental scientific, moral, and political importance.

The question and answer actually given simply reflect the fact that Protestant churchgoers tend (statistically speaking, as always) to come from groups tending, for reasons having nothing to do with Christianity or churchgoing, to be more prejudiced (rural Southern Fundamentalists, as opposed to urban nonbelievers, for example). This no more demonstrates that churchgoing increases prejudice than the fact that Japanese churchgoers are shorter than Canadian nonchurchgoers demonstrates that going to church makes you short.

The important question that the answer seems to address but does not is the effect on prejudice of churchgoing when all other variables are held steady. In other words, one does not want to compare churchgoers from Birmingham with nonchurchgoers from New York, but churchgoers from Birmingham with nonchurchgoers (matched for race, income, class, residential area, and the like) from Birmingham (or churchgoers from New York with nonchurchgoers from New York). It is the answer to *this* question that is likely to demonstrate whether churchgoing has the effect of increasing prejudice, decreasing it, or leaving it unaffected.

Q. The number of federal government employees has grown sharply over the past two decades.

A. The number of federal civilian officials has remained almost constant for twenty years, although the number of state and local-government officials has, risen significantly.

Comment: The intuition of the student (and the rest of us) is that bureaucracy has burgeoned. That this intuition derives from our experience with state and local bureaucracies, and does not accurately reflect the federal situation, is interesting, but, at best, only mildly surprising. It is the state and local bureaucracies with which people have the most daily experience, experience that leads them to correctly believe that bureaucracy in general has increased significantly.

Q. Exposure to pornography makes people more likely to commit sex crimes.

A. Studies of sex offenders show that they are less likely than non-offenders to have been exposed to pornography. Far from encouraging sex crime, pornography seems to provide some people with an alternative outlet.

Comment: The answer does not address, much less refute, the question. It addresses the issue of the relative exposure to pornography of offenders and non-offenders. The issue described in the question—the issue of the causal role of pornography—is this: Do offenders who read pornography commit a greater number of (or the same number or fewer) crimes than do offenders who do not read pornography (or who read less pornography)? That the non-offender, who perhaps lacks a necessary condition that must complement pornography if one is to become an offender, reads as much pornography as the offender (or even more) is irrelevant. One would not deny that curry makes an ulcer worse simply because curry will not give an ulcer to one who lacks the other necessary conditions for the development of an ulcer.

Q. One thing that is found in every society is romantic love.

A. Romantic love may seem a part of "human nature" to us, but in many societies it is unknown and in many others it is regarded as ridiculous or tragic.

Comment: The issue raised in the question is whether there are societies in which romantic love is unknown (not whether there are societies in which it is negatively sanctioned). That some societies ridicule romantic love or see it as tragic demonstrates that these societies *do* recognize romantic love.

That many societies do not institutionalize romantic love (seeing it as a threat to social stability) is a point that is true, important, and probably unknown by most students. However, the test question is not concerned with societies that recognize romantic love yet negatively sanction it, but with alleged societies that are so successful at socializing their members that romantic love never rears its head.

I have spent the past decade and a half studying cross-cultural regularities, and like many others I have come to strongly distrust claims of the absence in a society of an emotionally rooted behavior that is found in every other society. Such claims are almost invariably made on the basis of secondhand references. When one looks to the ethnographies of societies said to lack a certain kind of behavior (in those cases where the sources are given), the description of those societies makes it clear that the behavior is *not* absent. On a very few occasions, a specialized ethnography concentrating on an entirely different subject will give no evidence of the behavior in question. However, when the behavior is negatively sanctioned (and therefore not exhibited openly), when the subject of the ethnography is, say, irrigation methods, and the behavior in question is romantic love— and when we know that this behavior can be observed in virtually all other of the world's societies, it is dubious to conclude that absence of a mention of the behavior in the ethnography is strong evidence that members of the society do not exhibit the behavior.

Q. On average, high-income people in the United States pay a greater proportion of their income in taxes than low-income people.

A. High-income people pay roughly the same proportion of their income as low-income people do. The reasons are that the rich can use many tax loopholes and that sales and other indirect taxes take a relatively larger percentage of poor people's income.

Comment: There are two problems with this answer, even if we accept that it is empirically correct. First, if my students are representative, and I suspect they are, then most students do not only not register surprise at the answer, but in fact are surprised that the rich don't pay a *smaller* percentage of their incomes because they can buy lawyers who can find loopholes and because the system favors the rich. Second, even if the students did believe that the rich pay a higher percentage, their belief would be a function of their equating "taxes" with income taxes, not the sales and indirect taxes required to make this question "work."

Q. Husbands are more likely to kill their wives in family fights than wives are to kill their husbands.

A. Husbands and wives are equally likely to kill one another; although husbands are usually stronger, wives are more likely to resort to lethal weapons.

Comment: This certainly is a surprising "fact," one that will surprise students as much as will the "fact" that there are more Chinese in New Jersey than there are in China. These two "facts," however, have about equal truth content. According to a recent FBI Uniform Crime Report, husbands kill their wives about three times as often as wives kill their husbands.

Q. The amount of money spent on a school's equipment and facilities has a strong effect on the academic success of its pupils.

A. The amount of money spent on a school's facilities seems to have little influence on pupil achievement. Performance is primarily related to family and social class background.

Comment: One might question whether the student is all that surprised by the answer. The cynic might have doubts whether the research on which the answer is based possessed the methodological sophistication and rigor necessary for disentangling the factors of income, social class, and the tendency of schools with high-income students to both spend more money and achieve academic success. Nonetheless, it takes only the slightest generosity to give this question a passing grade.

Q. A substantial portion of people on welfare could work if they really wanted to.

A. Less than 2 percent of people on welfare are adult males who have been out of work for several months. Nearly all are children, old people, handicapped people, or mothers who are obliged to stay at home to look after their families and have no other source of income.

Comment: If we ignore possible quibbles about precise percentages, this answer is correct in its claim that most people on welfare are in the groups listed. For some students, the question probably accomplishes the test's goal of surprising them with a correct answer. However, at least as many (in my experience) are aware that a relatively small percentage of welfare recipients are malingerers or cheaters. In fairness it should be said that this may not have been true when the question was originally written and, if we again wish to be generous, we might give this question a passing grade.

Q. The income gap between blacks and whites has narrowed in recent years.

A. Despite civil rights and other legislation, the income gap between blacks and whites has actually widened in recent years; black workers are generally less skilled than white workers and less skilled workers suffer more in times of depression.

Comment: While the flaw here is somewhat less deep than that in the next question (to which it is similar), the belief that seems to be under attack is not the belief that this answer challenges. The strong belief of the student is that a black and a white in the *same position* earn more nearly equal incomes than they did formerly. This belief is correct. That blacks are the first to be laid off in times of "depression" (by which I assume is meant recession; there has not been a depression in fifty years) is a point worth making, but hardly one that will surprise a student.

Q. The income gap between male and female workers has narrowed in recent years.

A. The income gap between male and female workers has widened rather than narrowed; women hold few high-paying positions and the average working white woman earns less than the average working black man.

Comment: This is the test's quintessential question. It elicits the "incorrect" answer from—and therefore surprises—the student by introducing a construct ("income gap") with which the student is unfamiliar. It thereby seems to capture and refute the strong belief on which the student bases his "incorrect" answer. However, the strong belief is that, after twenty years of the women's movement, a man and a woman occupying the same position (and having equal credentials) receive more-nearly equal incomes than they did formerly. This belief is entirely correct. In other words, to the student, the term "income gap" refers to a man and a woman in the same position. The fact that the "income gap" referred to by the question—the average incomes of all full-time male and female workers— has increased does not challenge any deeply held belief of the student and is not likely to surprise him. It is particularly unlikely to surprise him when he realizes that the "income gap" referred to in the question has increased as a result of the same forces that have led to a decrease in the difference in incomes of a man and a woman in the same position: Women have joined the work force in large numbers and, since one joining the work force earns an entry-level income, these new female workers bring down the average income of working women and increase the "income gap" between the sexes.

Q. Human beings have a natural instinct to mate with the opposite sex.

A. Human beings do not have an instinct to mate with the opposite sex. Our sexual preferences are entirely learned; in fact, if an instinct is defined as an inherited complex behavior pattern, human beings do not have any instincts at all.

Comment: This answer commits three errors in two sentences: (1) While the causation of heterosexuality and homosexuality is far from understood, it has for a decade become increasingly apparent that there is a physiological component that interacts with environmental factors to generate sexual direction. I know of no researcher who any longer holds that the causation of sexual direction is entirely environmental. (2) Even if one rejects this and goes so far as to see the issue as entirely undecided, the question is a poor one, for the student feels —correctly—that his answer is as likely to be correct as is that of the test. (3) As is so common in sociology, there is an attempt to instill in the student's mind a rejection of the possibility that physiological factors play an important role in determining human behavior. The first-day student is hardly likely to know that, if "instinct" is defined as requiring "complex behavior patterns," there are still physiologically rooted tendencies and predispositions other than "instincts" that clearly affect human behavior (i.e., a predisposition is clearly involved in sexual arousal, even though this predisposes one to actions whose specific characteristics are socially determined).

A severe critic might add a fourth error: It is questionable whether the term "learned" means much at this level of interaction of physiology and environment; just as the term "causation" tends to lose its meaning, or, at the very least, its fertility, at the quantum level, so does "learning" lose its meaning at deep levels.

Q. For religious reasons, most American Catholics oppose birth control and are less likely than Protestants to enter interfaith marriages or to be divorced.

A. More than 80 percent of American Catholics favor birth control; Catholics are more likely than Protestants to enter interfaith marriages and Catholics have a higher divorce rate than Protestants.

Comment: A scratch single, a long fly out, and a strikeout on three called change-ups.

It is unclear from the Roper poll on birth control whether the 80 percent figure refers to Catholic approval of birth control for everyone or just for non-Catholics. More important, it is likely that the beginning student equates "favors" with "uses," and it is only Catholic usage that would surprise the student. (It is axiomatic in sociology that actual behavior often fails to reflect stated opinion.) Nonetheless, it *is* probable that most beginning students underrate Catholic use of birth control.

There is somewhat less than meets the eye in the fact that a Catholic is more likely to enter an interfaith marriage than a Protestant. Most Catholic interfaith marriages are to Protestants and most Protestant interfaith marriages are to Catholics. Since there are twice as many American Protestants as Catholics, it is hardly surprising that a higher percentage of Catholics intermarry (i.e., that a Catholic is "more likely" to intermarry).

The "fact" about Catholics having a higher divorce rate than Protestants is as astonishing as it is untrue. Protestants have a much higher divorce rate.

Index

abnormal behavior, 49
abnormal causes, 49, 60n
aggression, 91, 93, 96, 97, 109, 111, 115,
  116, 138, 141, 147n, 182, 183
AIDS (Acquired Immune Deficiency
  Syndrome), 67, 96
Amazonian society, 117n, 172
American Astronomical Society, 158
American Psychiatric Association, 48, 49
Austen, Jane, 110

behaviorism, 22
Bell, Alan P., 61n–62n, 68, 70n
Benbow, Camilia Persson, 109, 120n,
  147n
Bernard, Jessie, 118n, 174
bisexuality, 62n
black dominance, 121, 123, 124, 153
Blumberg, Rae Lesser, 81
Bok, Bart J., 158, 162
Bontoc society, 81
Bouchard, Claude, 128n
Bower, B., 120n
Bribri society, 80

capitalism, 85, 172
Chapman, Rex, 124
College Board, 142
college performance, 131, 132, 133, 134,

135, 140, 142, 144
Common-Sense Sociology Test, 205,
  206–212
competition, 170
coprophilia, 51, 60n, 68, 70n
creationism, 157

Darwin, Charles, 157
Darwinian theory, 156, 178
deference, 117n
democracy, 19
descriptivism, 193, 194
"deterrence," 25, 26, 30, 31, 33, 39, 42,
  43, 44
discrimination, 48, 91, 92, 108, 109, 113,
  135, 152
dominance behavior, 78, 94, 100, 117n,
  170
Duberman, Martin, 48, 51
Durkheim, Emile, 206

Educational Testing Service, 142
Edwards, Harry, 126–127
egalitarianism, 74, 75, 76, 81, 118n
Erhardt, Anke A., 119n
Ehrlich, Isaac, 27
Einstein, Albert, 23, 161, 165
environmentalism, 22, 41, 98, 99, 100,
  124, 127

Equality Between Men and Women in Sweden, 117n
Equal Rights Amendment, 106
Eratosthenes, 21
evolutionary theory, 93, 157, 170

Fausto-Sterling, Anne, 79
"feedback," 98, 99, 101, 126
female androgens, 100
female dominance, 117n
feudalism, 85
Fisher, Seymour, 56, 61n, 191n
Flaubert, Gustav, 110
freedom of speech, 19, 38
Freud, Sigmund, 16, 37, 87, 110, 177, 190
Freudian theory, 54, 59, 60n, 65, 66, 68, 87, 156, 177–190, 191n
    explanation of homosexuality, 55, 56, 58, 65, 186, 188
Friedman, Milton, 23
Gabb, M., 118n
Galileo, 160
Gallico, Paul, 128n
Gandhi, Indira, 73
gender identity, 96, 97
"G intelligence," 143, 144, 145
Goffman, Erving, 206
Gould, Stephen J., 79
gravity, 171
Greenberg, Roger P., 56, 61n, 191n

Haldane, John, 98
Henslin, James, 60n
hermaphrodites, 100, 165
hermeneutics, 171
homosexual behavior, 48–49, 50, 52–53, 54, 58, 60n, 61n–62n
    Asexuals, 62n
    Close-Coupled, 62n
    Dysfunctionals, 62n
    female homosexuals, 62n
    Functionals, 62n
    "latent homosexuality," 61n, 183, 184
    Open-Coupled, 62n

Homosexualities, 61n, 70n
Hook, Sidney, 184, 185, 191n
Hooker, Evelyn, 57, 67, 70n
hormonalization, 97, 98, 100, 101, 102, 118n
humanitarianism, 49

Iban society, 80
income gap, 210, 211
Inevitability of Patriarchy, The, 61n, 72, 74, 77, 78, 79, 80, 81, 82, 83, 86, 88, 92, 93, 94, 95, 96, 102, 105, 174, 176n
inferiority, 105, 127
intelligence, 142, 143, 145
"interaction," 98, 99
"internal resistance," 41, 42
intolerance and pain, 58
I.Q. tests, 94, 116, 142, 143, 144, 145
Iroquois society, 81

Jacklin, Carol Nagy, 120n
Javanese society, 80
Jerome, Lawrence E., 158, 162
Journal of Projective Techniques, 70n

Kamin, Leon, 79, 118n
Karlen, Arno, 49, 60n
Kenuzi Nubians, 80
Kinsey Institute, 61n
!Kung society, 81

Lazerowitz, Morris, 179–180, 191n
Leiderman, P. H., 119n
Levin, Margarita, 170
Lewontin, Richard, 79, 92, 118n, 119n

Maccoby, Eleanor, 110, 112, 120n
Male and Female, 117n
male attainment, 74, 75, 83, 84, 85, 88, 89, 90, 92, 102, 103, 105, 106, 107, 108, 119n
male dominance, 74, 75, 76, 83, 84, 86, 87, 88, 89, 90, 91, 92, 93, 94, 95, 96, 99, 100, 101, 102, 103, 104, 106,

107, 109, 110, 114, 118n, 119n, 147n, 172, 173
"male paradigms," 171
male physical strength, 85, 87, 100, 105, 147n
Male Homosexuals, 62n, 70n
Man and Woman, Boy and Girl, 119n
Marquesas society, 80
Marx, Karl, 23
Marxism, 22
maternal instinct, 85, 90
matriarchy, 117n, 172
Mbuti society, 81
McDonald's, 85
Mead, Margaret, 75, 77, 117n–118n, 173–175
Meir, Golda, 73
Mennea, Pietro, 122
Mill, John Stuart, 104
modernization, 86, 106–107
Molina, Robert, 128n
Money, John, 96, 97, 119n
moral imperative, 198
motivation, 89, 90, 92, 103, 104, 134, 144, 190
Moynihan Report, 40

Nagle, Ernest, 179, 191n
natural rights, 203n
"nature vs. nurture," 71
necrophilia 50, 51, 52, 59, 60n, 68, 70n
"negative sanction," 42, 51, 53, 57, 58, 60n, 67, 68, 70n, 209
Newton, Isaac, 23
normality, 47, 48, 50, 51, 52, 54, 55, 59, 60n, 61n, 62n, 68, 70n
Not in Our Genes, 79, 118n

Oakley, Charles, 124
"Objections to Astrology," 157, 158
Oedipus Complex, 88, 184, 185, 189
overdetermination, 183–184
Oxford English Dictionary, 196n

Pap, Arthur, 184

phenomenology, 171
pleasure principle, 178
Popper, Karl, 177, 184, 185
pornography, 32, 208
"positive sanction," 42, 52, 53, 58, 62n, 65, 67
postdiction, 185, 186, 188
prejudice, 48, 53, 91, 92, 108, 109, 152, 207–208
prescriptivism, 193, 194, 195, 196n
Psychoanalysis, Scientific Method, and Philosophy, 191n
Psychobiological Approaches to Social Behavior, 119n
Psychology of Sex Differences, The, 120n

Quine, W. V., 165

racial differences, 94
racism, 121, 127
reaction formation, 183
reconceptualization, 173
Reith, John E., 125
repression, 184, 185
Roper poll, 212
Rose, Steven, 79, 118n
Rothbard, Murray, 23
Russell, Bertrand, 165
Russell, Bill, 153

Sagarin, Edward, 60n
Sanday, Peggy Reeves, 86
Schacter, Stanley, 99, 100, 119n
Scholastic Aptitude Test, 110, 131–148
Scientific Credibility of Freud's Theories and Therapy, The, 191n
Scientific Evaluation of Freud's Theories and Therapy, 61n
Sears, R., 191n
Semang society, 80
semiotics, 171
Sex and Temperament in Three Primitive Societies, 77, 117n–118n, 173
sex differences, 65, 72, 94, 95, 96, 111, 114, 115, 119n, 137, 138, 140, 146n,

147n, 174, 175
sex drive, 89
sex preferences, 65
sexual differentiation, 98, 103, 141
"sexual oppression," 54
Shakespeare, William, 188
Shapiro, David, 119n
Skinner, A., 118n
socialism, 85
socialization, 84, 172
Social Science Research Council Bulletin, 191n
sociobiology, 93, 94
Sociological Theory: 1984, 81
Sociology of Sex, The, 60n
Soviet Union, 76, 93
Spencer, Herbert, 156
Sport and Human Genetics, 128n
Stanley, Julian C., 109, 120n, 147n
Status of Women in Pre-Industrial Society, The, 118n
Stone, D., 118n
Structure of Science, The, 179
sublimation, 184, 185
"suggestibility" of hormones, 99–100
superiority, 105, 108, 110, 121, 123, 127, 128n, 133, 137, 138, 140, 142, 148n
Supreme Court, 203n
"survival of the fittest," 178, 191n

Tasaday society, 81
Tchambuli society, 174, 175
territorial imperatives, 94
territoriality, 94
Thatcher, Margaret, 73
Thurnwald, Richard, 118n
transference, 178

unconscious disposition, 184
unconscious feeling, 184
United States, 17, 58, 72, 76, 93, 108, 121, 122, 209
universality, 78, 79, 81, 84, 87, 88, 92, 93, 99, 101, 102, 103, 108, 118n, 119n, 172, 173

van den Haag, Ernest, 28
Vico, 206
Vivas, Eliseo, 190

WAIS, 110
Webb, Spud, 123
Weber, Max, 206
Weinberg, Martin S., 58, 61n–62n, 68, 70n
Whyte, William King, 80, 118n
Williams, Colin, 58, 62n, 68, 70n
Williams, Donald C., 179–180, 191n
Wittgenstein, Ludwig, 165